The Politics of Translation in the Middle Ages and the Renaissance

D0743695

MEDIEVAL AND RENAISSANCE TEXTS AND STUDIES

VOLUME 233

The Politics of Translation in the Middle Ages and the Renaissance

Edited by
Renate Blumenfeld-Kosinski
Luise von Flotow
Daniel Russell

Arizona Center for Medieval and Renaissance Studies
Tempe, Arizona
2001

National Library of Canada Cataloguing in Publication Data

Main entry under title:

The politics of translation in the Middle Ages and the Renaissance

(Perspectives on Translation)
Includes bibliographical references.

ISBN 0-7766-0527-5

1. Translating and interpreting—Europe—History—To 1500. 2. Translating and interpreting—Europe—History—16th Century. 3. Civilization, Medieval. 4. Renaissance.
5. Literature, Medieval—Translations—History and criticism. 6. European literature—
Renaissance, 1450-1600—Translations—History and criticism. I. Russell, Daniel II. von
Flotow, Luise, 1951- III. Blumenfeld-Kosinski, Renate, 1952- IV. Series.

P306.P64 2001   418'.02'0902   C2001-900512-1

Cover illustration

In 1476, Margaret of England (1446-1504), the wife of Charles the Bold of Burgundy, commissioned a copy of the French translation of the *Consolation of Philosophy* (*De Consolatione
Philosophiae*), a Latin work written by Boethius (480-524). Called "the last of the Romans,"
Boethius had translated works by Aristotle and Ptolemy and wrote the *Consolation* while
in prison awaiting execution. The French version was produced by Jean de Meung (1240-c.
1305), poet and translator. The manuscript, illuminated by a Bruges artist, was copied
in Ghent by David d'Aubert. The dedicatory picture shown here depicts Jean de Meung, in
what is probably a courtyard, presenting his translation to Duchess Margaret. She and her
ladies-in-waiting are wearing elegant court dress. *Copyright:* Thüringer Universitäts- und
Landesbibliothek, Friedrich-Schiller-Universität Jena, ms. El. f.85, f.13ᵛ.

Medieval and Renaissance Texts and Studies series (No. 233)
Arizona Center for Medieval and Renaissance Studies
Tempe, Arizona
ISBN 0-86698-275-2

© University of Ottawa Press, 2001
542 King Edward, Ottawa, Ont. Canada K1N 6N5
press@uottawa.ca   http://www.uopress.uottawa.ca
ISBN 0-7766-0527-5
ISSN 1487-6396

Printed and bound in Canada

Acknowledgements:

This volume could never have been published without the indispensable confidence, financial support, and editorial and production assistance of many individuals and institutions. The editors would like first to thank the Universities of Pittsburgh and Ottawa for making such undertakings possible.

In particular our thanks go out to Jean Delisle who found a home for our work in the "Perspectives on Translation" series that he edits for the University of Ottawa Press, and to Vicki Bennett, editor-in-chief of that Press, and her staff, for their efforts in shepherding the work through the long process of bringing it to the public.

Financial support for its publication was forthcoming from the Faculty of Arts Publication Fund of the University of Ottawa and from The Richard D. and Mary Jane Edwards Endowed Publication Fund in the Faculty of Arts and Sciences at the University of Pittsburgh. The Medieval and Renaissance Studies Program and the Department of French and Italian at the University of Pittsbsurgh provided constant support in ways too numerous to count. Finally, the University of Pittsburgh Center for West European Studies provided the funding necessary for Andrew Petiprin, a French and History major at the University of Pittsburgh, to provide enormous assistance in preparing camera-ready copy of the manuscript. Andrew, with his computer expertise and careful attention to the manuscript, contributed greatly to the successful and timely publication of this volume.

To all, our deepest thanks.

R. B.-K., L. v. F., D. R.
Pittsburgh, May 2001

Table of Contents

Translation in the Politics of Culture

Luise von Flotow
University of Ottawa

Most writing can be shown to be "political" in some sense, conforming to the context in which it is produced, deliberately transgressing it, reflecting upon it, or aiming at a particular readership in order to convince, seduce or otherwise exert influence. Most reading, too, is conducted in a political context in which a written text may be suppressed, ignored or awarded prizes. Texts that reach the public, as well as those never published, are embedded in the social, political and cultural processes of their day. Translation, the careful reading and deliberate rewriting of a text, can be viewed as doubly political; not only was the first text embedded in and influenced by certain political configurations, but the second text, the rewritten version, adds yet another layer of politics, that of the new, translating culture and era.

Politics, in the widest sense of the term, and translation are activities that have always been linked—in the present as much as in the Middle Ages and the Renaissance. Yet for many years, the cultural, political and ideological aspects of rewriting/translation, as well as the importance and ubiquity of these activities, have been obscured by other interests: among them, a strong focus on national literatures and national "genius," which precluded the study of translation; notions about writing as creative work and translation as an always-foiled attempt at achieving equivalence, which rendered translation a second-class art; "formalist" questions about how to define translation or establish criteria for a "good" translation, which produced subjective evaluations; and, since the 1950s, the hopes placed in machine translation, which fired linguistic approaches to translated texts. These interests largely ignored the cultural importance of translation in creating and transferring knowledge, and the ideological and political role it plays in the translating culture, all of which pushed the study of translations, in particular of literary translation, to the periphery of academic pursuits.

Over the course of the last twenty years there has been a renaissance in translation studies, a new focus on its roles in certain cultures at certain periods. A loose association of researchers and academics, located, not surprisingly, in "translating" cultures such as Israel, the Netherlands, Belgium, Germany and Canada, inaugurated the "cultural turn" in translation studies, which has now spread throughout Europe and is making headway in the United States, South America, India and South Africa. The dynamism of this development is doubtless supported by international and national politics, such as the official multilingualism of the European Union and the exchange of personnel across its language borders; the official bilingualism of Canada; and in the greater economic and political forces of globalization. Translation in these scenarios is vital, and the study, analysis and teaching of translation have taken on new importance. In literary translation studies, the field has also benefitted from the post-structuralist/postmodernist debates around originality, authorship and authority, which have served to open the way for the study of influence, of *métissage*, and for new voices in the field: women, postcolonial writers and critics, gay, lesbian and queer thinkers.

While translation studies as a discipline is decidedly heterogeneous, with scholars developing many different areas of research, one common thread seems to be the idea of systems. The cultural productions of a particular society are part of a system that consists of many, possibly conflicting, and certainly competing, subsystems: "a differentiated and dynamic 'conglomerate of systems' characterized by internal oppositions and continual shifts."[1] Scholars studying translation within this "polysystem approach" locate their texts in the political, economic and cultural contexts from which they derive and into which they move; they examine the forces and processes that may have influenced them and seek to understand the interaction of source and translating culture in the texts. Translations are not evaluated as "good" or "bad," nor is the possibility or impossibility of translation at issue; instead, texts designated and accepted as translations in a certain culture are studied in context, and the context always includes politics.[2]

Such work in translation studies is also beginning to be done by scholars focussed on the Middle Ages and the Renaissance. They, too, have renewed their interest in translation and politics over the course of the last decade. Rita Copeland's 1991 study of rhetoric, hermeneutics and translation in the Middle Ages is clearly concerned with texts in systems and the political and ideological issues that impinge upon interpretive practices. She writes in her conclusion, "If the tradition of translation I have considered here can be understood through its historical placement in the academic systems of rhetoric and hermeneutics, it also carries the ideological import of those systems, and it transfers their ideological tensions to another plane, the confrontation between Latinity and vernacularity" (Copeland 1991, 223). Copeland's terminology alone—systems, tensions, ideological import, confrontation—reveals her interest in understanding translation, rewriting and commentary as activities carried out within constantly shifting spheres of influence and power. Similarly, the articles generated by the Cardiff Conferences and collected in publications edited by Roger Ellis have been increasingly focussed on contextualizing translation and understanding the political import of operating both within one context and between two. Ruth Evans' introduction to *The Medieval Translator IV* (1994) provides a powerful argument for links between translation studies and medieval studies (Evans 1994, 20-45). Evans deplores the narrow field in which medieval studies has historically been situated, and sees translation studies as a wider disciplinary and interdisciplinary field where medieval translation may "achieve greater academic visibility and contribute to the redrawing of the historical maps of 'translation' " (Evans 1994, 23). But she also wants to encourage medievalists to pay attention to categories they have tended to ignore, "such as 'the role of ideology in the shaping of a translation.' "[3] For her, "translation is a powerful site of cultural transformation...in which new modes of thinking through the notion of 'difference,' which is at the heart of the problematic of translation, are born" (Evans 1994, 36). Appropriately, many of the articles in the collection are clearly in line with translation studies approaches, examining the cultural, political and systemic contexts within which translation was done and the roles it played.

The important shift from Latin to the vernacular that took place via translation and commentary in the late Middle Ages is the focus of an important section of the recent *The Idea of the Vernacular. An Anthology of Middle English Literary Theory* (Wogan-Browne et al. 1999, 314-30). Here, writing in the vernacular, whether in translation or other texts, is also described as being situated in complex cultural fields and implying a deliberate and often strategic choice over Latin. Current studies of these texts in the vernacular are increasingly concerned with translation as a "site where cultural relations of dominance and subservience may be played out" (317). Translation plays a central role in discussions around the concept of *translatio studii et imperii*, and the means by which cultural value and authority were transmitted. Translation is involved in the transfer of literary texts and structures of thought as well as the translation of political power. Yet, as the authors of this material point out, the concept/practice of *translatio studii et imperii* can be understood either as "an endorsement of the authority of the past as a model and source for the present or, conversely, as an account of how 'modern' culture seeks to displace the past" (318), both describing and denying change. Dante's proclamation on the illustrious nature of the vernacular, *De vulgari eloquentia*, for example, was written in Latin and refers to Latin as a language that unites Europe. However, it also seeks to displace Latin, uniting the scattered Italian dialects instead. And while writers using Middle English may be less assertive than Dante, they, too, adopt attitudes of deference to the authority of Latin and assertiveness with regard to the vernacular, which they are shaping as a literary language. Beyond the realm of literary considerations, however, translation and writing in the vernacular are deliberate strategies around a "politics of access" (323): Translation in late medieval England is at the center of contentious issues about who should be able to read what.

Finally, late twentieth-century approaches to gender and identity are also surfacing in recent works that take translation as their focus in texts of the Middle Ages and the Renaissance. These were inaugurated by Margaret P. Hannay's anthology *Silent but for the Word: Tudor Women as Patrons, Translators, and Writers of Religious Works* (1985) with its articles on women translators, young Elizabeth I, Elizabeth More, Mary Sydney Herbert, that seek out the subject positions these women assume in their translations. Here, translation is explored as a form of self-expression in a political and cultural environment that placed heavy restrictions on writing and publication by women. Jocelyn Wogan-Browne (1999, 46-65) also focuses on the translator's subjectivity in her study of the female translator of Anglo-Norman hagiography, whom she sees as engaged in a process of generation and the creation of new life rather than an assault on or "dismemberment of the source text," (51) implying that male translators might have favored the latter approach. Most recently, Jane Chance takes a more political approach as she traces the systematic and deliberate misrepresentation and misappropriation of Christine de Pizan's writings in their contemporaneous English translations through strategies as diverse as the assertion of authorship by the male translator, the masculinization of female deities and illustrations that change the gendered power relationships between figures Pizan includes in her work (Chance 1998, 161-64). Translation is shown to be more than a struggle for meaning in these texts; it is also a struggle over gendered meaning.

The texts collected in the present volume discuss moments of translation selected from a broad historical period. These are linked by the connection between translation and politics that each piece demonstrates. And although no reference is made to contemporary translation studies scholars, the work clearly follows the "cultural turn" in translation studies. Interestingly, several articles take up a new topos in translation studies, one that neither Copeland nor Evans is explicitly concerned with—interventionist power exercised by the individual translator. Increasingly, translated texts are being considered the work of individuals who are as anchored in their time and context as any writer, and who, therefore, contribute—often unconsciously—to the politicization of a text. Whereas translators were once seen as transparent conduits at best, or traitors at worst, current work recognizes their interventionist power and discernment. In this collection of articles, Andrew Taylor, for example, shows how the marks of Reginald Pecock's self-assured and assertive personality are visible in his commentaries on biblical texts, which led to his indictment by church authorities, and Kenneth Lloyd-Jones comments on the personal ambition, opportunism and other foibles of Etienne Dolet—traits that are reflected in his translations as well as his public stance as translator. Translation is a cultural phenomenon produced by individuals with a certain personality as well as an agenda, and it is closely linked to the political and often economic or personal situation of the translator. The translator is an agent and plays an active, performative role, always in a political context. Oumelbanine Zhiri's article demonstrates to what extent the work of Leo Africanus is deliberately Europeanized by his translator and editor, who wished to make the work more meaningful for European readers "needing" to use Europe as a point of comparison in this text on Africa; Zrinka Stahuljak shows that although Froissart, the chronicler of the Hundred Years War, may insist on his neutrality, there are underlying aspects that call this position into question—among others, his decision to translate certain English accounts of the war and leave others in original French; finally, Dolores Buttry's close analysis of Wace's translation of the *Historia Regum Britanniae* shows that the translator imposes his own personal principles in refusing to pander to the new audience of Norman nobles wishing to be flattered and entertained. His personal concerns conflict with the political context, however, and lead to hostility at the hands of his patron and demotion.

While the translator's personal agenda is an important topos in this collection of work, the passage of time and the movement of a text from one order of thought to another is shown to be equally important for understanding the changes a text undergoes in translation. Philip Hendrick argues that Montaigne's version of Sebond adapts the certainties of scholasticism to a view of faith as "unfathomable mystery" and is an implicit plea for tolerance at a time of raging religious wars.

Similarly, Kenneth Lloyd-Jones points to Erasmus' rejection of Ciceronian style as being at least partially motivated by moral questions that became urgent in the face of religious strife—the esthetic demands of Ciceronian Latin could not do justice to the moral message of Christian Latin. In another vein, David A. Lopez' article on Alfred's translation of Boethius' *Consolation of Philosophy* shows how the passage of time and the movement of the text through time have erased the text's original political point. The work is no longer current as a political document but has become universalized in the translation.

Translation in the more metaphorical sense of adapting older materials to a new context is discussed in Adam McKeown's work on *Titus Andronicus*. Specifically, Shakespeare's juxtaposition of "sweet words and bloody images" is viewed as an attempt by Elizabethan society to come to terms with a foreign (Latin) element. This coming to terms is, however, consistently hampered by mis-translation, as Elizabethan audiences translate the Latin *pietas* as English "piety." Referring to the teaching and translation practices of Elizabethan schoolmasters, McKeown clearly anchors his analysis of the problematic adaptation of the story of Titus Andronicus to the Elizabethan stage in the cultural context of the time.

Throughout this volume of texts, then, translation is treated as a form of writing, the production of texts carried out in a certain cultural and political ambiance, and for identifiable, though not always stated, reasons. Further, every translator acts as an individual within this ambiance and may incorporate personal views, a personal agenda, in the treatment of the text. No translation is an innocent, transparent rendering of the original. Every translation reveals aspects of its context and invites the study of this transfer of materials over time and place, and from one order of thought or one system to another.

Notes

1. See Hermans citing Even-Zohar (1985, 11).
2. Many recent publications attest to the vitality of the field. See Snell-Hornby (1986); Brisset (1990); Lefevre (1992); Venuti (1992); Berman (1995); Simon (1996); von Flotow (1997); Bassnett and Trivedi (1999).
3. Here, Evans cites Lefevre (1992).

Works Cited

Bassnett, Susan, and Harish Trivedi, eds. *Post-colonial Translation*. London and New York: Routledge, 1999.

Berman, Antoine. *Pour une critique des traducteurs: John Donne*. Paris: Gallimard, 1995.

Brisset, Annie. *Sociocritique de la traduction*. Ed. du Préambule. Quebec, 1990.

Chance, Jane. "Gender Subversion and Linguistic Castration in Fifteenth-Century English Translations of Christine de Pizan." In *Violence Against Women in Medieval Texts*. Ed. Anna Roberts. Gainesville: University of Florida Press, 1998.

Copeland, Rita. *Rhetoric, Hermeneutics and Translation in the Middle Ages: Academic Traditions and Vernacular Texts*. Cambridge: Cambridge University Press, 1991.

Evans, Ruth. "Translating Past Cultures." In *The Medieval Translator IV*. Ed. Roger Ellis and Ruth Evans. Exeter: University of Exeter Press, 1994.

Even-Zohar, Itamar. *The Manipulation of Literature. Studies in Literary Translation*. Ed. Theo Hermans. London and Sydney: Croom Helm, 1985.

Flotow, Luise von. *Translation and Gender. Translating in the "Era of Feminism."* Manchester: St. Jerome Publishing; Ottawa: University of Ottawa Press, 1997.

Hannay, Margaret P. *Silent but for the Word: Tudor Women as Patrons, Translators, and Writers of Religious Works*. Kent, Ohio: Kent State University Press, 1985.

Lefevre, André. *Translation, Rewriting and the Manipulation of Literary Fame*. London and New York: Routledge, 1992.

—. *Translation/History/Culture*. London and New York: Routledge, 1992.

Simon, Sherry. *Gender in Translation. Cultural Identity and the Politics of Transmission*. London and New York: Routledge, 1996.

Snell-Hornby, Mary. *Übersetzungswissenschaft—Eine Neuorientierung (Zur Integration von Theorie und Praxis)*. Tübingen: UTB, Francke Verlag, 1986.

Venuti, Lawrence, ed. *Rethinking Translation. Discourse, Subjectivity, Ideology*. London and New York: Routledge, 1992.

Wogan-Browne, Jocelyn. "Wreaths of Thyme: The Female Translator in Anglo-Norman Hagiography." In *The Medieval Translator IV*. Ed. Roger Ellis and Ruth Evans. Exeter: University of Exeter Press, 1994.

—. "The Notion of Vernacular Theory." In *The Idea of the Vernacular. An Anthology of Middle English Literary Theory*. Ed. Jocelyn Wogan-Browne et al. University Park, Pa.: Pennsylvania State University Press, 1999.

Introduction: The Middle Ages

Renate Blumenfeld-Kosinski
University of Pittsburgh

How far back should we go to speak of medieval translation? When were writers first aware of the specific problems presented by a society using a learned language—Latin—as well as a number of vernaculars? One could start with Saint Jerome, who already in the fourth century in his translations from Greek to Latin addressed one of the major points of contention for the medieval—or, for that matter, any—translator: whether a translation should be faithful to the letter of the original text or to its sense. While he translated the Bible as accurately, or word for word, as he could, he argued that non-biblical texts should be translated "non verbum e verbo, sed sensum exprimere de sensu" [not word for word, but according to the sense] (Pratt 1991, 3). For medieval scholars, this problem of faithful translation took shape slowly because most of the early translations from Latin into various vernacular languages were adaptations, recasting the original text or even combining it with others. Some of these adaptations were almost indistinguishable from other exercises within the *trivium,* such as "commentary, amplification, or paraphrase" (Buridant 1983, 95). One of the earliest terms used to designate translation was *transferre,* evoking the Greek *metafero.*[1] In Old French, *translater* appears in early Bible translations. Other common expressions are *mettre* or *torner en romanz, espondre en romans* (harking back to the idea of explanation or commentary), or *transporter/transposer/traire du latin en romans* (evoking the idea of [cultural] movement). Certainly, the early methods of—and terms for—translation were as varied as the motivations behind it.

Charlemagne, with whom Claude Buridant begins his important study of medieval translation, saw the Christianization of the entire empire and the surrounding areas as one of the important points on his political agenda. Many of the translation projects he initiated and commissioned were tied to this desire of spreading the Christian message to those only capable of understanding the vernacular (1983, 85). The activities at the abbeys of Reichenau and St. Gall thus made available texts for the edification of relatively uneducated people and at the same time restored Latin to a level consonant with the rebirth of classical ideals in the Carolingian Renaissance. As W. D. Elcock observes, "The real restoration of literary Latin was brought about through the personal interest and energy of Charlemagne" (1975, 337). It was thus one powerful ruler who initiated two important cultural developments: a commitment to translation into the vernacular coupled with a concern for the quality of Latin, which distanced the written Latin of the Church and schools further and further from the spoken Vulgar Latin of the earliest Middle Ages. These two activities, then, contributed to the widening gap between learned Latin and the vernaculars of the many regions of the Carolingian empire, making translations ever more necessary. Two generations after Charlemagne, the Strassburg Oaths, sworn between two of the emperor's grandsons (Charles the Bald and Louis the German) against the third (Lothaire) in 842, bear testimony to the importance of translation, this time in a distinctly political context: The trilingual oaths were supposed to ensure that each party promised to uphold the same principles in their alliance against Lothaire. And because the soldiers themselves were required to swear the oaths (they are the *christianes folches* and *christian poblo* in the German and French versions), the use of the vernacular was of the utmost political importance.[2]

Another ruler, Alfred the Great in the ninth century, was responsible for commissioning and executing a series of important translations into Old English. At the other end of our period, we find an important group of translators in fourteenth- and fifteenth-century France working on explicit orders of their rulers, Charles V and Charles VI. Given this commitment on the part of various monarchs to translations into the vernacular, we must pose the question of the political aspects of these enterprises: What could be the ideological underpinnings of these cultural activities? How could translations be politically useful?

Two of the areas where medieval monarchs and aristocrats found useful material in ancient Latin texts were the establishment of the legitimacy of their rule (especially in the case of new dynasties taking over) and precepts for government and kingly virtue. Thus Alfred the Great, the subject of David A. Lopez' essay in this volume, supported an extensive educational reform program of which a crucial part was translations of such texts that were "needful for all men to know," such as Pope Gregory's late-sixth-century *Pastoral Care* and the *Dialogues.* The meditations on human tyranny and divine rule that Alfred emphasizes in his translation of Boethius' *Consolation of Philosophy* were certainly apt for the troubled times of his own rule. The transposition from the time of Theoderic to his own necessitated certain changes, but the basic questions were shown to be as crucial for a ninth-century king in England as they were for the sixth-century philosopher imprisoned in Pavia.

The first wave of translations into Old French (specifically Anglo-Norman) appears in the second half of the twelfth century, probably at the instigation of Henry II, who established the Angevin dynasty in England in 1154. The romances of antiquity, the anonymous *Roman de Thèbes,* the *Roman d'Enéas* and the *Roman de Troie* (by Benoît de Sainte-Maure), are adaptations of Vergil's *Aeneid,* Statius' *Thebaid* and the late antique accounts of the Trojan War by Dares and Dictys respectively.[3] The oldest of these texts, the *Roman de Thèbes,* with its stark depiction of parricide and fratricidal war, could function as a warning against the kind of disorders that preceded the accession of Henry II and persisted under his rule in the form of various rebellions fomented by his sons. Interestingly, one can see different messages adapted to the political circumstances of the different periods in Henry's reign and beyond in the various versions of the *Thèbes.*[4] The prose version appears as part of the vast *Histoire ancienne jusqu'à César,* commissioned by Roger IV, castellan of Lille, in early-thirteenth-century Flanders. This text "conceived of the classical past as a vast prologue to the history of Flanders" and helped to assure the self-definition and shape the political identity of the nobility of that region vis-à-vis the powerful French king Philip Augustus.[5] Classical history in the vernacular was now accessible to the non-clerical educated classes and was "intimately tied to issues of political power and authority" (Spiegel 1993, 117).

The *Roman d'Enéas* and the *Roman de Troie* fit into the political program of Henry II in that they glorify the founding of an empire and illustrate the spread of civilization eastward, a phenomenon encap-sulated in the myth of *translatio studii.* One of the historians working for Henry II was Wace, who in 1155 translated Geoffrey of Mon-mouth's *Historia Regum Britanniae* into Anglo-Norman.[6] The *Roman de Brut,* similarly the romances of antiquity—though not based on a classical source—fit into the political preoccupations of Henry II's new reign. The travels of Aeneas' grandson Brutus ended in Britain, which can thus lay claim to illustrious ancestry. David Rollo has recently explored the intimate relationship between claims to legitimacy and vernacular translation in this period (Rollo 1998). He highlights the subversiveness of some of the efforts of Wace and later of Benoît de Sainte-Maure—not necessarily perceived by their patron! In some instances the translator may undercut the ostensible celebration of his patron's lineage and claim to the new land; in others, he may simply introduce a shift in emphasis. Thus Geoffrey of Monmouth, writing just one generation before Wace, had subscribed to different ideological aspects of wars of conquest than did Wace. In her subtle reading of the changes wrought by Wace in his translation, Dolores Buttry shows in this volume that a new spirit of compassion and comprehension of people's suffering in these kinds of wars characterizes Wace's *Roman de Brut*.

On the one hand, these texts are meant to celebrate the heroism of invaders and the new "Britishness" of Henry II: The *Roman de Brut* "couched in a language limited to the francophone masters of the land,...at once marginalizes the Anglo-Saxons to irrelevance and makes the glories of the past the sole possession of one ethnicity," that of the Continental invaders (Rollo 1998, 21). But Wace also undermines this message by showing that the king is, in fact, an alien in his new country, which is confirmed by his and his entourage's French language. The "true" language of Britain is, according to Wace, a kind of Grecian dialect derived from the language of the long-ago Trojan settlers (Rollo 1998, 147). This problem of linguistic identity persisted into the fourteenth century and played a role in the Hundred Years War.

It was in the late thirteenth and fourteenth centuries that a new and important wave of translations appeared in France, where concerns for legitimate rulership and kingly virtue came to the fore in the translations made in the reign of Philippe le Bel (d. 1314). Paul Chavy underlines the political nature of the king's translation projects: "Le roi Philippe le Bel encourage systématiquement la vulgarisation par dessein politique, pour dépouiller un peu plus les clercs de leur privilèges" (1974, 559). On the other hand, it was, of course, the clerks who would undertake the translation projects in the first place. For the first time, we see "true translations and not adaptations"[7]—though not yet of the accuracy of the later fourteenth century—of Cicero's *Rhetorica ad Herennium*, some of Seneca's letters and parts of Livy. The translator of Cicero, a certain Johan d'Antioche, explained that he did not wish to alter much of Cicero's text for this would be "vice de presumpcion et d'orgueil" [a vice of presumption and pride]. But since each language has its own characteristics, sometimes the translator had to add something because of the "grant oscurté" [great obscurity] of the base text.[8] Jean de Meun, translating *Boethius* for Philippe le Bel, also meditated on his method. He asks his audience for forgiveness if he added or subtracted words or sentences:

Car se je eusse espons mot a mot le latin par le françois, li livres en fust trop occurs aus gens lais et li clers, neis moiennement letré, ne peussent pas legierement entendre le latin par le françois.

[For if I had rendered the Latin word for word in French, the book would be too obscure for laypeople, and the clerks, even though they are quite learned, could not easily understand what the Latin says through the French].[9]

Rita Copeland argues persuasively that Jean's insistence on his royal patron's title "roy des François" highlights the conjunction of *translatio studii* and *translatio imperii* and thus demonstrates that "the intellectual superiority of the French could translate into formidable political intelligence" (1991, 135). The translation into French, in fact, signals nothing less than "the transfer of ancient learning from clergy to court" (Copeland 1991, 135). Thus beginning with Philippe III (d. 1285) and continuing under Philippe le Bel and Jean le Bon (d. 1356) "se dégage une sorte de politique culturelle" (Lusignan 1987, 140), which targets texts for translation that were important to the perfection of the monarchic system, such as Giles of Rome's *De regimine principum.* The exemplarity of Roman history could now be exploited by educated laypeople. Thus, "the most important secular translation commissioned by [Jean le Bon] was Pierre Bersuire's French version of Livy's *History of Rome*" (Sherman 1995, 4), a translation that, together with Simon de Hesdin's 1375 translation of *Valerius Maximus*, would provide a treasure trove of moral and political exemplars to later writers such as Christine de Pizan (d. ca. 1430).

Under Charles V (d. 1380) we find the greatest activity of translation and, as a consequence, a great enrichment of the French vocabulary, including a large number of political terms (Brucker 1997, 73). In prefaces and glosses the translators reflected to varying degrees on their labors, establishing important criteria for modern views of translation. Indeed, as Charles Brucker (1997) has shown, a whole typology of approaches to translation—from literal transposition to free adaptation—can be derived from this material. The translators also provided, as Serge Lusignan argues, "un support idéologique" for the king's political and cultural aspirations (1987, 134). Nicole Oresme, one of the brilliant scholars employed by Charles V, insisted in his preface to the translation of Aristotle's *Ethics* that if past princes and their councilors had heeded Aristotle's lessons, their kingdoms would have lasted longer and done better (Lusignan 1987, 135). But so that rulers can indeed profit from these texts, they must be available in their vernacular. This transmission of learning is an obligation the translator has to carry out. He must translate these useful books "en françois et baillier en françois les arts et les sciences" (into French and make available the arts and sciences in French) (Sherman 1995, 9).

Oresme's important translation of Aristotle's *Politics*, whose manuscripts Claire Richter Sherman studies in her beautiful volume, forged a new political vocabulary. This phenomenon can be observed already in the translations of Brunetto Latini (d. 1294), whose encyclopedic work *Le Trésor* (written in French) owes much to Eustratius' commentary on Aristotle's *Nichomachian Ethics*. He also translated Cicero's *Rhetoric* into Italian and, as Cristiana Fordyce shows in her essay for this volume, adapted some of the political terminology to the conditions of his own time, for example, translating *respublica* as *comune* and "reversing the Aristotelian forms of perfect government."

It was, in fact, typical for medieval Italian translators to place more emphasis than French translators on works that could serve as models for rhetoric and poetic language (Monfrin 1963, 185). The great Roman historians such as Sallust, Livy, Valerius Maximus, Lucan and Suetonius were translated into Italian mostly in the fourteenth century, as were moral works such as Cicero's *De senectute* and Aristotle's *Ethics*, and the key work for an understanding of medieval dream visions and allegory, Macrobius' *Commentary on the Dream of Scipio.* But in addition we find translations of works that we do not find in France, mostly important rhetorical treatises, including, for example, the pseudo-Quintilian's *Declamations* (Monfrin 1963, 186).

All these translations, as were those in France, were prepared for specific noble patrons. The wisdom of rulers is both enhanced and demonstrated by their commissions of translations. But, interestingly, as Lusignan observes of these royally supported translations, "aucune proposition universelle ne vient en justifier l'entreprise" (1987, 151). The passages, mostly in prefaces, reflecting on the mechanics and philosophy of translation limit themselves to a particular work, translator and patron (1987, 151). This is not to say, however, that there was no general and public consciousness of the importance of different languages and translation.

This consciousness was expressed particularly forcefully early in the Hundred Years War. Froissart describes an ordinance proclaimed by the English King Edward III that stipulated that all lords, barons, knights and "honnestes hommes de bonnes villes mesissent cure et dilligence de estruire et aprendre leurs enfans la langhe françoise par quoy il en fuissent plus able et plus coustummier ens leur gherres" [honest burghers should diligently have their children instructed in and taught the French language so that they would get used to it and would be more capable in their wars].[10] A French-speaking army would presumably be more likely to beat the French on their home turf.

Froissart himself wrote, of course, in French, which he saw as a kind of universal language that might transcend the national divisions more and more visible during the Hundred Years War. He considered himself a fairly neutral reporter of what he saw in his travels and what was reported to him by reliable witnesses. Yet, as Zrinka Stahuljak observes in this volume, Froissart never guarantees the accuracy of the translations of the testimonies given to him by speakers of other languages: "Froissart's silence on the issue of linguistic translation can be attributed...to [a] feeling of loss of unity, cultural and linguistic." Thus French can no longer lay claim to being a universal and neutral language, and Froissart's "apprenticeship of neutrality" is doomed. The mere fact of Froissart's writing in French—as was the case for Wace in twelfth-century England—stakes out an ideological position.

Returning to the linguistic ability of the English, we can observe that there is more to it than a capacity to vanquish the French while speaking their language. In his translation of Aristotle's *Politics*, Oresme adds an important criterion to the definition of political unity: language. Indeed, it is unnatural for a people to have a ruler who does not speak their language: "Et pour ce est ce une chose aussi comme hors de nature que un homme regne sus gent qui n'entendent son maternel langage... L'en ne doit pas avoir roy d'estrange nation" [And it is thus unnatural that a man should govern a people who does not understand his mother tongue. One should not have a king from a strange nation].[11] The linguistic aspect thus feeds into new definitions of national identity fostered by the Hundred Years War. Edward's claim to the French throne could be refuted because he could never be a "natural" ruler of the French.[12]

Thus the English wanted to preserve their mastery of French for political reasons, but at the same time they felt themselves to be under linguistic attack. In 1377, Chancellor Robert Ashton

> reminded members [of Parliament] that the French were once again preparing for war. With the Spaniards, Scots, and other enemies the French "make us surrounded on all sides so that [they] can destroy our lord the king and his realm of England, and *drive out the English language*." This repeats Edward III's speech to the Commons, where he claimed that the French King Philip was resolved to destroy the English language and to occupy England.[13]

Was the war one for linguistic supremacy? Given the rather sparse production of texts in English before the fourteenth century, this anxiety seems somewhat curious. In fact, this period was propitious for translations from the French. In light of Ashton's remarks, one could see translation as a politically charged but peaceful—and socially more inclusive—activity. Among the texts translated at this time were chivalric romances meant for a French aristocratic audience; they now reached a lower social class and the translations were modified accordingly (Coleman 1981, 41). Book ownership also became somewhat more democratic, and a layman could very well own several books. Janet Coleman cites the 1388 inventory of Simon de Burley, who

> possessed nine French romances and only one (now unknown) book in English..., one [work] on the government of kings and princes which was, most likely a French translation of Giles of Rome's *De Regimine Principum*, a battered unnamed book of philosophy, a French translation by the twelfth-century Peter Comestor—the *Biblia Scholastica*—and one volume in Latin covered in black (1981, 18).

Thus Simon is typical of the educated trilingual classes of fourteenth-century England.

Given this trilingual ability in England, we have to ask whether Edward III would really have been a "roy d'estrange nation" for the French. Did he, indeed, speak no French? This is highly unlikely. But it is important to note that linguistic arguments played such an important role in the polemics of the Hundred Years War. England was also the site of another battle of language and translation: the persecution of the Lollards, based, in part, on their use of English religious texts translated from Latin. Of course, translating the Bible and other sacred texts was nothing new in Europe. We saw that this had begun already under Charlemagne and Alfred the Great, who supported translations of and helped disseminate religious texts in the vernacular. In France, the thirteenth century saw a number of Bible translations.[14] In England and Germany as well, there were plenty of translations and adaptations of the various books of the Bible. Two extremely pious men of the thirteenth and fourteenth centuries bear witness to the desirability of the use of the vernacular in devotion. Gautier de Coincy (d. 1236), the ardent admirer of the Virgin Mary and collector of her miracles, justifies his translation of Latin *miracula* by insisting that he wants to make accessible to ladies and to those ignorant of the *lettre* the marvelous deeds of the Virgin. Had these accounts remained confined to Latin, they would have been "enseveli" [buried] and thus useless for lay devotion (Gros 1998, 78-79). And Philippe de Mézières explains his use of French in *Le Livre de la vertu du sacrement de mariage* (1385-89) by claiming that even Saint Paul prayed to God "en son langage vulgar a et maternel" [in his vernacular mother tongue] (1993, 393). Therefore "combien que le latin soit le plus beau langage du monde...toutefois chascune creature naturelment s'entent mieulx en son propre langage que en autre quelconque langage forainement acquis" [although Latin is the most beautiful language in the world, people naturally understand things better in their own language than in another that they acquired elsewhere] (1993, 393). This is why Philippe offers prayers to the Virgin in French. Note that Philippe, a great polemicist of the Hundred Years War, also uses the argument of "nature" in his plea for a vernacular religious language. The use of vernacular translations was thus not only acceptable, but desirable in lay devotion.

In England, it was not the use of a vernacular Bible that got the Lollards into trouble, but rather the fact that the lower classes (and women!) now had direct access to the Scriptures. It was feared that this access would "foster sedition" (Coleman 1981, 209) because it would lead to well-founded criticism of existing power structures. But there was no going back to the exclusive use of Latin. Rather it was a question of rescuing the use of the vernacular from the heretics. This is what the fifteenth-century Bishop Pecock of Chichester hoped to accomplish with his vernacularization of scholastic theology. While he believed that laypeople were capable of following a rather demanding course of study in order to understand complex problems of theology, he did not recommend that a layman should do so without proper guidance—a position thoroughly misunderstood by his critics, as Andrew Taylor shows in this volume.

Translation could thus never be a neutral act. Secular rulers as well as religious leaders were heavily invested in this activity, which made hitherto exclusive texts available to a much broader audience. While some groups wanted to preserve their privileges of Latin learning in order to safeguard their roles as intercessors with the divine, others succeeded in exploiting the translations of Latin texts for their own purposes: for example, laying claim to legitimate rule by inventing illustrious lineages, vouched for by the authority of the ancient text. Thus if we speak of translation, we must necessarily also speak of the politics of translation.

Notes

1. The following terminological discussion is based on Buridant (1983, 96-99).
2. For a detailed linguistic analysis of the oaths, see Elcock (1975, 346-56).
3. See Schöning (1991) on these texts (with an extensive bibliography).

4. On these questions, see Blumenfeld-Kosinski (1984).
5. See Spiegel (1993, 116).
6. On Geoffrey, see Hanning (1966, chap. 5) and Rollo (1998, chap. 3). See also Blacker (1994).
7. Monfrin (1963, 168). See also Monfrin (1964).
8. Monfrin (1963, 169). See also Lusignan (1987, 143-45) for an analysis of Johan d'Antioche's methods. At one point d'Antioche invites his critics to see if they can do better than he—advice one would like to give some book reviewers of translations.
9. Quoted by Copeland (1991, 133). The translation is my own. Copeland's translation "the clerks, who are no less lettered" (than the lay readers?) seems to contain a *contresens*.
10. Quoted by Lusignan (1987, 107).
11. Quoted by Lusignan (1987, 109).
12. On the concept of nature in the political thought of the period, see Krynen (1982).
13. Coleman (1981, 52). Coleman's emphasis.
14. See Berger (1884).

Works Cited

Berger, Samuel. *La Bible française au moyen âge: Etude sur les plus anciennes versions de la Bible écrites en prose de langue d'Oil*. Paris: Imprimerie Nationale, 1884.

Blacker, Jean. *The Faces of Time: Portrayal of the Past in Old French and Latin Historical Narrative of the Anglo-Norman Regnum*. Austin: University of Texas Press, 1994.

Blumenfeld-Kosinski, Renate. "The Earliest Developments of the French Novel: The *Roman de Thèbes* in Verse and Prose." In *The French Novel. Theory and Practice*. French Literature Series 10 (1984): 1-10.

Brucker, Charles. "Pour une typologie des traductions en France au XIVe siècle." In *Traduction et adaptation en France à la fin du moyen âge et à la Renaissance*, ed. Charles Brucker, 63-79. Paris: Champion, 1997.

Buridant, Claude. "Translatio medievalis. Théorie et pratique de la traduction médiévale." *Travaux de linguistique et de littérature* 21 (1983): 81-136.

Chavy, Paul. "Les premiers translateurs français." *French Review* 47 (1974): 3, 557-65.

Coleman, Janet. *Medieval Readers and Writers, 1350-1400*. New York: Columbia University Press, 1981.

Copeland, Rita. *Rhetoric, Hermeneutics, and Translation in the Middle Ages: Academic Traditions and Vernacular Texts*. Cambridge: Cambridge University Press, 1991.

Elcock, W. D. *The Romance Languages*. 2nd rev. ed. London: Faber and Faber, 1975.

Gros, Gerard. "'Por ses myracles biau rimer...': Etude sur le projet hagiographique de Gautier de Coinci." *Revue des sciences humaines* 251 (1998): 72-87.

Hanning, Robert. *The Vision of History in Early Britain: From Gildas to Geoffrey of Monmouth*. New York: Columbia University Press, 1966.

Krynen, Jacques. "'Naturel.' Essai sur l'argument de la nature dans la pensée politique française à la fin du Moyen Age." *Journal des savants* (avril-juin 1982): 169-90.

Lusignan, Serge. *Parler vulgairement: Les Intellectuels et la langue française aux XIIIe et XIVe siècles*. 2nd ed. Paris: Vrin, 1987.

Monfrin, Jacques. "Humanisme et traductions au moyen âge." *Journal des savants* (1963): 161-90.

—. "Traducteurs et leur public en France au moyen âge." In *L'Humanisme médiéval dans les littératures romanes du XIIe au XIVe siècle*, ed. Anthime Fourrier, 247-64. Paris: Klincksieck, 1964.

Philippe de Mézières. *Le Livre de la vertu du sacrement de mariage*. Ed. Joan B. Williamson. Washington: Catholic University of America Press, 1993.

Pratt, Karen. "Medieval Attitudes to Translation and Adaptation: The Rhetorical Theory and the Poetic Practice." In *The Medieval Translator II*, ed. Roger Ellis, 1-27. London: Center for Medieval Studies, Queen Mary and Westfield College, 1991.

Rollo, David. *Historical Fabrication, Ethnic Fable and French Romance in Twelfth-Century England*. Nicholasville, Ky.: French Forum Publishers, 1998.

Schöning, Udo. *Thebenroman – Eneasroman – Trojaroman: Studien zur Rezeption der Antike in der französischen Literatur des 12. Jahrhunderts*. Tübingen: Niemeyer, 1991.

Sherman, Claire Richter. *Imaging Aristotle: Verbal and Visual Representation in Fourteenth-Century France*. Berkeley and Los Angeles: University of California Press, 1995.

Spiegel, Gabrielle. *Romancing the Past: The Rise of Vernacular Prose Historiography in Thirteenth-Century France*. Berkeley; Los Angeles; London: University of California Press, 1993.

Introduction: The Renaissance

Daniel Russell
University of Pittsburgh

Translation during the Renaissance was an extremely important activity, but it was an activity much different from translation as we understand it today. As in ancient Rome, the goal of the translation was not to replicate, with as much reproductive accuracy as possible, the original text and the intent with which the author had produced it. On the contrary, the goal was usually to appropriate the text being translated for the needs of the target culture, and sometimes this goal was aggressively expressed in military metaphors (Friedrich 1992, passim; Heidegger 1975, 23). This activity of appropriation was best expressed, however, in the term *translatio*, which did not necessarily mean "translation" but the transfer of a text, a tradition or a right from one society or culture to another. In fact, as we see in Oumelbanine Zhiri's study of Leo Africanus' *Description of Africa* (1550), *translatio* did not even need to involve translation in the modern sense at all: It could remain at the level of editorial intervention.[1]

Zhiri studies G. B. Ramusio's edited version of Leo's geographical and historical account to demonstrate how the act of *translatio* could have far-reaching political and cultural consequences. In this case, the political aim was, at least implicitly, or perhaps even subconsciously, to reaffirm European cultural hegemony. It also made Leo's text more familiar, and hence acceptable, to its target audience by accommodating it to the cultural habits of the intended audience at that time; this was another aim of much Renaissance translation. In cases like this one, editorial practice erased the anomalies of foreign cultures until such a time as philology finally made this rather cavalier practice intellectually unacceptable. Then, theories of cultural relativity had to be developed to account for such discrepancies; a primitive stage in this process is evident in Montaigne's essay "Des cannibales," and it reaches full maturity in eighteenth-century relativism.

The techniques and political implications of such "editing" or "intralingual translating" were perfectly clear to Renaissance humanists, as Kenneth Lloyd-Jones demonstrates in his discussion of Erasmus' exercise in his dialogue known as the *Ciceronianus* of "translating" a religious text from "Christian" Latin to the "Ciceronian" Latin of Nosoponus. The exercise, as Lloyd-Jones shows, turns a Christian text into a pagan one, and in Erasmus' times this was a dangerous political act, as Etienne Dolet, one of Erasmus' Ciceronian opponents, was soon to discover. And Dolet, for one, must have used the practice in an aggressively self-conscious way.

Such appropriation continued unabated from antiquity to the Renaissance, and its implications, as Erasmus' text reveals, were often religious and thus had far-reaching political implications. Vergil's fourth eclogue is a case in point. As Edwin D. Floyd shows so interestingly, the process by which later Christians saw and understood this text as a prophecy of the coming of Christ probably began in late antiquity with interpretations like the Greek translation that Floyd discusses. Translation was absolutely essential in determining the way a text was received, and translations like this one suggest why Vergil's eclogue was viewed in the Renaissance as a text to be revered, used as a text for divination, and, finally, one to be parodied as such by Rabelais (*Tiers Livre*, chaps. 10-12). Sometimes, as with Montaigne's translation of Raimond Sebond's *Theologia Naturalis*, the translation edited out theological points and positions no longer acceptable to an audience whose view of the Christian world had changed since its composition some two hundred years earlier in a somewhat different culture. This is the kind of work that Philip Hendrick and Edward Tilson highlight in their complementary studies of Montaigne's translation of this work that is so central to our understanding the longest and one of the most important chapters in his *Essais*.

Ramusio's modifications to his edited version of Leo's text, or, indeed, the changes in any other text submitted to the same process, bring to light two problems that determined the way translation was understood, and the purposes to which it was put, in the Renaissance. First, it is clear that the author did not, in this system, possess the kind of authority that he or she would have in the post-Romantic world of the nineteenth and twentieth centuries. Hence, translators obviously felt it less imperative to attempt to replicate the style and intentions of the author in the "translated" text. In any case, doing so would often have been next to impossible, as translators attempted to turn texts from a sophisticated and "copious" Latin into a French or any other vernacular that was lacking the vocabulary and refined and polished stylistic techniques necessary to make that kind of translation possible. Indeed, translations like Barthélemy Aneau's literal version of Alciato's emblems (1549) were quite daring experiments intended to show that

French could possess the clarity, precision and brevity of Latin (Norton 1984, 115-22). To attain these linguistic goals in French, the Pléiade poet Joachim Du Bellay advised aspiring poets in his *Deffence et illustration de la langue francaise* (1549) to use translation as a means of enlarging the vocabulary and developing the stylistic suppleness of French. There is nothing new here: Not only does this advice echo Aneau, it also echoes one of the reasons Wolfgang Hunger undertook the German translation of Alciato's emblems, which Chretien Wechel published in 1542. Not only did such exercises contribute to broadening the semantic and stylistic dimensions of a vernacular language, but they also played into the cultural politics of societies competing for the mantle of successor to the great classical civilizations of antiquity.

The second problem this work highlights is the paradox that lies at the heart of the very act of translation. On the one hand, translation transfers a text, not only from a foreign language, but also from a foreign culture, into the target language and culture. This difference makes translation necessary and impossible at the same time. Hence, Ramusio's editing betrays Leo's text while making it more accessible to the target audience of educated, or at least literate, Europeans. Translation, as Roman Jakobson claimed (149), following Franz Boas, has no difficulty transferring what one language *may* say into another, but only with what it *must* say. As a result, the translation is always a different work from the original.

Translation in the Renaissance was also made more problematic by the lack of agreement over what words meant. There was, in short, no single accepted "dictionary" for sixteenth-century French. Until the early seventeenth century, the only available lexicons were works like John Palsgrave's *Esclaircissements de la langue francoyse* (1530), Robert Estienne's French/Latin and Latin/French dictionaries of 1538/39 and Maurice de La Porte's *Les Epithètes* of 1571. Hence, each translation was something of a personal reading of the text being translated, and it often ranged far from the style and intent of the original. Sometimes, such "translations" produced masterpieces like Du Bellay's famous sonnet "Si nostre vie est moins qu'une journée" (1, 122), in the second edition of *L'Olive* (1550), his first sonnet sequence; it is often considered a mere translation of a sonnet by Bernardino Daniello—but what a difference!

Sometimes, as with Amyot's Plutarch, still in print in a Gallimard Pléiade edition, such translations were so highly successful at integrating the text into the target culture that they produced a canonical version, the vulgate, so to speak, of an ancient classic for centuries to come. Vulgates, and what I have come to think of as the "vulgate effect," are what integrate foreign texts into the target culture. Vulgates capture the spirit of the original and combine it with the spirit of the target culture in such a way that it is a new work. As such, they reinforce the prevailing ideology of the target culture by annexing to it a treasure from another culture and thus advance the political agenda of a ruling class at home. A famous example from the Renaissance would be, I think, the King James Bible, long the "vulgate" of English-speaking people.

How did translation work in practice in the French Renaissance? An interesting and revealing scenario may be found in Pierre de Ronsard's delicate little *chanson* "Le Printemps n'a point tant de fleurs," from his *Nouvelle Continuation des Amours* of 1556. Editors usually label this charming poem a paraphrase of one of Marullus' neo-Latin epigrams. Marullus, in turn, had borrowed the conceit from Ovid (*Ars amatoria*, 2, 519ff). In a series of lines structured in a pattern of anaphoric and isocolonic repetition, the poem claims that nature and a variety of well-known places do not possess as much of the produce that helps to characterize them "Que je porte au cueur, ma maitresse,/Pour vous de peine et de detresse." Following Marullus, Ronsard writes in his original version:

> Ni la mer n'a tant de poissons,
> Ni la Secile de moissons,
> Ni l'Afrique n'a tant d'arennes,
> Ni le mont d'Ide de fonteines…(7, 249-50)

Marullus' Italian setting remains intact here, but a year later Ronsard changed "Secile" into "Beauce," "l'Afrique" into "Bretaigne" and "le mont d'Ide" into "Auvergne," as he progressively adapted his text in subsequent editions to another place and another culture.

Like any poet, Ronsard was adapting his material to the cultural setting of an audience closer to him and to his own experience. This was a common practice during the Renaissance when most people were as culturally place-bound as their medieval ancestors. But increased travel drew the attention of the more sophisticated and powerful elite to works from different cultural spheres. This produced a kind of tension, and internationally active printers responded by transporting successful works from one culture to another through the vehicle of this kind of translation. To take the example of two emblem books by Guillaume de La Perrière and Georgette de Montenay, they both underwent considerable change in translation as they moved, one across the Channel to England and the other into German post-Reformation culture. As Mary V. Silcox has shown, when Thomas Combe "translated" La Perrière's *Theatre des bons engins* into English (ca. 1593), he was generally quite faithful to the sense and sometimes even the wording of the original. However, by substituting an English verse form, and by replacing features of French life with English details and concerns, he changed the tone and directed the work to a different, more middle-class audience interested in moral education rather than humanist learning. In a similar way, Marion Moamai has shown how an anonymous German translator changed Georgette de Montenay's *Emblemes, ov devises chrestiennes* of 1571 from a militantly Reformist work of the time of the French religious wars, and probably directed to the nobility, into a tract of conventional morality for middle-class German burghers of the first quarter of the seventeenth century, long after they thought religious disputes had largely been settled—even though the Thirty Years War was on the horizon! In both cases, publishers in tune with the cultural politics of different communities adapted the works to make them culturally "vraisemblables" in the target audience.

Cultural and political appropriation through translation was as current and common in the late European Renaissance as it had been during the Roman Empire. It clearly had its place in the schools and other didactic and pedagogical venues. It would appear that Chretien Wechel designed and published the first authorized version of Alciato's emblems to be used as a schoolbook for young students (Russell, 114). The rationale here was probably that pictures provided a "translated" version of the text, but Wechel quickly began to publish bilingual editions, French and Latin, or German and Latin, to make it even easier to read Alciato's model epigrams. When Wolfgang Hunger published his German translation in 1542, he claimed in his (Latin) preface that he was interested, in the first instance, in improving his own written German style.

When Barthélemy Aneau published his translation of Alciato's emblems, the second in less than fifteen years, he had some very specific aims. In his dedicatory epistle he counsels the young Scottish nobleman to whom he dedicates his work to use the bilingual edition to help him improve his no doubt shaky command of French. But the boy would have had a hard time trying to compare any two versions. While Aneau did try to follow the Latin closely, most "translations" of the emblems are homely paraphrases at best. Du Bellay may have counseled translation as a way of enriching the vocabulary of French, but equivalences were not easy to find. The "illusion of interchangeability," as Glyn P. Norton puts it, caused all sorts of problems of the kind Adam

McKeown studies in the transfer of the word *pietas* to "piety" and "pity" in *Titus Andronicus*. The result was often the kind of confusion we find here, but in other instances, a new word was created that ultimately enriched the vernacular.

In the end there was no translation in Renaissance Europe that would meet modern standards of "interchangeability," nor was there often much effort to produce one. Generally, any "literal" translation was made simply to show that the vernacular was capable of the concision and precision of Latin, that is, that the vernacular was just as good as the standard with which it was being compared. It would appear that the reason for this approach to translation lies in the conception of the author in the pre-modern, or early modern, period. The author in those times did not have the originating authority that he or she came to have in the post-Romantic period. The *auctor* was a mere name attached to a text and drew his or her authority only from the text; the name implied no specific intention and left the work open to appropriation for other localized needs in other cultures.

Notes

1. This would amount to what Roman Jakobson has characterized as "intralingual" translation as opposed to "interlingual" translation or what we ordinarily think of when we use the term.

Works Cited

Drysdall, Dennis L. "Defence and Illustration of the German Language: Wolfgang Hunger's Preface to Alciati's *Emblems* (text and translation)." *Emblematica* 3, 1 (1998): 137-60.

Du Bellay, Joachim. *Oeuvres poétiques*. Ed. Henri Chamard. Vol. 1: New edition by Yvonne Bellenger. Paris: Nizet, 1982.

Erasmus, Desiderius. *The Ciceronian: A Dialogue on the Ideal Latin Style*. Trans. Betty I. Knott. In *Complete Works of Erasmus*. Vol. 26. Toronto: University of Toronto Press, 1986.

Friedrich, Hugo. "On the Art of Translation." In *Theories of Translation*, ed. Rainer Schulte and John Biguenet, 11-16. Chicago: University of Chicago Press, 1992.

Heidegger, Martin. "The Origin of the Work of Art." In *Poetry, Language, Thought*, trans. Albert Hofstadter, 17-87. New York: Harper Colophon Books, 1975.

Jakobson, Roman. "On Linguistic Aspects of Translation." In *Theories of Translation*, ed. Rainer Schulte and John Biguenet, 144-51. Chicago: University of Chicago Press, 1992.

Moamai, Marion. "Dame d'honneur and Biedermann: The German Translation of Georgette de Montenay's *Emblemes, ov devises chrestiennes.*" *Emblematica* 4, 1 (1989): 39-62.

Norton, Glyn P. *The Ideology and Language of Translation in Renaissance France and Their Humanist Antecedents.* Travaux d'Humanisme et Renaissance 201. Geneva: Droz, 1984.

Ronsard, Pierre de. Oeuvres completes. Ed. Paul Laumonnier, STFM, Vol. 7. Paris: Didier, 1959.

Russell, Daniel. *Emblematic Structures in Renaissance French Culture.* Toronto: University of Toronto Press, 1995.

Silcox, Mary V. "The Translation of La Perrière's *Le Theatre des bons engins* into Combe's *The Theater of Fine Devices.*" *Emblematica* 2, 1 (1987): 61-94.

Erasmus, Dolet and the Politics of Translation[1]

Kenneth Lloyd-Jones
Trinity College

It would seem that almost anything we might say of politics can equally be said of translation, whether we have in mind the Aristotelian sense of man as a political animal, Bismarck's conviction that "Die Politik ist keine exacte Wissenschaft" [Politics is not an exact science[2]], or the praxis of politics as the art of the possible. Politics engages the interplay of power relationships, the negotiations and compromises necessary for their resolution and—ideally at least—the search for the communal goal we call polity; so does translation. The Renaissance inherited from the ancient world, along with much else, the rhetorical sense of language as a suasive means to an ideological end and thereby of translation as a political enterprise. In the hope of laying some conceptual groundwork for the essays that follow, my intention here is to focus on a seminal aspect of the question, one that serves to concretize some aspects of the humanist understanding of language, with particular regard to the nature of imitative writing and translation, and that engages us in the politics of the transmission of culture: the polemic between Erasmus and Etienne Dolet.

It was a commonplace notion in the classical world that important relationships exist between whatever we are talking about and the language we use to that end. This ancient differentiation, commonly known as the *res-verba* question, may be taken to signify the difference between "what is meant" and "what is said." In our own time, a number of writers have also looked into this distinction, but perhaps few more bleakly than Samuel Beckett or Eugène Ionesco. Whereas thinkers from the classical period through the Renaissance and beyond conceived of the *res-verba* relationship as an arrangement of deep structures underlying meaningful communication, it would sometimes appear that "saying" and "meaning" may today be regarded as all but mutually exclusive. We might recall, as an example of this disjuncture, Ionesco's

La Leçon, in which the murderous professor asks his pupil to translate into Romanian the phrase, "Les roses de ma grand-mère sont aussi jaunes que mon grand père qui était Asiatique" [The roses of my grandmother are as yellow as my grandfather who was Asian] (Ionesco 1954, 82). Innocently (and it is revelatory that for such innocence she will soon thereafter be strangled, her voice—her only medium of both saying *and* meaning—permanently silenced), the pupil asks, "Comment dit-on roses, en roumain?" [How do you say "roses" in Romanian?], and the professor replies, in an assertion that allows of no counterargument, "Mais 'roses,' voyons" [But "roses," of course]. There can be only one way to *say* "roses" (or "roses") in any language, and that is "roses" (or "roses"...), but what we mean, when we say, clearly depends on the language in which we say it. A rose by any other name might smell as sweet, but the kind of "gift" it represents depends entirely, for example, on whether the offer is made in English or in German: "A gift" can delight, but "das Gift" [poison] can kill.

It is no accident that Ionesco invokes translation here, since it is, in fact, in our efforts to replicate original meaning in fresh language (to put old *res* into new *verba*) that we are brought up against what Glyn P. Norton has called the "translative dilemma" (Norton 1984, 59). If meaning is a function of the particular language being spoken, then alteration of language surely risks alteration of meaning. This realization is not, of course, solely the discovery of our contemporaries: Cicero, in his efforts to bring over Greek philosophy into Latin, constantly struggled with the numerous problems ensuing from the fact that his target language, Latin, could not quite say (and so could not quite mean) what the Greek original could simultaneously both say and mean. One of his most far-reaching statements in this respect is in the *De optimo genere oratorum* [*On the best kind of orators*], a treatise probably meant as a preface to his translation of two Greek speeches by Aeschines and Demosthenes. These versions are no longer extant, and there is some doubt as to whether Cicero actually ever did them. However that may be, it is his statement of translative methodology that matters here:

> ...nec converti ut interpretes, sed ut orator, sententiis isdem et earum formis tamquam figuris, verbis ad nostram consuetudinem aptis. In quibus non verbum pro verbo necesse habui reddere, sed genus omne verborum vimque servavi. Non enim ea me adnumerare lectori putavi oportere, sed tamquam appendere (*De optimo genere oratorum*, 14).

> [...and I have rendered them not as a translator, but as an interpreter, with their ideas—and their forms—as well as their figures of speech—made suitable to the usages of our own language. I have not

held it necessary to render word for word, but I have conserved the general character of the words and their expressive force. In point of fact, I have not thought it my task to dole them out one by one to the reader, but rather to provide him with equivalent weight.]

The importance of this passage lies not only in Cicero's rather off-hand distinction between *interpres* and *orator*, but also in his requirement that the rhetorical features of the source text be reflected according to the rhetorical norms of the target language. It is important, however, to note that *interpres* is to be taken here as "translator" (of words) and *orator* as an "interpreter" (of meaning), i.e., one who seeks not to speak merely so as to convey, but, in fact, so as to persuade. An "*interpres*-translator" seeks to insert himself minimally into whatever it is he is carrying over from source to target, interposing himself as the most faceless go-between possible, whereas the "*orator*-interpreter" consciously fashions his version in order to convince us as to what he believes the original means. Cicero's distinction thus reflects a primary sense of obligation to the target language and *its* public, engaging Latin's own rhetorical resources and his own capacity to interpret eloquently, and a secondary sense of obligation to the Greek original as the enshrinement of authorial intent: "translation into," as it were, rather than "translation out of." Translation, once it involves anything beyond the most basic search for lexical equivalency, requires interpretation: The translator must address his personal, subjective sense of what the original means.[3] Cicero's metaphor of the original, not as a treasure that the translator doles out piece by piece, but rather as something for which he must provide "equivalent weight," is not significantly different from Walter Benjamin's celebrated notion that a translation must "[incorporate] the original's mode of signification" (Benjamin 1992, 79). The translator's business is not to convey what the original says (once he changes the *language* of the original, how can he?), but rather its "mode of signification"—the nexus of *what* it means and *how it says* what it means.

Furthermore, in defining his translation as the enterprise of an interpreter, dedicated to oratorical, persuasive effect, Cicero brings to the fore the importance of rhetoric in a manner that had major repercussions for his Renaissance successors. Thinkers like Erasmus came to recognize, in their turn, the unavoidably hermeneutic dimensions of translation and would find in the recourse to rhetoric an interpretive strategy that made of translation a form of *imitatio*, of duplicative writing, in which the rhetorical resources of the target language were factors carrying, at the very least, "equivalent weight" to those of the source text. Much of the humanist theorizing of translation sees it as an essentially rhetorical enterprise, and in this it draws its inspiration from Cicero's claim to have translated oratorically. It was not only Cicero's theoretical position, however, but also his own practice that was to prove highly instructive here—as we may see, for example, from the way (or ways, rather) in which he translated the complexity of the Greek word *logos*.[4] Sometimes *verbum* will do, sometimes *sermo*, or *dictio*, or *dictus*, or *vox* [respectively, "a word, as expressing an idea," "anything that one says," "the action of speaking," "the action of saying" and "the human voice, as the instrument of speech or other utterances"[5]]. But most pregnantly of all, in the *De Inventione*, when dealing with the *logos* that is at the root of our transformation from uncultured wild beasts into cultivators of *societas*, *civitas*, and, above all, *humanitas* ["sociableness," "civic-mindedness," "the prevalence of humane values over brutishness"], Cicero interprets it as *ratio atque oratio* [both reasoning and a saying] (*De Inventione*, 1.2). Our very humanity stems from the fact that we have been persuaded into civilization by a *logos* in which the distinction between "saying" and "meaning" is effaced in a seamless, rhetorically eloquent unity of discourse and idea. This fundamental consideration not only lay at the heart of much of the Roman sense of human society, but was to play an essential role in the deeply rooted humanist sense of community. The notion of the social and cultural importance of translation as primarily a target-driven activity was predicated on and shaped by the specificity of the community for which the interpretative activity was being undertaken—an ideal rooted in civic humanism, and one that clearly emerges from the prefaces and certifications of royal privilege appended to so many French Renaissance translations, such as Louis LeRoy's versions of Plato in the 1550s (Lloyd-Jones 1998, 25-40).

All reflection on translation requires consideration of the nature of language itself, how we apprehend and how we comprehend it, and the notion that no language has meaning until we interpret it permeates the thought of Erasmus (Rummel 1985; Hoffmann 1994). In particular, as Manfred Hoffmann has shown, Erasmus is a "rhetorical theologian" whose hermeneutic is shaped by the conviction that "the biblical text is divine speech of persuasion [which] follows rhetorical rules. Therefore, the exegete must be able to recognize the linguistic clothing of the theological content" (Hoffmann 1994, 56-57)—in other words, to distinguish the *verba* from the *res*. "Like his beloved church Fathers, Origen, Jerome and Augustine," Hoffmann continues, "Erasmus took rhetoric to be the handmaiden of theology" (Hoffmann 1994, 212). Since God has revealed Himself in ways that invite, even require, human translative interpretation through biblical exegesis, the only way open to us in this mighty endeavor is through the rhetorical characteristics of language: Whatever God said, we have only human language to say what we think He meant. But this obligation to put into our own words, to "translate" interpretively, inevitably makes for ambiguities in light of the nature of language itself:

> Language...communicates by mediating and uniting, creating community through consensus and concord. Or it may disrupt by separating and dividing, causing disagreement and destruction. Orderly speech corresponds to the order of the universe. Vicious speech creates disorder.... Ultimately, language places human beings in the company of God or the devil (Hoffmann 1994, 213).

Given this ambiguous potential, then, the care that must be brought to our attempts at the articulation of meaning is of crucial importance, and this is as true of biblical exegesis as it is of any other interpretive endeavor. When we interpret, whether we do so within the same language or by moving from one language to another, we engage in an act of attempted duplication that is, in fact, a form of imitative composition. Seen this way, translation involves negotiating the tension between the translator's sense of obligation to the original (in rhetorical terms, his construal of the nature of *imitatio*) and his sense of the degree to which he can address his own understanding of the original and speak in his own name (in rhetorical terms, the degree of *inventio* deemed congruent with his interpretative, as opposed to his translative, function). For Erasmus, as Hoffmann shows so clearly, there can be no such thing as dispassionate, philological translation. All translation calls for *inventio* and for *imitatio*. Human language by its nature embodies meanings, and thus the translator can never be a faceless go-between: Far from being a blank pane of glass through which our view of the original passes unaltered, the translator is more comparable to the prism, which refracts, for better or for worse, the light that passes through it, but which can never be neutral. When that light is the Word of God, then it is only too clear how the prism of human hermeneutic (whether through intralingual interpretation or through interlingual translation) must be carefully considered, given its ability to bring us to salvation— or to damnation.

It will surprise no one that some of Erasmus' most powerful discussions of this fearsome potential of language are featured among his theological writings, but a text with the rather academic subtitle of *Dialogue on the Ideal Latin Style* of 1528 [6] might seem, on the face of it, a much less likely candidate for such a topic. The fact is, however, that nowhere more than in his *Ciceronianus* (as this text is also known) does Erasmus bring greater brilliance, verve and passion to the demonstration of his thesis. At the start of the *Ciceronianus*, two companions, out for a stroll, catch sight of an old friend, formerly the life and soul of every student party but now reduced to a gaunt and haggard shell of his former self. These days, Nosoponus (*nosos*, "disease"; *ponos*, "toil") displays the symptoms of a repulsive disease, which, bearing as it does a close resemblance to syphilis, is so new that it does not yet have a modern name, only a Greek one, "*zelodulea*, 'style-addiction'" (Knott 1986, 342). Nosoponus is suffering from the disfiguring disease of Cicero-nianism, a malady indelibly associated in Erasmus' mind with the kind of Latinity he had observed with horror during his time at the papal court in Rome. This paralyzing disease has afflicted those humanists who, in Erasmus' opinion, are engaged in forms of imitative writing, which can only lead us away from God and into the arms of the devil— namely, those scholars who, in their desire to restore the Latin language to a classical purity that they considered some ten or twelve centuries of evolution to have dimmed and spoiled, had developed what Erasmus believed to be a highly dangerous approach to the imitation of the style of Cicero.

Nosoponus has made the mistake of assuming that it is possible to amputate language from the thought that it serves to articulate, and his cult of Cicero is purely on the level of semantic and syntactical imitation, with no concern for Cicero's principles and values. He tells his friends, at great length, how he works: For the past seven years, he has read no other author but Cicero and has locked away all the other books he owns lest they pollute the purity of his single-minded devotion. He has learned virtually the whole of Cicero's vast output by heart, and copied into a huge lexicon every single word, in every single form in which it occurs in Cicero's writings. A second, even larger volume catalogs all of "Cicero's characteristic expressions in alphabetical order" (Knott 1986, 346), and a third monster categorizes all the *clausulae*, "the rhythmical patterns Cicero uses to begin or end his phrases, clauses and periods" (Knott 1986, 347). Thus, when Nosoponus writes Latin, he can be sure of being as Ciceronian as possible, since he will only use words and forms that are sanctified by their presence in Cicero's writings. To accomplish his monumental task, Nosoponus has severed his connection with human society and renounced as many distracting passions as possible, even abjuring matrimony and family life, and living on no more than "ten very small raisins [and] three sugared coriander seeds" a day (Knott 1986, 353).

As a result of his fear of doing anything un-Ciceronianly, Nosoponus can now barely bring himself to use his Latin at all. But whenever he absolutely has to, he writes no more than half a dozen sentences, each of which takes him at least a week to craft, since he scours his three lexicons at least ten times for each word lest he commit a solecism. Thus, as his friends soon point out, he embodies a concept of language that subjugates everything personal and original to mindless aping and that negates the function of language as our only means of saying what we mean. Nosoponus' Latinity denies the primordial role of language as communication, focussed as it is entirely on the need of the Self to express and not at all on the need of the Other to be reached. We may compare it to a solipsistic radio broadcast in a dead world: There is surely emission, perhaps even transmission, but there is no reception. There is saying, but there is no meaning: There is *oratio*, but no *ratio*. A certain need for self-gratification is met, but no concept of community is validated.

Erasmus' argument has two major components. First, there is the straightforwardly esthetic or stylistic argument: Modern times and modern sensibilities call for modern modes of expression, and it is both anachronistic and stylistically improper to use Ciceronian Latin to argue today's issues. Good style calls for us not to freeze Latin into an excessively reverential kind of rigor mortis, but to grant it all the spontaneity and capacity for growth of any truly living language whose function is to mean, not merely to say.

The second component of Erasmus' condemnation of Ciceronianism goes infinitely further than the mockery of stylistic inanities. This aspect of Erasmus' argument is anchored in the immediate, in the religious problems of his time, but its implications are extraordinarily far-reaching. His fundamental objection to Ciceronianism can be stated quite plainly: To express the mysteries and truths of Christianity while limiting oneself to the language of pagan Latinity is, of necessity, to fall into the promotion of pagan values oneself. Writing in 1528, just eleven years after Martin Luther's break with the Roman Catholic Church, Erasmus contemplates a Christendom increasingly divided: The advocacy of pre-Christian, Ciceronian Latin—the language of a writer and a culture from whom God in His wisdom had chosen to withhold the benefits of revealed Truth—can only exacerbate the intellectual disarray, spiritual turmoil and international dissensions now shattering the humanist and Christian communities. Whether we share Erasmus' concern for Christianity or not, there can be no gainsaying his understanding of the intellectual and spiritual consequences of the very language we elect to use. Under the cover of comic discourse, Erasmus demolishes the notion that there is "what we say" (our *ratio*) and "how we say" (our *oratio*) by showing that the "what" and the "how" are one. Nothing is ever "just a matter of words."

To illustrate his point, one of the companions composes a Latin passage of flawlessly orthodox Christian narrative, which he then proceeds to "translate" into Ciceronian Latin. Erasmus thus manages to change a perfectly Christian text into a pagan one. First, the unproblematic original, in "Erasmian," Christian Latin:

> Iesus Christus, uerbum et filius aeterni Patris, iuxta prophetias uenit in mundum,ac factus homo, sponte se in mortem tradidit, ac redemit ecclesiam suam, offensique Patris iram auertit a nobis, eique nos reconciliauit, ut per gratiam fidei iustificati, et a tyrannide liberati, inseramur ecclesiae, et in ecclesiae communione perseurantes, post hanc uitam consequamur regnum coelorum (Gambaro 1965, lines 1959-1965).

> [Jesus Christ, the Word and the Son of the eternal Father, according to the prophets came into the world, and having been made man, of his own free will surrendered himself to death and redeemed his church; he turned aside from us the wrath of the Father whom we had offended, and reconciled us to him, so that, being justified by the grace of faith and delivered from tyranny, we might be taken into the church, and persevering in the communion of the church, might after this life attain the kingdom of heaven (Knott 1986, 389).]

Even the most conservative theologians would be hard-pressed to find a threat to orthodoxy here. Now, the self-same "ideas" put into the language that Cicero would have had to use, and to which, of course, has little we might call Christian about it:

> Optimi Maximique Iouis interpres ac filius, seruator, rex, iuxta uatum responsa, ex Olympo deuolauit in terras, et hominis assumpta figura, sese pro salute Reipublicae sponte deuouit diis manibus, atque ita concionem siue ciuitatem siue Rempublicam suam asseruit in libertatem, ac Iouis Optimi Maximi uibratum in nostra capita fulmen restinxit, nosque cum illo redegit in gratiam, ut persuasionis munificentia ad innocentiam reparati, et a sycophantae dominatu manumissi, cooptemur in ciuitatem, et in Reipublicae societate perseuerantes, quum fata nos euocarint ex hac uita, in deorum immortalium consortio rerum summa potiamur (Gambaro 1965, lines 1965-1976).

> [The interpreter and son of Jupiter Optimus Maximus, our preserver and king, according to the oracles of the seers winged his way from Olympus to earth and, assuming the shape of man, of his own free will consigned himself to the spirits of the dead to preserve the republic; and thus asserting the freedom of his assembly or state or republic, quenched the thunderbolt of Jupiter Optimus Maximus, directed at our heads, and renewed our good relations with him, in order that, being restored to innocence by the generous gift of our

persuasion, and manumitted from the lordship of the denouncer, we might be co-opted into the citizenship of the state and, persevering in the society of the republic, might, once the fates summon us to depart this life, achieve the sum total of all things in the company of the immortal gods (Knott 1986, 389).]

To promote the language of pagan Latinity, at a time when Christendom was increasingly rent asunder by the Lutheran schism, was both misguided and fraught with danger—all the more so when this "Ciceronian" Latin masqueraded as a vehicle for the expression of Christian truths. As one of the companions is ultimately moved to protest,

> It's paganism, believe me...sheer paganism that makes our ears and minds accept such an idea. The fact is that we're Christians only in name.... We have Jesus on our lips, but it's Jupiter Optimus Maximus and Romulus that we have in our hearts.... We must destroy this paganism, tear it out, expel it from our minds, bring a truly Christian heart to our reading (Knott 1986, 394).

At the very moment when the most persuasive voices are needed for the restoration of Christian unity and the spreading of God's Word, Erasmus was certain that the exclusive cultivation of the language of even the greatest pagan thinker could only be highly damaging to the Christian faith. As he so brilliantly demonstrates, to ponder the nature of translation: All language is, by its very nature, a translation of something, whether we mean the passage from brain to tongue, or ear to brain, or from one language to another. No discourse is exactly and wholly replicable, for there can be no translation without interpretation: To say is to mean, and to say anew is to mean anew.

When Erasmus published his devastating attack on the "Ciceronians," a young Frenchman was enrolled at the University of Padua, studying with one of Europe's most distinguished practitioners of Ciceronian Latin, Simon de Villeneuve (Villanovanus). Villeneuve was himself the student and protégé of the recently deceased Christophe de Longueil (Longolius), a Flemish humanist widely hailed as the most accomplished Ciceronian of his time. This Frenchman was Etienne Dolet, and although we cannot be certain of when exactly he read Erasmus' dialogue (published, as we have noted, by Froben in Basel in March 1528), we may be sure that he devoured it as soon as he could, and probably within the year. Nothing was to affect Dolet's subsequent intellectual and personal life as much as this encounter with Erasmus' thinking on the translative nature of language, an encounter that led not only to Dolet's career as one of the French Renaissance's most important humanist scholar-printers, but also ultimately to his conviction by the Sorbonne Faculty of Theology on charges of blasphemy, and, shortly thereafter, in 1546, to his public hanging and the burning of his corpse (Christie 1899; Worth 1988; Longeon 1990). After several attempts by the authorities to indict him for what was held to be the publication of scandalous and blasphemous editions, the charge that was finally made to stick was that of having translated a text, erroneously thought at the time to be by Plato—the dialogue we now know as the *Axiochus*—in such a manner as to deny the immortality of the soul. Where the pseudo-Plato had written that there was no point in fearing death for while we are alive, it still lies ahead of us, and once we are dead, it is behind us and we can no longer be affected by it, Dolet had translated the concluding "and after death you will not be" by the words "et après la mort tu ne seras rien du tout." It was the addition of those two little words, "rien *du tout*" [nothing *at all*] that sealed Dolet's appalling fate, and the journey that led to the noose and the flames of the Place Maubert in 1546 can be said to have started with his reading of Erasmus' *Ciceronianus* soon after its appearance in 1528.

Dolet must have seized on Erasmus' dialogue with a mixture of genuine conviction and bare-faced opportunism, as a means of making a name for himself. (And here, we must never underestimate the extraordinary power of the humanist yearning for the validation of posterity, a deeply rooted motivation that went far beyond the conventional human impulse for reputation and respect.) Immediately upon reading Erasmus' text, Dolet must have determined to secure his own immortality by engaging in a polemic with the most famous man of letters in all of Europe. While the immediate justification for his onslaught lay chiefly in Erasmus' mildly critical reference to the revered Longolius and in his having failed to include a number of French humanists in the small list of those whose Latinity he could approve, Dolet seized on this rather slim pretext to justify his own entry into the world of letters. Furthermore, he decided to do so in a manner that would at once vindicate his own deeply held belief in the value of Ciceronian imitation, demonstrate his own superb competence as a Latinist and prove to the world that the great Erasmus had finally met his match: He would engage Erasmus precisely on the terrain of the interpretive, translative function of language.

Whatever Dolet's intentions, fate was to rearrange his plans. He probably began work at once on his answering dialogue, in which he set out to pay back Erasmus in his own coin in an exuberantly clever, although quite brutally ad hominem, text. But whether it was conceived or started in 1528, or later, Dolet did not have the opportunity to publish his riposte until 1535: This would be his dialogue *On the Imitation of*

Ciceronian style, against Erasmus of Rotterdam, and in support of Christophe de Longueil (Dolet 1535). By the time the dialogue was published, Erasmus was ailing and soon to be on his deathbed. It is, however, worth noting—in spite of the seven years' interval since his own publication and Erasmus' evident surprise at the resurgence of what must have seemed an old quarrel by then—that his concern over where our compulsion to translate interpretively can lead us remains as deep and as powerful as ever. His letters reveal not only his irritation at the fact that he felt he had been willfully misunderstood and misrepresented by his assailant, but also his unremitting conviction that such promoters of Ciceronianism were actively engaged in the work of the devil. In March 1535, he writes: "Now they say that a sour book has been published against me in Lyon, authored by some Etienne Dolet or other, whose speeches and letters are more likely to make you throw up than to inspire you. I've never met him, and if I did, I'd have no inclination to answer him" (ed. Allen 1947, no. 3005). Just over a year later, some six weeks before his death, he answers a consoling letter from Melanchthon with a reference to Dolet's name as a pun on the Latin word for "stench" and declares his conviction that "there can be no doubt that Satan, who would prefer all of us to be Ciceronians rather than Christians, is behind this song and dance.... For such a thing of scant worth does Satan, envious of Christ, excite these poor creatures!" (ed. Allen 1947, no. 3127).

Dolet's dialogue, also known as the *Erasmianus* (no doubt because Erasmus' was known as the *Ciceronianus*), was probably the first in order of specific conception (although second in order of publication) of a series of four major compositions: the *Orationes* (Dolet 1534), the *Erasmianus* (Dolet 1535), the two volumes of *Commentarii Linguae Latinae* (Dolet 1536 and 1538) and *La Maniere de bien traduire d'une langue en aultre* (Dolet 1540). It can be held that all of these works flow from Dolet's encounter with the Erasmian notion of language as something requiring an approach on the interpretive or translative level—a sense of what I have called elsewhere "the hermeneutic imperative" (Lloyd-Jones 1995, 27-43). By 1528, Dolet may well have begun the accumulation of thousands of what we would nowadays call "3 by 5 file cards" on which he must have collected the various examples of correct Latin usage (in which Cicero naturally occupies the place of honor) and which were to form the basis of his two massive volumes *Commentaries on the Latin Language*. As to when he undertook the drafting of what we may consider to be the last of his specific responses to Erasmus' notion of language, no particular date seems to suggest itself. But before we turn to this fundamental text in the history of Renaissance translation theory, *La Maniere de bien traduire d'une langue en aultre* [*How to translate well from one language to another*], we need to evoke the first, relatively unexpected opportunity that fate granted Dolet in his translation battle with Erasmus, namely the chance to give a public speech in Latin at the University of Toulouse in the fall of 1533.

After completing his curriculum at the University of Padua, Dolet spent some time furthering his studies at the University of Venice and serving as Latin secretary to the French ambassador to the Venetian Republic. By 1532, he had moved on to the study of jurisprudence at one of the most important European centers of the time, the University of Toulouse, where he rapidly become embroiled in the turbulent tensions between the religious, civil and university powers struggling for dominance in the city. Toulouse was not only the birthplace of the Inquisition (which was busily burning religious dissenters at the stake by the time of Dolet's arrival). It was also an important intellectual and cultural crossroads at which the new learning promoted by humanists of all persuasions was locked in combat with the most theologically scholastic and scientifically conservative forces of the time, to the point that Toulouse had become—and was to remain, until the French Revolution, as such authors as Voltaire would attest—synonymous with the most vicious intolerance and the most repressive cruelty. The annals of the *parlement*, the *sénéchaussée* and the university Senate of the 1520s and 1530s are replete with edicts and counteredicts as the civil powers endeavored to control and constrain the university, in which there was increasing evidence of a dangerous new liberalism at work. Endless decrees were promulgated attempting to suppress student demonstrations in the name of public order—decrees that inevitably resulted more than anything else in the provocation of further riots and generalized mayhem on the part of the students themselves (Dawson 1923).

Already noted as a distinguished Latinist, Dolet was elected in the summer of 1533 to be that year's official orator of the guild of French students at the university ("French" meaning from north of the River Loire, Toulouse being the capital of the still semi-autonomous province of Languedoc). Town and gown relations were in a particularly bad way that summer, and even the king, Francis I, who had undertaken a tour of his provinces to thank them for having raised the ransom money to have him released from Madrid after his capture at Pavia, had cut short his royal visit and fled. Thus it was that Dolet—burning with humanist ambition, eager to avenge the double injustice of the civil and ecclesiastical authorities who were opposing freedom of speech and liberty of conscience among the students and that of Erasmus for his earlier attack against an ethic and against teachers whom he cherished— mounted the podium on October 9, 1533. His posture could not fail to bring to mind that of Cicero himself. He, too, had been called upon to defend the values of the Republic (the civic state in Cicero's case, the Republic of letters in Dolet's) against the onslaught of uncouth barbarians whose ignorance of correct Latinity (i.e., of Ciceronian style) was merely the outer manifestation of their contempt for the communal values of *societas* and *humanitas*—values that depended on good language, persuasive oratory and ethical hermeneutic to protect and preserve them.

Dolet's speech, which amounts to some twenty pages in its published form, is, in fact, a masterpiece of Ciceronian imitation, perfectly organized according to the canons of deliberative oratory; it constitutes a ringing defense, through its faithful adherence to Ciceronian style, of all that is noble and good in the domain of Ciceronian ethical and social values. As such, it provides a brilliant refutation of Erasmus' onslaught of 1528 (Lloyd-Jones 1991, 439-447). It also managed to offend, mightily, both the civil authorities in Toulouse and the guild of local Gascon students, who found themselves more than a little insulted by Dolet's insistence on their manifest and universally acknowledged inferiority to the students of France. It was immediately decided that Dolet had to be answered, and some four to six weeks later, the Gascon orator Pinache spoke publicly against him. This speech is now lost, but we may suppose it to have been highly offensive in Dolet's regard. Never one to allow a personal affront to pass unanswered, he consequently gave, toward the end of the year, a second speech of personal rebuttal in which he demolished Pinache and his benighted supporters, the Toulouse authorities, the Gascon nation and all anti-humanist (and thus anti-Ciceronian and anti-French) barbarians in general, with such violence that he was very shortly thereafter arrested and thrown into prison. He was released after a couple of days, thanks to the intervention of powerful protectors whom both his undoubted intellectual brilliance and the connections he had made while working for the ambassador to Venice had secured for him. He then found himself banished from Toulouse under penalty of death, and he left the despised city in the spring of 1534. It was, in fact, his intention to return to Padua, but ill health and probably the need to earn his living caused him to stop off in Lyon on the way and to take temporary employment there as a proofreader for the German humanist publisher-printer Sébastien Gryphe (Sebastianus Gryphius).

It was while working for Gryphius that Dolet probably took the opportunity to indulge in some creative moonlighting and produced his first published work, a volume containing the revised speeches (now, with the safety of some 200 intervening miles, called *Orationes Duae in Tholosam* [*Two Orations against Toulouse*]) and a selection of his Latin poems and epistles. No doubt realizing that if he left Lyon, at that time the center of the French publishing industry, he would forgo such easy access to printing shops and booksellers, Dolet then gave up his plan to return to Italy, produced within a year his riposte to Erasmus and settled in Lyon for the remaining twelve years of his life to become one of the most important native-born editor-publishers of his generation.

We may only marvel at how this brilliant but headstrong and self-destructive man made quite sure, through the selection of the texts he translated and published, and the prefaces that he appended to them (as well as his own original compositions in French and in Latin), that he was never for long out of the gun sights of the authorities, and in particular those of the Sorbonne, whose single-minded pursuit of him led ultimately to his dreadful fate in 1546. Of particular interest here, though, is Dolet's response to Erasmus' ideas on language, imitative writing, interpretation and translation—a response that comes chiefly into focus on the theoretical level in the formulation of the principles of good translation outlined in his *Maniere de bien traduire* of 1540.

Dolet's *Orationes*, *Erasmianus* and *Comentarii Linguae Latinae* can all be seen as representing a massive and heroic effort on the level of praxis to argue his case against Erasmus, by means of a series of persuasive demonstrations of the social and ethical good that ensues when such imitation is practiced at the level of both language and thought, of both *oratio* and *ratio*. Erasmus has indeed shown, with his translation of Christian Latin into pagan Latin, that our need to interpret can have serious, even dangerous, political and moral consequences. But the heart of their disagreement lay perhaps less in some bedrock of truth than in the difference between a moral and an esthetic conception of the issues. For Erasmus, to translate Christian truths into the language of pagan Latinity was to paganize those ideas, whereas for Dolet good Latinity meant imitating the best model, and that model could only be Cicero. The best Latin style was Ciceronian, and all else was anachronism or solecism. But certainly, for both humanists, the touchstone of all matters lay in classical rhetoric. This emerges clearly from the tantalizingly fragmentary hints as to what Dolet had projected to be a major work, his *Orateur Françoys*, to which he made a fleeting allusion in the *Maniere de bien traduire*. But as far as we know, he never produced the *Orateur Françoys*. If, in fact, any version of it actually existed, it probably went into the flames to which his body was consigned, along with as many of his imprints and manuscripts as the authorities could get their hands on, after his hanging in 1546.

It is in Dolet's listing of five points for good translation as he presents them in his *Maniere de bien traduire d'une langue en aultre*, a text that remains to this day remarkably understudied and undervalued, that the full nature of his response to Erasmus may be sensed. It is immediately apparent that Dolet, in his turn, sees the translator as primarily obligated to his target rather than to his source—and this is worth remembering when we recall the argument of many of Ciceronianism's critics, to the effect that its practitioners were locked into the dead fixity of the past rather than responsive to the needs of a living community still enjoying potentiality (Cave 1979, 127 and following):

> En premier lieu, il fault que le traducteur entende paraictement le sens et matiere de l'autheur qu'il traduict: car par ceste intelligence il ne sera jamais obscur en sa traduction....

> La second chose qui est requise en traduction, c'est que le traducteur ait parfaicte congnoissance de la langue de l'autheur qu'il traduict: et soit pareillement excellent en la langue en laquelle il se mect à traduire....

> Le tiers poinct est qu'en traduisant il ne se fault pas asseruir iusques la que l'on rend mot pour mot... (Dolet 1540, 13-15).

> [In the first place, the translator must understand perfectly the meaning and subject matter of the author he is translating, for such understanding will prevent him from ever being obscure in his translation....

> The second thing that is required in translation is that the translator have perfect knowledge of the language of the author he is translating, and that he have an equally excellent grasp of the language into which he is about to translate....

> The third point is that, when translating, we must not enslave ourselves to the point that we provide a word for word rendition....]

In each of these points, intellectual competence and a complete grasp of *what* is being said and of *how* it is being said are allied in the name of the clarity and persuasive force of the target version. This same consideration emerges even more strongly from the final two points:

> La quatriesme reigle que ie veulx bailler en cest endroict, est plus a obseruer en langues non reduictes en art, qu'en autres. I'appelle langues non reduictes encores en art certain et repceu: comme est la

Françoyse…et autres vulgaires. S'il aduient doncques que tu traduises quelque liure Latin en icelles…il te fault garder d'vsurper mots trop approchants du Latin….Contente toy du commun, sans innouer aucunes dictions follement, et par curiosité reprehensible… (Dolet 1540, 15-16).

[The fourth rule that I wish to establish here applies more to those languages still awaiting artistic development, than to others. By languages still awaiting complete universally recognized artistic development, I have in mind such languages as French…and the other modern languages. If it should happen that you are translating some Latin book into one of these languages…you must guard against using words that are too close to Latin…. Content yourself with everyday usage, and do not, out of reprehensible affection, invent insane and newfangled forms of expression….]

It is important to note this stress on the need to recognize that modern vernaculars may not yet have the rhetorical resources and *copia* of the classical tongues, and thus to avoid recourse to outlandish neologisms and, as Norton has it, "all innovation that violates the integrity of the common language" (Norton 1984, 213). It is also worth noting that Dolet implicitly privileges, as had Cicero in the *De optimo genere oratorum*, the need to cultivate equivalency of rhetorical effects between source and target versions. The politics of translation in Renaissance France would result, particularly after the call for national linguistic renovation proposed by the Pléiade in 1549, in a deliberate program of vernacular cultural enhancement, in which esthetic norms dictated by what sat most naturally with the national language were to govern the development of neologisms and the principles of linguistic borrowing. Joachim du Bellay and Pierre de Ronsard would owe much to Dolet's pioneering in this regard, and they acknowledged as much in the *Deffence et illustration*, less than three years after his death, hailing him as "[un] homme de bon jugement en notre vulgaire" [a man of good judgement in our national language] (Du Bellay 1549, 86).

But it is Dolet's fifth point, seeking, like so much else in humanist thinking, to guarantee the future by anchoring it in the best of the past, which speaks most directly to the central issue:

Venons maintenant à la cinquiesme reigle…laquelle est de si grand' vertu, que sans elle toute composition est lourde et mal plaisant. Mais qu'est-ce qu'elle contient? rien autre chose que l'obseruation des nombres oratoires: c'est assçavoir vne liaison et assemblement des dictions auec telle doulceur, que non seulement l'ame s'en contente, mais aussi les oreilles en sont toutes rauies…d'yceulx nombres oratoires ie parle plus copieusement en mon orateur: parquoy n'en feray icy plus long discours (Dolet 1540, 17-18).

[Let us now come to the fifth rule…which is so important that, without it, all writing is heavy and displeasing. What does this rule involve? Nothing less than fidelity to the flow and rhythms of Classical oratory: that is to say, linking and putting the words together with such harmony as not only to gratify the spirit but also to delight the ear…. I will deal at greater length with this question in my *French Orator*, and so will say no more about it here.]

Intolerance and fanaticism never afforded him the opportunity. But it is no accident that we have here a further echo of the principles of Ciceronian rhetoric, involving, as Norton says, "both a harmonic principle, an emission of pleasure to the ear, and a structural principle based on the actual linkage of words" (Norton 1984, 213). Ciceronianism is nothing if not the arrangement of words in the service of ideas—the desire to reflect "the original's mode of signification." As Cicero himself notes, in his *De optimo genere oratorum*:

Optimus est enim orator qui dicendo animos audientium et docet et delectat et permovet. Docere debitum est, delectare honorarium, permovere necessarium (*De optimo genere oratatorum*, 3).

[So the best orator is the man who, when he speaks, manages to instruct, to delight and to persuade the minds of his listeners. To instruct is a duty he owes to his listeners; to delight is a free gift he brings to them; to persuade them is a necessity.]

And in his *Orator*, he further stresses this point:

Erit igitur eloquens…is qui in foro causisque civilibus ita dicet, ut probet, ut delectat, ut flectat. Probare necessitatis est, delectare suavitatis, flectere victoriae… (*Orator*, 69).

[And so the eloquent man…is the one who, before the legislature or in a court of law, will speak in such a manner as to demonstrate, to delight, to sway. To demonstrate is a matter of necessity, to delight is a matter of pleasure, and to sway is how he wins his cause….]

Delighting the ear responds to the esthetic element of classical rhetoric: *delectare*; gratifying the spirit requires an intellectual component: *docere*. Both are necessary, since the *logos* is composed of both *ratio* and *oratio*, and all translation involves creative interpretation, itself incorporating that blend of *inventio* and *imitatio* that accomplishes the persuasive function of rhetorical practice: *permovere*. With his investment in the *nombres oratoires*, Dolet stakes a claim for the rhetorical dimensions of translation. And the practice of rhetoric is nothing if not a political undertaking.

Whatever we may finally conclude regarding the polemic between Erasmus and Dolet, it seems fair to say that they both understood the extent to which any translative act is unarguably a rhetorical undertaking, even if they were to disagree over whether it constituted primarily a moral or an esthetic activity. But perhaps in the long run, this is something of a distinction without a difference. It was always the case that the three-fold thrust of classical rhetorical practice was seen as an attempt to gratify us in order that we should learn something worthwhile, representing a value by which we could be honestly persuaded and to which we could be sincerely committed: *delectare, docere, permovere*. It was for this very reason, after all, that Aristotelian rhetoric held that "it is certainly better that the decent person reveal himself to be trustworthy than that his speech be letter-perfect" (Aristotle III.17.12). Similarly, Roman theoreticians like Cato, Cicero and Quintilian insisted that rhetoric and moral worth were not to be separated, for the orator was to be a *vir bonus dicendi peritus* (a good man skilled in the art of speaking). At one level, it is true that Dolet, in both the *Orationes* and the *Erasmianus*, makes a stronger claim for the rhetorical skills rather than the moral principles of the orator (Chomarat 1981, 819 and following), but a wider reading of his arguments suggests that this was, at least in part, a polemical means of distancing himself from Erasmus (Lloyd-Jones 1993, 9-19). On a more fundamental level, their common reverence for the modes of classical rhetoric and the importance they accorded to them in their own theory of translation suggest that the two humanists, so different in so many ways, were closer than they may have thought.

For both Erasmus and Dolet, the principles of classical rhetoric confirmed the notion that language is both a "saying" and a "meaning," and they understood that nothing reveals this to be so more powerfully than our attempts at translation. Translation is a rhetorical transaction: That this transaction is mediated less by what we say than by what we mean (and are taken to mean) is why political motives and purposes can never be far from the heart of the translative enterprise.

Notes

1. This essay is based on a plenary lecture delivered at the conference on "The Politics of Translation in the Middle Ages and the Renaissance" held at the University of

Pittsburgh in April 1997. It is thus meant to serve as a general introduction to this volume of essays.

2. All translations, unless otherwise noted, are my own.

3. The traditional distinctions between "literary" translation and "technical" translation are, of course, assumed here: In the latter category (as, say, in the case of instructions for handling explosives), creative originality on the part of the translator is highly undesirable!

4. "(a) the word, or that by which the inward thought is expressed, Lat. oratio; and (b) the inward thought itself; Lat. ratio": An Intermediate Greek-English Lexicon, 476-477.

5. These translations represent the primary definitions of the Latin words in the Oxford Latin Dictionary; other translations are, of course, possible, depending on the precise interpretation being sought.

6. Dialogus, cui titulus Ciceronianus, sive De optimo genere dicendi. All following quotations are taken from the edition by A. Gambaro, cited as Gambaro (1965); translations are taken from the annotated translation by Betty I. Knott, The Ciceronian: A Dialogue on the Ideal Latin Style, cited as Knott (1986).

Works Cited

An Intermediate Greek-English Lexicon (founded upon the seventh edition of Liddell and Scott's Greek-English Lexicon) (1889). Oxford: Clarendon Press, 1980.

Oxford Latin Dictionary. Ed. P. G. W. Glare et al. Oxford: Oxford University Press, 1983.

Aristotle. Art of Rhetoric. Trans. and ann. J. H. Freese. Cambridge, Mass., and London: Heinemann, 1982.

Benjamin, Walter. "The Task of the Translator." In Theories of Translation, ed. Rainer Schulte and John Biguenet, 71-82. Chicago: University of Chicago Press, 1992.

Cave, Terence. The Cornucopian Text: Problems of Writing in the French Renaissance. Oxford: Clarendon Press, 1979.

Chomarat, Jacques. Grammaire et Rhétorique chez Erasme. 2 vols. Paris: Les Belles Lettres, 1981.

Christie, R. Copley. Etienne Dolet, the Martyr of the Renaissance. London: Macmillan, 1899.

Cicero. De optimo genere oratorum. Trans. and ann. H. M. Hubbell. Cambridge, Mass., and London: Heinemann, 1976.

—. Orator. Trans. and ann. H. M. Hubbell. Cambridge, Mass., and London: Heinemann, 1971.

Dawson, John. Toulouse in the Renaissance. New York: Columbia University Press, 1923.

Dolet, Etienne. Orationes Duae in Tholosam (Lyon: S. Gryphius [?], 1534). Ed. and trans. Kenneth Lloyd-Jones and Marc van der Poel. Geneva: Droz, 1992.

—. Dialogus, De Imitatione Ciceroniana, adversus Erasmum Roterodamum, pro Christophoro Longolio (Lyon: S. Gryphius, 1535). Ed. E. V. Telle. Geneva: Droz, 1974.

—. Commentarii Linguae Latinae. 2 vols. Lyon: S. Gryphius, 1536 and 1538.

—. *La Maniere de bien traduire d'une langue en aultre. D'avantage de la punctuation de la langue françoyse, plus des accents d'ycelle.* (Lyon: E. Dolet, 1540). Reprint, Paris: Techener, 1830.

Du Bellay, Joachim. *La Deffence et illustration de la langue françoyse* (Paris, 1549). Ed. Henri Chamard. Paris: Didier, 1948.

Erasmus, Desiderius. *Opus Epistolarum Des. Erasmi Roterodami.* Ed. P. S. Allen, H. M. Allen and H. W. Garrod. Vol. 11. Oxford: Oxford University Press, 1947.

—. *Dialogus, cui titulus Ciceronianus, sive De optimo genere dicendi.* (Basel: Froben, 1528). Ed. and trans. A. Gambaro. Brescia: La Scuola Editrice, 1965.

—. *The Ciceronian: A Dialogue on the Ideal Latin Style.* Trans. and ann. Betty I. Knott. (Complete Works of Erasmus Vol. 28). Toronto: University of Toronto Press, 1986.

Hoffmann, Manfred. *Rhetoric and Theology: The Hermeneutic of Erasmus.* Toronto: University of Toronto Press, 1994.

Ionesco, Eugène. *La Leçon. Théâtre I.* (1954). Paris: Gallimard, 1965.

Lloyd-Jones, Kenneth. *"Une étoffe bigaré...*Dolet critique du style érasmien" In *Acta Conventus Neo-Latini Torontonensis,* ed. A. Dalzell et al., 439-447. Binghamton, N.Y.: Medieval and Renaissance Texts Society, 1991.

—. "Imitation et Engagement chez Dolet." In *Etudes sur Etienne Dolet, le théâtre au XVIe siècle, le Forez, le Lyonnais et l'histoire du livre, publiées à la mémoire de Claude Longeon,* ed. Gabriel-André Pérouse, 9-19. Geneva: Droz, 1993.

—. "Erasmus and Dolet on the Ethics of Translation and the Hermeneutic Imperative." In *International Journal of the Classical Tradition* 2-1 (1995): 27-43.

—. "Belles Fictions & Descriptions Exquises...: Translative Strategies for Christianizing Greek Thought in the Renaissance." In *Religion and French Literature* (FLS, vol. 25). Ed. Buford Norman. Amsterdam: Rodopi, 1998.

Longeon, Claude. *Hommes et Livres de la Renaissance.* Saint-Etienne: Presses de l'Université Jean-Monnet, 1990.

Norton, Glyn P. *The Ideology and Language of Translation in Renaissance France, and Their Humanist Antecedents.* Travaux d'Humanisme et Renaissance, 201. Geneva: Droz, 1984.

Rummel, Erika. *Erasmus as a Translator of the Classics.* Toronto: University of Toronto Press, 1985.

Worth, Valerie. *Practising Translation in Renaissance France: The Example of Etienne Dolet.* Oxford: Clarendon Press, 1988.

Eusebius' Greek Version of Vergil's *Fourth Eclogue*

Edwin D. Floyd
University of Pittsburgh

Abstract

As it adjusted the syntax and vocabulary of the Latin original, a fourth-century Greek translation of *Eclogue 4* veered pretty consistently toward a messianic interpretation and so helped shape subsequent reading of Vergil's poem along such lines. The most readily accessible dimension thus added to *Eclogue 4* involves Homeric resonances, reused from a Christian perspective. Occasionally, though, the translation goes beyond Homer to other archaic material; nowadays, we can best approach some of this other material through Indo-European poetics. From its blending of various traditions, the translation emerges as a work that is literarily both interesting and sophisticated, and at line 62, it can even play a role in establishing Vergil's text and meaning.

The Greek translation

Composed around 40 BC, Vergil's *Eclogue 4* was subsequently read as an inspired prophecy of the birth of Jesus Christ some forty years later. Today such an interpretation is not so popular, but actually, through a majority of the generations that have read it, the specifically Christian interpretation was dominant. It was fostered by the prestige of Vergil, inasmuch as Christian readers wished to connect themselves with the greatest of Roman poets. Conversely, though, the messianic interpretation of *Eclogue 4* also fed into medieval and later readers' continued admiration of Vergil, as seen, for example, in the fact that Vergil is Dante's guide through much of the *Divine Comedy*. As late as the eighteenth century, Pope produced, in English, a poem called "Messiah," based on Vergil, and Johnson then put Pope's poem into Latin; both Pope and Johnson were clearly writing with an eye toward

(1) the Roman original and (2) a Christian interpretation of the Latin text.

In the West, either the Latin text of *Eclogue 4* or the occasional Western vernacular adaptation of it was what was naturally read. Probably the most specific source, though, for reading Vergil in Christian terms is to be found in a fourth-century Greek translation, cited by Eusebius. Repeatedly, the translation adopts a messianic view of *Eclogue 4*, and its stance is likely to have influenced bilingual Greek-Latin readers, familiar with both the Latin text and its Greek translation.[1]

In the very first line, for example, the deprecating tone (presumably intended by Vergil), which is introduced by *paulo* [slightly] in *paulo maiora canamus* [let us sing of slightly greater things], is absent from the Greek μεγάλην φάτιν ὑμνήσωμεν [let us sing a great song]. Vergil's own form of expression serves well to contrast the program of *Eclogue 4* with other pastoral poetry, without, however, actually transgressing the bounds of pastoral. Its modification in the Greek version, though, suggests that this will be a poem with explicitly greater aspirations and correspondingly deeper meaning.

A comparable point is the rendering, in line 4, of "Cumaean song" as "Cumaean prophecy." Vergil's own word *carminis* might indeed imply "prophecy"; in fact, this nuance is confirmed by the high incidence of future verb forms in the poem (about 35 specifically future forms, along with various imperative and subjunctive forms, in just 63 lines). As with line 1, though, the translator seems concerned to place the poem in as serious a context as he can; correspondingly, he uses μαντεύματος [prophecy], instead of a more general word such as ἀοιδή [song].

Slightly greater adjustment is involved in the handling of line 6. Vergil's two coordinate clauses, *iam redit et Virgo, redeunt Saturnia regna* [already the Virgin returns, Saturnian kingdoms return], do not actually connect the Virgin and child very closely. The translation, though, neatly remedies the problem (for the *interpretatio Christiana*) by using a subordinating construction, ἥκει παρθένος αὖθις, ἄγουσ' ἐρατὸν βασιλῆα [the Virgin comes again, bringing a lovely king]. Dependent now on παρθένος [Virgin], the participle ἄγουσ' [bringing] has as its object βασιλῆα [king]: Not only does the Virgin return, but she actually brings something. Or rather, she brings someone, inasmuch as, in the process of making this adjustment in Vergil's syntax, the translator also changes Vergil's abstract noun *regna* [kingdoms] to the phrase ἐρατὸν βασιλῆα [lovely king].[2]

Traditional allusions

Another adjustment from Vergil's Latin comes in line 26, as Vergil's single word *parentis* [of a parent] becomes the noun-adjective phrase πατρός τε μεγιστου [and of the greatest father]. The added "ornamental" epithet μεγιστου primarily stresses the high position of the child's father; however, it could also suggest a comparison with Zeus himself, in view of Homer's usage of Ζεῦ πάτερ...μέγιστε [Zeus, greatest father] at *Iliad* 3.276 and elsewhere. Within the pagan-Christian interface, which is assumed in the translation, then, there is an identification of the child as the son of God.

At line 49, on the other hand, a divine reference is ostensibly toned down. The Latin here refers to Jupiter by name, in the phrase *magnum Iovis incrementum* [great increase of Jupiter], but the translator leaves out the actual name of the pagan divinity at line 49. Even as he does so, though, he actually makes the divine background of the son more explicit. For one thing, his word ἐριβρεμέτao [loud-thundering] is a Homeric epithet of Zeus, found (as ἐριβρεμέτεω) at *Iliad* 13.624. Also, the preceding word πατεός [father's] specifies his relationship with the child, in a way that Vergil's more mysterious phrasing (*Iovis ... incrementum* [increment / increase of Jupiter]) does not.

Still another form of adjustment is exhibited at line 61, as the translation renders Vergil's *decem menses* [ten months] as πολλοὺς λυκάβαντας [many lukabantes]. Appearing just twice in Homer (along with sporadic occurrences in later authors such as Apollonius of Rhodes), the Greek noun is a rare and poetic word. Parallel to the allusions to *Iliad* 3.276 at line 26 and to *Iliad* 13.624 at line 49, then, the translator's use of λυκάβαντας gives an elevated cast to his version.

According to the Homeric scholia, the word λυκάβας means "year." Such a sense might theoretically be possible in a messianic poem, as referring to the eternally pre-ordained conception of Christ through "many years." Both the Vergilian original and the Greek translation, however, focus fairly literally on the mother's pregnancy. Consequently, "years" does not seem so feasible as the sense intended for λυκάβαντας in the translation. Probably the best solution comes from consideration of Dio Chrysostom 7.85.1, where the word λυκάβας, as used at *Odyssey* 19.306, is taken as meaning "month." In view of this passage, then, one could imagine the translator of Vergil saying that his familiarity with epic usage transcended the schoolbook knowledge contained in the Homeric scholia; instead, he could say, he was following a tolerably well-known rhetorician such as Dio.[3]

Additionally, the legitimacy of "month" as a meaning of *lukābaw* is confirmed by the Indo-European root **luk-* [light]. From this, one can extrapolate an underlying meaning for λυκάβας as "course of light," i.e., λυκα [light] + βας [going], with the second part of the compound (which does not otherwise have any very convincing function) falling readily into place as a derivative from βαίνω [go]. Theoretically, such a compound, derived from "light" and "going/course," could refer to various calendrical terms, including "year"; however, the most likely meaning would be "month," as proposed by Koller (1973). That is, the original sense would have been "from one month to another," with an overall semantic development parallel to the derivation of Latin *luna* [moon] from the root **luk-* [light].

Another instance of relative freedom in the translation, combined with a plausible rationale for this freedom, comes in line 19, as the Latin phrase *hederas...cum baccare* [ivy with cyclamen] is rendered as κριθὴν ἠδὲ κύπειρον [barley and galingale]. The variation in vocabulary is considerable, but one can surmise a reason for it in the fact that the Vergilian original presents a potentially confusing array of ideas; first, we have the essentially decorative ivy and cyclamen, and then edible substances, namely, colocasium (the root of which was eaten) and acanthus (used medicinally), followed in lines 21-22 by lactating goats with distended udders. At the cost of taking some liberties with vocabulary, the translator instead gives us a more consistent focus on edible substances, starting off with barley and galingale instead of ivy and cyclamen. Moreover, he does so within what can be heard as a very traditional framework. The result, in line 19, is a neat example of what Watkins, in his recent book on Indo-European poetics, calls a "merism," i.e., a "bipartite phrase" of which the "parts share most of their semantic features, and together serve to define globally a higher concept" (Watkins 1995, 45). Typical merisms are Hittite phrases meaning "barley and spelt," "grains and grapes" and the like, along with Greek "wheat and barley," found at *Odyssey* 9.110. Like these, the translation of *Eclogue* 4.19 expresses a global concept, namely, "food for men and horses," through its use of "barley" and "galingale" respectively, and it correspondingly has an archaic ring to it, appropriate to the spirit, if not the letter, of the Vergilian original.

How did the translator know Indo-European?[4]

But, of course, our fourth-century translator of Vergil must be several millennia removed from proto-Indo-European. How then could there be an Indo-European background for the merism exemplified at line 19? For that matter, how legitimately could we put his use of λυκάβαντας at line 61 into any Indo-European etymological perspective?

The answer, surprising as it may seem, is that there was a demonstrably long preservation of ancient Indo-European poetic traditions in many of the daughter languages. In the case of Celtic poetry, for example, Watkins writes as follows of its close similarities with Vedic India: "Despite the enormous differences in tone and cultural outlook the system, the structural position of the poet in each society, is remarkably similar in India and Ireland, and the Irish system remained basically static over the 1000 years from the beginning of our documentation to the collapse of the Celtic world" (Watkins 1995, 75). A similar pattern is also demonstrable in Germanic, especially in *Beowulf*, to which there are more than forty references in his index (Watkins 1995, 599).

The pattern of a lengthy preservation of Indo-European poetic traditions can also be noted in first millennium AD Greek authors such as Gregory of Nazianzus, Nonnos and Cometas. Gregory, for example, at 893.14 (the numbering is from Migne, *Patrologia*, vol. 37), refers to the forbidden fruit in Eden as ἀνδροφόνος (man-slaying, deadly). The specific usage is, of course, Christian rather than proto-Indo-European in origin. If we turn to Sanskrit, though, we find that *nrhan*, cognate with Greek ἀνδροφόνος, is used to refer to the distinctly sinister god Rudra (the predecessor of the modern Siva) at *Rig-Veda* 4.3.6 and to a deadly instrument (the Marutas' thunderbolt) at 7.56.17. Another Indo-Iranian language, Avestan, uses the same combination of "slay" and "man" (in the form *jeneram*) to refer to evil women who could threaten the happiness of a marriage at *Yasna* 53.8; for these Indo-Iranian uses, see Schmitt (1967, 123-127). All three of the Indo-Iranian uses are very neatly combined by Gregory in the context of 893.14. First, the Christian poet uses the phrase ἀνδροφόνοιο φυτοῦ [murderous plant] to refer to the apple tree itself as an instrument of doom, and then this is explained, in the immediately following lines, 894.1-2, by the combinations δυσμενέος δόλος [an enemy's craft], alluding to Satan, and παρφασίης τ' ἀλόχου [and a wife's persuasion], referring to the deadly woman, Eve. It is also easy to find a *tertium comparationis* between Indo-Iranian and Christian Greek. At line 98 of the Hesiodic *Shield of Herakles*, for example, the deadly war god Ares (a kind of Greek analog of Vedic Rudra) is given the epithet ἀνδροφόνος, at

Pindar, *Pythian* 4.252 the deadly Lemnian women, parallel to the women of *Yasna* 53.8, are so referred to, and Tyrtaios, *fr.* 19.9 mentions a "man-slaying spear," on a par with the murderous thunderbolt of *Rig-Veda* 7.56.17. It must be from passages such as these, standing within the Greek tradition itself (and not from Indo-Iranian passages), that the fourth-century AD writer Gregory derived his own usage of ἀνδροφόνοιο at 893.14.

A similar pattern is observable in the case of Greek ἱμάσσειν [to lash], cognate with Hittite *ishimas* [rope, cord]. The Hittite term is used in the narration of a god's dealing with a monstrous opponent, and the Greek cognate is used in much the same way in a number of passages in Nonnos, *Dionysiaca*. There is also another occurrence of the verb at his *Paraphrasis of John* 6.88 (paraphrasing, more or less, *John* 6.22), where the context is the divine Jesus' walking on water and so exhibiting control over forces of nature, much like the Hittite Storm God when dealing with the serpent Illuyankas or the Greek Zeus when dealing with Typhoeus. Nonnos' relatively "late" use of the pattern, though, is not isolated within Greek. More than a millennium previously, there are instances of the pattern in Homer, Hesiod and the *Homeric Hymns,* and it must be sources such as these, rather than Hittite ones, on which the fifth-century AD writer drew.[5]

The reuse of ancient formulas also continues well into the medieval period. Cometas (ninth century AD), for example, twice uses a very ancient formula κλέος ἄφθιτον [fame unwithering / imperishable], at *Anthologia Graeca* 15.40, lines 29 and 57. In Cometas' first use of κλέος ἄφθιτον, in line 29, the speaker is Jesus, referring to his intention of acquiring imperishable fame through raising Lazarus from death, and at line 57, with which the poem concludes, the story is summarized in terms of the multitude praising God's imperishable fame, demonstrated through His son's activities. In part, Cometas' usage of κλέος ἄφθιτον is based on a well-known Homeric passage, *Iliad* 9.413. In the Homeric passage, though, the focus of the phrase is specifically on the hero Achilleus' posthumous fame, rather than either contemporary praise or a physical conquest of death. Inasmuch as the *Iliad* passage is not really very close, in either content or ethos, to Cometas' usage, the latter must also be considered against the pattern of various other early Greek examples of κλέος ἄφθιτον. Attractive alternative sources for Cometas' usage in *Anthologia Graeca* 15.40 are an inscription from near Delphi, referring to a craftsman's reputation, spread by Hera and Athena, and Hesiod, *fr.* 70.5, which describes the gods' granting physical immortality to either Ino-Lukothee or her son Melikertes; additionally, as Cometas reflects these archaic Greek uses, his use of κλέος ἄφθιτον also resembles a Vedic pattern of (1) festive celebration and (2) associated with the gods, which is found in association with a cognate formula *sravas...aksitam.*[6]

From the perspective of authors such as Gregory, Nonnos and Cometas, then, we can likewise view the Greek translator of Vergil as entering into a dialogue with inherited traditions. His use of λυκάβας, for example, reflects Dio Chrysostom's interpretation of *Odyssey* 19.306, and behind this there is an Indo-European etymology. His merism at line 19 could also preserve an archaic poetic figure of speech, even though the combination κριθὴν ἠδὲ κύπειρον is not specifically paralleled in Homer or, apparently, elsewhere in Greek. Complementing the more specifically Homeric allusions noted in Section 2 (Traditional allusions), such passages in the Christian translation of *Eclogue 4* would serve to suggest that despite apparent differences in detail, this translation gives a fundamentally correct interpretation of Vergil. In fact, these passages, even though they differ from the Latin original, could also imply that while the translation transcends the particular historical circumstances in which the Roman poet was constrained to write, it does so along lines that are poetically on a level with Vergil.[7]

A textual problem

Near the end of the poem, though, we seem to get a fairly elementary mistake by the translator rather than any subtle balance of different traditions. At line 62, the Latin refers to children not smiling on a parent. The Greek translation has the opposite: Parents are not smiling on a child. In this instance, then, it is not a matter of adding an "ornamental" epithet such as μεγίστου [greatest] at line 26 or using an obscure but poetically resonant word such as λυκάβαντας at line 61 in the immediate context of the parent-child reference; instead, in line 62, it is a matter of turning Vergil's meaning upside down. Would not this rudimentary misunderstanding of Latin grammar (or, at best, brazen disregard of it) seriously undermine the translator's standing with any ancient bilingual Greek-Latin reader who was more or less comfortable with both languages?

The answer is that the preceding paragraph misstated the case: The translation does not, in truth, do violence to the text that a bilingual Greek-Latin reader of the fourth century AD would have known. The manuscripts of Vergil all have the dative singular *cui* [to whom] and the nominative plural *parentes* [parents] in line 62. Accordingly, those who turn the text upside down are modern editors, who regularly change *cui* to nominative plural *qui* and *parentes* to dative singular *parenti.*[8]

Instead of the emended text, it is obviously the manuscript text of Vergil that the Greek dative singular σοί [to / on you] and nominative plural γονεῖς [parents] are intended to represent. The situation concerning the dative singular and nominative plural can be stated even more strongly. Despite modern critics' confident assertions to the contrary, the text with *cui...parentes* is not only that which was current in the fourth century, it is almost certainly what Vergil wrote.

Against the authenticity of *cui...parentes*, Coleman states that this, the manuscript reading, "gives easy grammar but feeble sense; a mother's smile hardly characterizes her child as exceptional nor would the absence of it, however unnatural it seems, obviously disqualify him from future greatness."[9] In Coleman's judgment, we must therefore jettison "easy grammar" for a reference to an unsmiling child. Most other modern critics have followed a similar line of reasoning.

It is not, however, really a drawback to the transmitted reading that it well nigh compels one to ask what sort of "unnatural" parents (rather than child) we are dealing with. In fact, once we ask this question, the manuscript reading becomes positively preferable—if we follow the analysis proposed by Berg (1974) and subsequently developed by Arnold (1994-95). According to this analysis, Vergil's imagery throughout *Eclogue 4* refers not to an actual child and parents, but rather to some sort of developing poetic program. Berg's own view is that we can see Vergil's future poetic career, as exemplified in the *Georgics* and *Aeneid* (and already, more or less, planned by Vergil), in the references to agriculture and warfare at lines 28-30 and 31-36 respectively, while Arnold, with some difference in focus (but still following the same basic correlation), regards these and other passages in *Eclogue 4* as instead referring to how both Vergil and others might develop Roman poetry.[10]

To be sure, this particular approach to *Eclogue 4* is pretty much ignored by both Coleman (1977) and Clausen (1994) in their commentaries, as well as by Penutelli (1995) in his survey of recent scholarship on the poem. There are, however, strong arguments in its favor. One important point is that the word *puer* [boy], which is used four times in *Eclogue 4* (lines 8, 18, 60 and 62) to refer to the child whose birth is celebrated in this poem, is elsewhere in the *Eclogues* used only of shepherds who are closely associated with poetry; for instance, Alexis, the object of Corydon's song at *Eclogue* 2.17 and 45, is so referred to. Another complementary argument is that the verb *incipio* "begin," three times associated with the *puer* in *Eclogue 4*, is elsewhere in the *Eclogues* always associated with poetic performance.

At *Eclogue* 3.58, for example, Palaemon, using the same imperative form *incipe* as is used to address the child at *Eclogue* 4.62, invites Damoetas to begin his poetic competition with Menalcas.

There is also another point, not developed by either Berg or his successor Arnold but yet of considerable significance. Whether, with Berg, we view *Eclogue 4* as specifically prefiguring Vergil's own future poetry or, with Arnold, as a more general poetic manifesto, the manuscript reading *cui non risere parentes* (on whom parents have not smiled) in line 62 gains considerably in plausibility. If the child is somehow poetry, then the parents are Vergil and/or the Muse. Correspondingly, the complaint that it is silly to imagine a parent who would have to be encouraged to smile at its newborn child simply disappears. The Muse should naturally be a severe critic of those whom she inspires, and her smile (as well as Vergil's own) would need to be cultivated. From this perspective, then, *cui non risere parentes* is actually preferable, as indicating that the Muse's approval is necessary for the future success of the child—poetry—which is referred to in the poem.[11]

Notes

1. The entire text of the Greek translation is printed, without much concern for meter, in Migne's stalwart *Patrologia*, vol. 20, cols. 1289-1302. A version with various emendations, mainly to remedy the meter, appears in Kurfess (1937, 284-285), and this is followed in Wlosok (1983, 76-79; Wlosok 1990, 456-459). Also, for a recent survey of scholarship on the Greek translation, see Rochette (1997, 276-277). Some lines from the Latin original, such as 2-3 and 11-12, are omitted in the Greek translation (at least as it has come down to us in Eusebius' citation). The result is that there are just 54 lines in the translation, though I shall follow the usual convention of simply giving the line number from the Vergilian original.
2. From a modern perspective, it might seem that the Greek translation sometimes veers fairly far from the original. Actually, though, it might be better characterized as aiming, within the parameters of ancient translations, distinctly toward the literal side. Most of the evidence, of course, is in the other direction, i.e., from Greek to Latin. (For a provocative treatment of Latin-to-Greek translation, see Fisher [1982]). At least in the case of Greek-Latin translation, it is clear that considerable liberties could be taken in the transfer between the two languages. In Germanicus' translation of Aratus' *Phainomena*, for example, the opening section of the Greek original, dealing with Zeus (lines 1-23), is replaced by a section dealing with Augustus' bringing peace to the Roman Empire; for an overall discussion of Germanicus' translation, see Possanza (in preparation). Rather than anything resembling Germanicus' very free handling of Aratus, the translation of *Eclogue 4* sticks mainly to minor verbal and syntactical adjustments, which yet have a fairly consistent, Christian agenda.

3. For the translator's use of λυκάβαντας (and for references to earlier treatments of the passage), see Wigtil (1978).
4. The question mark is intended to allude to Watkins (1995, 369), where he discusses Rix (1990). Dealing with authors such as Pindar, a whole millennium earlier than Nonnos, Rix had asked more or less the same question. Watkins counters with the following: "Pindar learned the formulas that vehicled in unbroken fashion the Indo-European poetic tradition just as he learned the language that continued unbroken the Indo-European linguistic tradition." Less attention has been paid to first millennium AD Greek in this connection, but basically the same arguments apply to Greek from this period as to Pindar.
5. For the occurrences of forms of ἱμάσσειν in Nonnos' *Dionysiaca*, see Watkins (1995, 459). Watkins' focus, though, is not so much on Nonnos (whom he more or less dismisses as "bizarre"), and he does not consider the parallel occurrence in the *Paraphrasis of John*.
6. See Floyd (1980) and Floyd (1999) for discussion of the correlation of κλέος ἄφθιτον and *sravas...aksitam* and of Cometas' usage of the Greek combination.
7. It may be relevant in this connection to note that Constantine makes the claim that Vergil wrote cryptically so as to avoid persecution in his own time; see Eusebius in Migne, *Patrologia*, vol. 20, cols. 1292-1293.
8. The emended text is printed by both Hirtzel (1900) and Mynors (1969), in their successive Oxford Classical Texts, as well as by Coleman (1977) and Clausen (1994) in their commentaries.
9. Coleman (1977, 148); his discussion continues on p. 149.
10. Berg (1974, 167-177, with notes, 209-211), followed by Arnold (1994-95). Also, Berg, n. 50, p. 210, mentions della Torre (1892) as a predecessor of his own (Berg's) approach to *Eclogue 4*, but I have not seen this nineteenth-century work.
11. The fact that Berg (1974, 50) assumes the correctness of the reading *qui...parenti* does not affect the potential importance of the manuscript reading for his argument. Rather, it simply reflects the extent to which modern scholars tend to assume the correctness of the now "standard" text. Even discussions of the Greek translation, in fact, seem to work on this assumption; Wlosok (1983, 75-79; 1990, 456-459), for example, cites the ostensible "original" (i.e., Mynors' 1969 Oxford text) and the Greek translations on facing pages, with just a note, p. 78 and p. 458, that the manuscripts have *cui non risere parentes*.

Works Cited

Arnold, Bruce. "The Literary Experience of Vergil's Fourth Eclogue." *Classical Journal* 90 (1994-1995): 143-160.
Berg, William. *Early Virgil*. London: Athlone Press, 1974.
Clausen, Wendell. "Virgil's Messianic Eclogue." In *Poetry and Prophecy*, by James L. Kugel, 65-74 and 203-204. Ithaca: Cornell University Press, 1990.
Clausen, Wendell. *A Commentary on Virgil, Eclogues*. Oxford: Clarendon Press, 1994.
Coleman, Robert. *Vergil: Eclogues*. Cambridge: Cambridge University Press, 1977.
della Torre, R. *La quarta egloga di Virgilio commentata secondo l'arte grammatica*. Udine, 1892.

Eusebius. *Constantini Imperatoris Oratio ad Sanctorum Coetum* in Migne, vol. 20, 1233-1316.

Fisher, Elizabeth A. "Greek translations of Latin literature in the fourth century A.D." *Yale Classical Studies* 27 (1982): 173-215.

Floyd, Edwin D. "Kleos aphthiton: An Indo-European Perspective on Early Greek Poetry." *Glotta* 58 (1980): 133-157.

—. "Cometas, On Lazarus: A Resurrection of Indo-European Poetics?" *Proceedings of the Tenth Annual UCLA Indo-European Conference: Los Angeles, May 21-23, 1998. Journal of Indo-European Studies Monograph Series* 32 (1999): 183-201.

Hirtzel, Frederick Arthur. *P. Vergili Maronis Opera.* Oxford: Clarendon Press, 1900.

Johnson, Samuel. "Translation of Pope's 'Messiah.'" In *Poems (The Yale Edition of the Works of Samuel Johnson,* vol. 6), ed. E. L. McAdam, Jr., with George Milne, 30-33. New Haven and London: Yale University Press, 1964.

Koller, Hermann. "Λυκάβας." *Glotta* 51 (1973): 29-34.

Kurfess, Alfons. "Die griechische Übersetzung der vierten Ekloge Vergils." *Mnemosyne*, ser. 3, vol. 5 (1937): 283-288.

Migne, J.-P. *Patrologia cursus completus: Series graeca.* Paris: Migne, 1857-1866.

Mynors, R. A. N. *P. Vergili Maronis Opera.* Oxford: Clarendon Press, 1969.

Penutelli, A. "Bucolics." In *A Companion to the Study of Virgil,* by Nicholas Horsfall, 27-62. London: Brill, 1995.

Pope, Alexander. "Messiah." In *Poems, vol. 1: Pastoral Poetry and an Essay on Criticism.* Ed. E. Audra and Aubrey Williams, 112-122. London: Methuen, 1961.

Possanza, Mark. *Translating the Heavens: Aratus, Germanicus and the Poetics of Latin Translation.* Unpublished manuscript.

Rix, Helmut. "Review of Studies in Memory of Warren Cowgill (1929-1985)." *Kratylos* 35 (1990): 41-48.

Rochette, Bruno. *Le latin dans le monde grec: Recherches sur la diffusion de la langue et des lettres latines dans les provinces hellénophones de l'Empire romain.* Brussels: Collection Latomus 233, 1997.

Schmitt, Rüdiger. *Dichtung und Dichtersprache in indogermanischer Zeit.* Wiesbaden: Otto Harrassowitz, 1967.

Watkins, Calvert. *How to Kill a Dragon: Aspects of Indo-European Poetics.* New York and Oxford: Oxford University Press, 1995.

Wigtil, David N. "A Note on Λυκάβας." *American Journal of Philology* 99 (1978): 334-335.

Wlosok, Antonie. "Zwei Beispiele frühchristlicher 'Vergilrezeption': Polemik (Lact., div. inst. 5, 10) und Usurpation (Or. Const. 19-21)." In *2000 Jahre Vergil: Ein Symposion*, by Victor Pöschl, 63-86. Wiesbaden: Otto Harrassowitz, 1983; also pp. 437-459 in Wlosok, *Res Humanae—res divinae.* Heidelberg: Carl Winter, 1990.

Translation and Tradition: Reading the *Consolation of Philosophy* Through King Alfred's *Boethius*

David A. Lopez
Deep Springs College

Comparative textual studies between original texts and later translations, such as those presented by my colleagues in this volume, have significantly improved scholars' understanding of many facets of ancient and medieval societies. In the process of examining how political motivations of the translators differed from those of the original authors, much insight has been gained into the broad relationships between text and society. In these studies, it has generally been assumed that differing political motivations *must* fundamentally alter the roles of the original and the translation. I would like to suggest here, however, that such a fundamental alteration is not *necessarily* a consequence of translation; it is possible, despite differing political motivations between author and translator, that both the original and the translation maintain essentially the same roles within their respective societies.

To demonstrate how this might be so, I will concentrate on Alfred's *Boethius*, a ninth-century translation from Latin into English of Boethius' sixth-century *Consolation of Philosophy*. Boethius composed the original about 524—ostensibly as an *apologia* for his actions—after having been imprisoned by Theoderic, the Arian Christian king of Ostrogothic Italy, under charges of treasonously plotting with orthodox senators in Constantinople to overthrow Theoderic (O'Daly 1991). Alfred's translation was made about 887, as part of a broad effort of educational reform undertaken to help reinforce royal authority and Christian administration in the West Saxon kingdom, in the face of nearly overwhelming Viking invasions (Otten 1964; Frakes 1988).

I shall demonstrate my thesis by addressing one question central to the interpretation of the original text that has not yet been answered in a satisfactory manner: namely, the nature of its relationship to Christianity. Of the six texts chosen by Alfred to compose the core library for his education reforms, the *Consolation* is the only one not explicitly Christian and orthodox; but Alfred, relying on a tradition of Boethius' orthodoxy, has little trouble making his version explicitly Christian. Alfred's reading of the *Consolation* as a Christian text despite its non-Christian appearance begs the question: Why is there no explicit Christianity in the *Consolation*?

Previous answers to this question have been shown to be untenable. It was once advanced that there might be two writers named Boethius, one a Christian, the author of the five theological tractates that bear that name; the other pagan, the author of the *Consolation*. It has since been proven through textual analyses that the author of the theological tractates was almost certainly the same person as the author of the *Consolation* (Rand, Stewart and Tester 1973). The suggestion was then entertained that this single Boethius became disillusioned with Christianity after his arrest and the failure of the Roman clergy to support him, and apostatized in prison; but as Henry Chadwick has successfully argued,

> If the *Consolation* contains nothing distinctively Christian, it is also relevant that it contains nothing specifically pagan, either.... [T]he *Consolation* contains no sentence that looks like a confession of faith either in the gods of paganism or in Christian redemption.... Everything specific is absent, and probably consciously avoided. The ambiguity seems clearly to be deliberate (Chadwick 1981, 249).

In formulating his own answer to the question, Chadwick ignores the possibility that the tradition of Christian interpretation of the *Consolation*, and particularly Alfred's translation of it, can profitably be considered.[1] The only solution that Chadwick can thus propose to account for the religious ambiguity of the text is an assertion of "humanism" for Boethius. Such an assertion does not, however, answer the question in a meaningful way. Boethius' humanism did not, after all, prevent him from being unambiguous in the theological tractates; why should it have done so in the *Consolation*?

A close comparison of the *Consolation* and Alfred's *Boethius* does, I believe, illuminate the nature of Boethius' ambiguity. Alfred in his translation connects the two themes of human tyranny and divine rule of the cosmos that recur [2] throughout the *Consolation*, themes with which modern scholarship has only dealt separately (O'Daly 1991, 75-98). But, I believe, precisely in the contrast between these two themes can be found the key to understanding the *Consolation*'s religious ambiguity and its relevance to the circumstances of its composition.

Boethius introduces the theme of divine rule quite early in the work. He insists first on the antiquity of the divine law:

> [N]ihil antiqua lege solutum linquit propriae stationis opus. Omnia certo fine gubernans hominum solos respuis actus merito rector cohibere modo (I.V.23-7).[3]

> [The action of each particular position leaves nothing absolved from ancient law. Governing all things to a certain end, you [i.e., God], the ruler, refuse to limit only the acts of man to a meritorious path.]

This "ancient law" governs every action of all things to a predetermined end. Moreover, the monarchical nature of the divine rule of the cosmos implies that monarchy is the best and proper form of rule within human society:

> Si enim cuius oriundo sis patriae reminiscare, non uti Atheniensium quondam multitudinis imperio regitur, sed εἰς κοίρανός ἐστιν, εἰς βασιλεύς [*Iliad* II:204], qui frequentia ciuium non depulsione laetetur, cuius agi frenis atque obtemperare iustitiae libertas est (I.5.4).

> [If indeed you recall from which country you are descended, not as in Athens long ago is it ruled by the power of many, but *One is its lord, and one its king*, who is pleased by the attendance, not the banishment, of subjects; to be guided by his bridle and to submit to his precepts is freedom.]

Divinity rules the cosmos just as a king rules his kingdom; humans are the subjects of both sort of king. Yet the status of mankind within the cosmos is exceptional: Humans are exempt from direct divine control, being free to choose between good and evil actions. Nevertheless, the divine king prefers his subjects to choose the good, which is true freedom, thus avoiding banishment.

Moreover, if true freedom lies in obedience to the ancient law of the divine king, so, too, true happiness:

> Nam nisi fallor, ea uera est et perfecta felicitas quae sufficientem, potentem, reuerendum, celebrem laetumque perficiat. Atque ut me interius animaduertisse cognoscas, quae unum horum, quoniam idem cuncta sunt, ueraciter praestare potest, hanc esse plenam beatitudinem sine ambiguitate cognosco. O te, alumne, hac opinione felicem, si quidem hoc, inquit, adieceris! Quidnam? inquam. Essene aliquid in his mortalibus caducisque rebus putas quod huius modi statum possit affere? Minime, inquam, puto idque a te, nihil ut amplius desideretur, ostensum est. Haec igitur uel imagines ueri boni uel imperfecta quaedam bona dare mortalibus uidentur, uerum autem perfectum bonum conferre non possunt (III.9.26-30).

["Now unless I am mistaken, that is true and perfect happiness which makes one sufficient, powerful, well-respected, widely-honored, and joyful. And so that you may know that I have understood more profoundly, I know that what can truly evince one of these is, since they are all the same, complete happiness without ambiguity." She replied, "O you pupil, happy by this opinion, if you but add this certain thing." "What is that?" I said. "Do you think there to be anything among these mortal and perishable affairs which could confer a state of this kind?" "Not at all do I think so," I replied, "and nothing of what is shown by you could be more fully proven." "Therefore these things are seen to give to mortals an image of the true good, or some imperfect good; but they cannot confer the true, perfect good."]

No earthly means can gain true happiness, but only imperfect images of happiness; for those who understand rightly, true happiness, like true freedom, can be found in seeking the divine and in obedience to the "ancient law."

Thus, for Boethius, the created world is an ordered and purposeful place in which humans act freely in ways either good or evil; only good actions lead to true freedom and happiness. Now Boethius juxtaposes to this theme of divine rule that of human tyranny. This rule, too, directs what is subject to it to a certain end, but the end is destruction and ruin, not freedom and happiness:

Nouimus quantas dederit ruinas urbe flammata patribusque caesis.... Celsa num tandem ualuit potestas uertere praui rabiem Neronis (II.VI.1-2, 14-15)?

[We know how much destruction he (i.e., Nero) caused, when the city (i.e., Rome) burned and her fathers perished.... Did exalted power suffice in the end to avert madness from the perverse Nero?]

Nero, the prototypical human tyrant, is here described as "mad" and "perverse." He burns his own city for amusement and murders the leaders of the empire as well as his own family. He cannot control his passions, and so his power is detrimental to him. This is, indeed, the case with all tyrants:

Qui se uolet esse potentem, animos domet ille feroces.... tamen atras pellere curas miserasque fugare querelas non posse potentia non est (III.V.1-2, 8-10).

[He who wishes himself to be powerful, let him rule (his own) savage passions.... (P)ower, however, is not able to banish fierce disturbances of mind, nor to chase out wretched complaints.]

The ruler who is in control of his passions can employ his power wisely.

The one who is not, however, does not gain from his power; his passions consume him and dictate the use of his power to him—to the detriment of his human subjects. Such, to Boethius, is the nature of tyranny.

For Alfred, these two themes from the *Consolation* are not merely juxtaposed, but interwoven; as I shall show, Alfred reads them as mutual commentaries: two sides of the same coin, as it were. Alfred closely follows his original in introducing the divine rule of God quite early in his text; but where Boethius stresses the antiquity of the divine laws, Alfred stresses the need of mankind to be obedient to them:

> Hwæt þe ealle gesceafta heorsumiaþond þa gesetnessa þinra beboda healdað. butan men anum se ðe oferheorð. Eala ðu ælmihtiga scippend and rihtend eallra gesceafta. help nu þinum earmum moncynne (Ch. IV).[4]

> [What! do all creatures obey you, and keep the institutions of your commandments, except man alone, who is disobedient? O, you almighty maker and governor of all creatures, help now your miserable mankind.]

For Alfred, as for Boethius, mankind alone has the potential not to obey the divine commandments. Alfred, however, further implies that mankind cannot remain obedient without the continual help of God.

Alfred does not stress the metaphor of divine governance as royal. In other respects, however, for Alfred the relationship between God and man is much as it is for Boethius. God desires mankind to choose to obey and rewards those who do while punishing those who do not. Alfred is somewhat more explicit than Boethius:

> [N]e sceolde þe eac nan man swelces to gelefan þær ðu gemunan woldest hwylcra gebyrda þu wære ond hwylcra burgwara for worulde. oþþe eft gastlice hwilces geferscipes ðu wære on ðinum Mode. ond on þinre gesceadwisnisse. þæt is þæt þu eart an þara rihtwisenra ond þara rihtwillendra. þa beoþ þære heofencundan Ierusalem burgware.... Swa hwa þonne swa þæs wyrþe biþ þæt he on heora ðeowdome beon mot. þonne bið he on þam hehstan freodome (Ch. V§1).

> [Nor could anyone thus believe it of you, when you would call to mind, of what families you were, and of what citizens, as to the world; or again, spiritually, of what society you were in your mind, and in your reason; that is that you are among those who think rightly and will rightly,[5] who are citizens of the heavenly Jerusalem.... Whosoever, then, is worthy of this, that he may be in their [i.e., the heavenly citizens'] service, he is in the highest

freedom.]

The choice to obey divine law is again equated with true freedom. Those who so choose are "right thinking" and citizens of the heavenly Jerusalem. Just as for Boethius, for Alfred true freedom and true happiness have the same source, obedience to divine laws; nor is it possible to achieve either true freedom or true happiness apart from the divine:

Ac þæs me ðincþ þæt þæt beo seo soþe ond seo fullfremede gesælþ. ðe mæg ælcum hire folgera sellan þurhwunigendne welan. ond ecne anweald. ond singalne weorþscipe. ond ece mærþe. ond fulle genyht. ge furþum þæt ic cweþe sie seo soþe gesælþ ðe an þissa fifa mæg fullice forgifan. forþam[6] ðe on ælcum anum hi sint ealle. forþam ic secge þas word ðe. for þy ic wille þæt þu wite þæt se cwide swiþe fæst is on minum Mode. swa fæst þæt his me nan man gedweligan ne mæg. Ða cwæþ he. Eala cniht. hwæt þu eart gesælig þæt þu hit swa ongiten hæfst. Ac ic wolde þæt wit spyredon git æfter ðam þe þe wana is. Ða cwæþ ic. Hwæt is þæt þonne. Ða cwæþ he. Wenst þu hwæþer ænig þissa andweardana gooda þe mæge sellan fulle gesælþe. Ða andswarode ic. ond cwæþ. Nat ic nan wuht on þys andweardan life þe swelc gifan mæge. Ða cwæþ he. Ðas andweardan god sint anlicnessa ðæs ecan godes. næs full god. forþam hi ne magon soþ god ond full god forgifan heora folgerum (Ch. XXXIII§3).

[But it seems to me[7] that that is the true and the perfect happiness, which can give to all its followers permanent wealth, and everlasting power, and perpetual dignity, and eternal glory, and full abundance. And moreover, I say that is the true happiness which can bestow any of these five; because in every one they all are. I say these words to you, because I am desirous that you should know that the doctrine is well fixed in my mind: so fixed, that no man can draw me aside from it. Then said he, "O, child, how happy you are, that you have so learned it! But I am desirous that we should still inquire after that which is deficient to you." Then said I, "What is that, then?" Then said he, "Do you think that any of these present goods can give you full happiness?" Then answered I, and said, "I know nothing in this present life that can give such." Then said he, "These present goods are images of the eternal good, not full good, because they cannot give true good nor full good to their followers."]

Alfred's translation at this point is very close to the original. Alfred's "right-thinking" people recognize the limited nature of happiness derived from worldly pursuits and the necessity of obedience to the divine laws for attaining true happiness. Those who do so can attain "everlasting power," the same power God Himself uses to rule the cosmos.

Alfred explicitly contrasts this power with that of tyrants. While Boethius insists that tyrants lack true power, Alfred admits that tyrants can have power of a sort, but of the wrong sort:

> Hwæt we witon hwelce wælhriownessa. ond hwilce hryras. hwilce unrihthæmedu. ond hwilc man. ond hwilce arleasnesse se unrihtwisa Casere Neron weorhte. se het æt sumum cyrre forbærnan ealla Rome burh on anne sið æfter þære bisene þe gio Trogia burg barn. hine lyste eac geseon hu seo burne. ond hu lange. ond hu leohte be þære oþerre. ond eft he het ofslean ealla þa wisestan witan Romana... Wenst þu þæt se godcunda anweald ne mihte afyrran þone anweald þam unrihtwisan Casere. and him þære wuhhunge gesteoran. gif he wolde... Nu ne was þær genog sweotol þæt se anweald his agenes ðonces god næs. þa se god næs þe he to com (Ch. XVI§4).

> [We know what cruelties, and what ruins, and what adulteries, and what wickedness, and what impiety, the unrighteous Caesar, Nero, wrought. He at one time gave order to burn all the city of Rome at once, after the example that formerly the city of Troy was burned. He was desirous also to see how it would burn, and how long, and how bright, in comparison with the other; and he besides gave order to slay all the wisest counselors[8] of the Romans.... Think you that the heavenly Power could not take away the power[9] from this unrighteous Caesar, and correct the madness in him, if he would?... Was it not them sufficiently evident, that power of its own nature was not good, when he was not good to whom it came?]

Nero is here presented in the same broad strokes as in Boethius' text: Wicked, mad, he burns Rome for amusement and murders his wise councilors. But Alfred's choice of vocabulary is much more closely tied to that of the passages already cited; while God is *rihtend* and the citizens of the heavenly Jerusalem are *rihtwise*, Nero is *unrihtwise*. Both God and Nero have *anweald*, but even Nero's "unrighteous power" is dependent on the forbearance of God in not removing that power from him. Nero is again the type of the tyrant, but his tyranny seems much more clearly opposed to the divine rule of the cosmos than is immediately apparent in the *Consolation*.

Still, for Alfred and Boethius, the nature of tyranny is the same:

> Ðe þe wille fullice anweald agan. he sceal tilian ærest þæt he hæbbe anweald his agenes modes. ond ne sie to ungerisenlice underþeod his unþeawum (Ch. XXIX§3).

> [Whoever desires fully to possess power, ought to labor first that he may have power over his own mind, and be not indecently subject to his vices....]

Like Boethius, Alfred claims that the tyrant who fails to control his passions will be unable to wield power justly; but Alfred adds that the ruler who can control his passions will have power "fully." This distinction between full power and other power recalls that between true freedom and mere worldly freedom, or between full happiness and mere worldly happiness. Alfred again makes more explicit the opposition between the two themes.

The connection between these two themes in Alfred's *Boethius* can more clearly be seen in his translation of the climactic poem *O qui perpetua*, in praise of the divine creator:

> Eala Dryhten. hu micel ond hu wunderlic þu earþ. ðu þe ealle þine gesceafta. gesewenlice ond eac ungesewenlice. wunderlice gesceope ond gesceadwislice heora weltst. ðu þe tida fram middaneardes fruman oþ ðone ende endebyrdlice gesettest. swa þæt te hi ægþer ge forð faraþ. ge eftcumaþ. þu þe ealle ða unstillan gesceafta to þinum willan astyrast. ond ðu self simle stille and unagendedlic ðurhwunast. forþamþe nan mihtigra þe nis. ne nan þin gelica. ne þe nan neodðearf ne lærde to wyrcanne þæt þæt ðu worctest. ac mid þinum agenum willan. ond mid þinum agenum anwealde þu ealle ðing geworctest. ðeah ðu heora nanes ne beþorfte.... Ne bisnode þe nan man. forþam ðe nan ær þe næs. þara þe auht oððe nauht worhte. Ac þu ealle þing geworhtest swiþe gode ond swiþe fægere. ond þu self eart þæt hehste god ond þæt fægerests. swa swa þu self geworhtest. þu geworhtest þisne middan geard. ond his welst swa swa ðu wilt. ond þu self dælst eall god swa swa ðu wilt.... Hwæt þu Drihten forgeafe þam sawlum eard on hiofonum. ond him þær gifst weorþlice gifa. ælcere be hire geearnunge. ond gedest þæt he scinaþ swiþe beorhte. ond ðeah swiþe mistlice birhtu. sume beorhtor. unbyrhtor. swa swa sterran. ælc be his geearnunga. Hwæt þu Drihten gegærderast ða hiofonlicon sawla ond ða eorþlican lichoman. ond hi on ðisse worulde gemengest. swa swa hi from ðe hider comon. swa hi eac to ðe hionan fundiaþ. Ðu fyldest þas eorþan mid mistlicum cynrenum netena. ond hi siþþan areowe mistlicum sæde treowa ond wyrta (Ch. XXXIII§4).

> [O Lord, how great and how wonderful you are! You who all your creatures visible and also invisible wonderfully have created, and rationally govern them! You who times, from the beginning of the middle-earth to the end, set in order, so that they both depart and return! You, who all moving creatures according to your will stir, and you yourself always fixed and unchangeable remain! No necessity taught you to make what you have made, but by your own will and by your own power you made all things, though you did need none of them.... No man set you an example, for no one was before you, who anything or nothing might make. But you have

made all things very good, and very fair, and you yourself are the highest good and the fairest. As you yourself did design, so you have made this middle-earth, and govern it as you will; and you yourself distribute all good as you will.... You, O Lord, have given to souls a dwelling in the heavens, and on them you bestow worthy gifts, to every one according to its deserving; and cause them to shine very bright, and yet with varied brightness, some brighter, some less bright, even as the stars, every one according to its desert. You, O Lord, bring together the heavenly souls and the earthly bodies, and unite them in this world. As they from you came hither, so shall they also to you hence tend. You filled this earth with various kinds of animals, and afterwards sowed it with various seed of trees and plants!]

Unlike the power of the tyrant who is enslaved to passion, the power of the creator in conceiving and directing all creation is explicitly rational, immutable and freely chosen. God is the archetype of goodness, the pattern after which everything else is made, and particularly human souls, which naturally desire to return to their source, despite the freedom of choice between good and evil inherent in the human will.

In this passage, however, Alfred has not interpolated the connection between the two themes of human tyranny and divine rule. The same explicitness exists in the original text:

O qui perpetua mundum ratione gubernas, terrarum caelique sator, qui tempus ab aeuo ire iubes stabilisque manens das cuncta moueri quem non externae pepulerunt fingere causae materiae fluitantis opus uerum insita summi forma boni liuore carens, tu cuncta superno ducis ab exemplo, pulchrum pulcherrimus ipse mundum mente gerens similique in imagine formans perfectasque iubens perfectum absoluere partes. Tu numeris elementa ligas, ut frigora flammis, arida conueniant liquidis, ne purior ignis euolet aut mersas deducant pondera terras... Tu causis animas paribus uitasque minores prouehis et leuibus sublimes curribus aptans in caelum terramque seris, quas lege benigna ad te conuersas reduci facis igne reuerti (III.IX.1-12, 18-21).

[O you who govern the world by constant reason, creator of earth and of heaven, who command time (i.e., measurable time) to come forth from eternity (i.e., undifferentiated time) and, remaining motionless, permit all things to move, whom external causes did not force to shape a work of floating matter, (a work) true to the innate form of the highest good, (a work) lacking malice; you command all things from a celestial pattern, itself most beautiful, regulating by mind the beautiful world, and forming (it) in like image, and commanding perfect parts to complete a perfect whole. You bind the elements by harmony, so that cold things unite with hot, and dry with wet; so that fire not emerge more bright, nor weighty things drag down the sunken lands.... Through equal causes, you bring forth souls and lesser lives, and, fitting (them) uplifted to swift chariots, you sow (them) in earth and sky; you cause them, turned towards you by a benign law, to be drawn back and returned through fire.]

Here, too, the power of the divine creator is explicitly contrasted to the inability of the tyrant to rule his passions. The creator conceives and directs through mind and reason. The creator is the form of the highest good, and therefore all creation is good, including the human soul, which, according to the divine law, naturally tends to return to its source.

Boethius in this passage, the centerpiece of the whole work (Chadwick 1981, 234-235), not merely juxtaposes but unites and interweaves the two themes of divine rule of the cosmos and impassioned human tyranny. The rational lawfulness of the divine *potentia* contrasts explicitly with the irrational destructiveness of tyrannical *impotentia*. The *Consolation* is a work concerned with virtue, and particularly with kingly virtue. The central theme of Alfred's *Boethius*, namely, *rihtwise anweald* versus *unrihtwise anweald*, is an interpretation of Boethius' text entirely justifiable from within the *Consolation*.

If, then, one reads these two themes in the *Consolation* as interwoven and opposed, rather than as merely juxtaposed, then certain other passages begin to take on greater significance. These passages suggest that the contrasting themes of just and unjust rule are not gratuitous, but rather invite the audience to derive conclusions that seem particularly relevant to Theoderic's new religious policies. Boethius, despite his disgrace and imprisonment, indicates to Theoderic that certain of his actions have more in common with tyrants like Nero than with the just rule of the divine. Alfred's treatment of these passages does not alter the fundamental purpose of the text in relation to society—that is, to establish a concept of proper human rule deriving from a parallel concept of divine rule, yet, lacking the same direct relevance to immediate circumstance, Alfred gives his work a more generalized meaning than does Boethius.

Boethius argues that since the divine ruler is good, and since all things created by goodness tend to the good, then nothing can fail to tend to the good and still remain in the state in which it was created:

Cum deus, inquit, omnia bonitatis clauo gubernare iure credatur eademque omnia, sicuti docui, ad bonum naturali intentione festinent, num dubitari potest quin uoluntaria regantur seque ad disponentis nutum ueluti conuenientia contemperataque rectori sponte conuertant? - Ita, inquam, necesse est; nec beatum regimen esse uideretur, si quidem detrectantium iugum foret, non obtemperantium salus. - Nihil est igitur, quod naturam seruans deo contra ire conetur? - Nihil, inquam (III.12.17-19).

["Since God," she said, "is justly believed to govern all things through the rudder of goodness, and all these things, as I have taught (you), hasten to the good through natural intention, can it be doubted that they are ruled voluntarily and turn themselves willingly to the command of the one setting them in order, just as things united to and commingled with their ruler?" I replied, "So it must be; and the rule would not seem good, if indeed it were a yoke of the sort which is refused, and not a salvation of the sort which is obeyed." "There is nothing, then, which might undertake to go against God while preserving (its own) nature?" "Nothing," I replied.]

The stark finality of the reply to Philosophia's second question leaves no doubt as to the fate of those who reject the harmonious order of the divine law. Such pointedness is striking. To disturb this harmonious order, as Theoderic's sudden reversal of his long-standing policy of religious toleration had done, must ultimately be self-defeating. Boethius here warns Theoderic against continuing the new, intolerant policy for the good of the kingdom as a whole.

For Alfred, however, this passage has a general, not a particular, meaning. Alfred makes this clear with an interpolation at the end of the passage:

Ne mæg nænne mon þæs tweogan þæt te eallra gesceafta agnum willan God ricsaþ ofer hi. ond eaþmodlice hiora willan wendaþ to his willan. Be þæm is swiþe sweotol þæt to God æghwær wealt mid þæm helman and mid þæm stiorroþre his godnesse. forþamþe ealle gesceafta gecyndelice hiora agnum willum fundiaþ to cumanne to gode. swa swa we oft ær sædon on þisse ilcan bec. Ða cwæþ ic. Hwi ne mæg ic þæs tweogan. forþamþe Godes anweald nære full eadiglic. gif þa gesceafta hiroa unwillum him herden. ond eft ða gesceafta næron nanes ðonces ne nanes weorþscipes weorþe. gif hi heora unwillum hlaforde herden. Ða cwæþ he. Nis nan gesceaft ðe he tiohhige þæt hio scyle winnan wiþ hire scippendes willan gif hio hire gecynd healdan wile. Ða cwæþ ic. Nis nan gesceaft þe wiþ hire scippendes willan winne. buton dysig mon. oððe eft ða wiþerwierdan englas (Ch. XXXV§4).

[No man can doubt this, that by the proper consent of all creatures God reigns over them, and bends their will conformably to his will. By this it is very evident that God governs everything with the helm and with the rudder of his goodness. For all creatures naturally of their own will endeavor to come to good, as we have often before said in this same book. Then said I, "Indeed I cannot doubt it, for God's power would not be entirely perfect if creatures obeyed him against their will: and again the creatures would not be worthy of any thanks or any honour if they unwillingly obeyed their lord." Then said he, "There is no creature which attempts to contend against its Maker's will, if it desire to retain its nature." Then said I, "There is no creature which contends against its Maker's will except foolish man, or again the rebellious angels."]

Boethius' stark "nothing" has become generalized. Alfred is willing to admit that mankind's freedom of choice does allow one to disregard the divine will, though not without consequences. His interpolated remark about foolish men and rebellious angels reduces the pointedness of the passage. The difference is significant, changing the passage's tone and affecting the audience on a different level, yet it has not altered the essential purpose of the passage.

Boethius further criticizes Theoderic's intolerance for its inevitable lack of success. While Theoderic may certainly injure his non-Arian subjects in their body or their possessions, he will never convince or convert the devout orthodox, like Boethius himself:

Quo vero quisquam ius aliquod in quempiam nisi in solum corpus et quod infra corpus est—fortunam loquor—possit exserere? Num quicquam libero imperabis animo? Num mentem firma sibi ratione cohaerentem de statu propriae quietis amouebis? Cum liberum quendam uirum suppliciis se tyrannus adacturum putaret ut aduersum se factae coniurationis conscios proderet, linguam ille momordit atque abscidit et in os tyranni saeuientis adiecit; ita cruciatus, quos putabat tyrannus materiam crudelitatis, uir sapiens fecit esse uirtutis. Quid autem est quod in alium facere quisque possit, quod sustinere ab alio ipse non possit (II.6.6-9)?

[Who indeed could stretch forth any rule on any other person, except over the body alone and what is inferior to the body—I mean possessions? Will you command anything to a free soul? Will you move a mind clinging to itself by firm reason from its state of inner repose? When the tyrant (i.e., Nearchus) thought that he would compel with torture a certain free man (i.e., Zeno) to betray those who knew of a conspiracy against him (i.e., Nearchus), he (i.e., Zeno) bit off his tongue and threw it in the face of the raging tyrant; tortured in this way, the wise man made virtuous what the tyrant thought a matter of cruelty. But what is there which one can do to another, which he cannot himself suffer from another?]

Whatever physical tortures may be employed, no right-thinking person, whose mind is set in the proper relationship with the divine, who possesses true freedom and true happiness, can ever be made to think wrongly. The ruler who attempts such a thing will only rage powerlessly while the virtue of the right-thinking increases. The striking shift from third to second person in the opening series of questions allows Boethius to speak dramatically to the intended audience: Will you, Theoderic, attempt, like Nearchus, this pointless thing?

Alfred again retains the content of the passage but changes the pointedness of tone to suit his wider audience:

> On hwæm mæg ænig man oþrum derian buton on his lichoman. oððe eft on heora welum. þe ge hataþ gesælþa. ne nan mon ne mæg þam gesceadwisan Mode gederian. ne him gedon þæt hit ne sie þæt þæt it biþ. Ðæt is swiþe sweotol to ongitanne be sumum Romaniscum æðelinge. se wæs haten Liberius.[10] se was to manegum witum geworht. forþam þe he nolde meldian on his geferan þe mid him sieredon ymbe þone cyning þe hie ær mid unrihte gewunnen hæfde. þa he þa beforan þone graman cyning gelæd wæs. ond he hine het secgan hwæt his geferan wæron þe mid him sieredon. þa forceaw he his agene tungan. and wearp hine ðær mid on ðæt neb foran. forþam hit gewearð þæt ðam wisan men com to lofe and to wyrðscipe þæt se unrihtwisa cyning him teohhoda to wite. Hwæt is þæt þe ma þæt ænig man mæge oþrum don. þat he ne mæge him don þæt ilce. ond gif he ne mæg. oþer man mæg (Ch. XVI§2).

> [Wherein can any man injure another, except in his body? Or again in their riches, which you call goods? No man can injure the rational mind, or cause it that it should not be what it is. This is very evidently to be known by a certain Roman nobleman, who was called Liberius. He was put to many torments because he would not inform against his associates, who conspired with him against the king who had with injustice conquered them. When he was led before the enraged king, and he commanded him to say who were his associates who had conspired with him, then he bit off his own tongue, and immediately cast it before the face [of the tyrant]. Hence it happened that, to the wise man, that was the cause of praise and honour, which the unjust king appointed to him for punishment. What is it, moreover, that any man can do to another, which he may not do to him in like manner? And if he may not, another man may.]

Alfred, too, claims that one's body and one's possessions are susceptible to injury but that the rational mind cannot be influenced by persecution. But Alfred puts the whole passage into the third person, condensing the initial questions and expanding the anecdote. The result mitigates the pointedness of the original. The tone of Alfred's translation is less dramatic, the significance more general.

Alfred reads the *Consolation* as an extended commentary on

virtue, and particularly on kingly virtue. The contrasting themes of divine rule of the cosmos and impassioned human tyranny, which are central in *Boethius*, are clearly present and connected in the original. Boethius, I believe, intended his work to be read in precisely this manner. Boethius, even disgraced and imprisoned, refused to lay aside the advisorial role, composing a work whose intended audience included Theoderic and the royal court. Boethius attempted to point out to Theoderic that the new policy of persecution and intolerance toward orthodox Christians by this Arian king was, in fact, unkingly, necessarily entailing negative consequences to the kingdom.

Herein lies the key to unlocking the problem of the *Consolation*'s religious ambiguity. As Chadwick and others have said, the ambiguity is almost certainly deliberate (Chadwick 1981, 249). Boethius was imprisoned precisely for a religious difference; tensions between orthodox and Arian were high. In order for the *Consolation* to be able to cross that divide, it necessarily needed to avoid reference to the religious nature of the quarrel. This Boethius accomplished splendidly. By relying solely on natural knowledge, by leaving aside the theological controversies inherent in any reference to revealed knowledge, Boethius created a text capable of being read both by his orthodox supporters and by Theoderic and the royal court.

Is, then, the *Consolation* a Christian text? Certainly there is nothing in it incompatible with Christianity. It was composed by a Christian; it was intended for a Christian audience, both orthodox and Arian; and it concerns broad problems of authority and virtue in a primarily Christian society. To this extent, I believe, the *Consolation* must be considered a Christian text.

The comparison of the two versions of the *Consolation* undertaken here has demonstrated how comparative translation studies need not necessarily assume that the different circumstances under which the original and its translation were composed create a fundamental difference in the nature of the text and its relationship with the society of its composer. Indeed, by avoiding this assumption, by reading the original text in light of the interpretation offered by Alfred's translation—an interpretation for which there is ample internal evidence in the *Consolation*—one is able to solve a persistent problem for modern scholarship concerning the original. Alfred's interpretation, and the tradition on which it is founded—which can be traced back contemporaneously to Boethius—should not too readily be dismissed in attempting to interpret the original. In this case, the existence of a translation that has not fundamentally altered the political underpinnings of the original offers more interpretive information than the original alone.

Notes

1. This tradition begins with Boethius' contemporary Cassiodorus; see, for example, Chadwick (1981); O'Donnell (1977); and especially Usener (1877). On the anonymous Saint Gall commentary available to Alfred, see especially Courcelle (1967). On whether Alfred actually made use of this commentary, compare, in the affirmative, Courcelle (1967), Bolton (1977, 33-78) and Donaghey (1964, 23-57); and in the negative, Wittig (1983, 157-98) and Bately (1984).
2. The major passages on human tyranny are I.3.10-11; II.V.13-8, 23-6; II.6.1, 6-9; II.VI.1-2, 13-8; III.4.2; III.IV.1-8; III.5.5-6; III.V.1-2, 8-10; IV.2.2, 23-4; IV.II.1-10; and on divine rule, I.V.23-7; I.5.4; I.VI.16-9; II.VIII.13-8; III.II.1-5; III.9.26-30; III.IX.1-21; III.12.17-9; IV.1.3, 7; IV.I.19-22; IV.6.55-6; IV.VI.34-48.
3. This and all further quotations from the *Consolation* are cited from Bieler (1957). According to standard usage, prose selections are cited by Book, Prosa and section number, with Roman, Arabic and Arabic numerals respectively; verse selections are cited by Book, Versa, and line numbers, with Roman, Roman and Arabic numerals respectively. Translations from the Latin are my own.
4. This and all further quotations from *Boethius* are from Fox (1970). Translations are according to Fox, except where noted, and except for the change throughout of "thee," "thou" and "thine" to "you" and "your."
5 Fox: ...that is that you are one of the just, and of those who will rightly...
6. Fox, in error: þorþam.
7. Fox, too strongly: But of this I am persuaded...
8. Fox, modernizing: senators.
9. Fox, figuratively: empire.
10. Fox, p. 355 n. 13, suggests that Alfred mistook the adjective *liberum* for a proper name.

Works Cited

Bately, J. "The Literary Prose of King Alfred's Reign: Translation or Transformation?" Inaugural Lecture of the Chair of English Language and Medieval Literature, King's College, University of London. Delivered March 4, 1980. Reprinted in *Old English Subsidia* 10 (1984).

Bieler, L., ed. *Anicii Manlii Severini Boethii Philosophiae Consolatio*. Corpus Christianorum, Series Latina XCIV. Turnholt: Brepols, 1957.

Bolton, D. K. "The Study of the *Consolation of Philosophy* in Anglo-Saxon England." *Archives d'histoire doctrinale et littéraire du moyen âge* 64 (1977): 33-78.

Chadwick, H. *Boethius: The Consolations of Music, Logic, Theology, and Philosophy*. Oxford: Clarendon Press; New York: Oxford University Press, 1981.

Courcelle, P. *La Consolation de Philosophie dans la tradition littéraire*. Paris: Études Augustiniennes, 1967.

Donaghey, B. "The Sources of King Alfred's Translation of the *Consolation of*

Philosophy." Anglia 82 (1964): 23-57.

Fox, S. *King Alfred's Anglo-Saxon Version of Boethius'* De Consolatione Philosophiae, *with a literal English translation, notes, and glossary.* New York: AMS Press, 1970.

Frakes, J. The Fate of Fortune in the Early Middle Ages: The Boethian Tradition. New York: E. J. Brill, 1988.

O'Daly, G. *The Poetry of Boethius.* Chapel Hill, N.C.: University of North Carolina Press, 1991.

O'Donnell, J. J. *Cassiodorus.* Berkeley: University of California Press, 1977.

Otten, K. *König Alfreds Boethius.* Tübingen: M. Niemeyer, 1964.

Rand, E. K., H. F. Stewart, and S. J. Tester. *Boethius: The Theological Tractates and the Consolation of Philosophy, with English Translation.* Cambridge: Harvard University Press, 1973.

Usener, H. *Anecdoton Holderi.* Bonn: C. Georgi, 1877.

Wittig, J. S. "King Alfred's *Boethius* and its Latin Sources: A Reconsideration." *Anglo-Saxon England* 11 (1983): 157-98.

Authority Refracted: Personal Principle and Translation in Wace's *Roman de Brut*

Dolores Buttry
Clarion University

The twelfth-century Norman chronicler, Maistre Wace, is perhaps the best illustration of the pitfalls of the medieval system of patronage.[1] As is well known, Henry II became so dissatisfied with the *Roman de Rou* that he replaced Wace as "court historian" with "Beneeit" (probably Benoît de Sainte-Maure). Several reasons have been advanced for this fall from grace: Jean-Guy Gouttebrouze relates it to the climate of hostility between ruler and clergy that would culminate in the death of Thomas à Beckett (Gouttebrouze 1991, 289). Other obvious reasons are Wace's insistence on using English sources as well as Norman ones to tell the tale of the Norman Conquest, thus weakening the official Norman version. Wace provides unflattering portraits of some of Henry II's ancestors and presents Robert Curthose as the legitimate Norman/English heir after the death of William Rufus. It is easy to see in the *Rou* the author's own predilections (or prejudices). He is a cleric and descended from nobility,[2] proud of his lineage and emphasizing the importance of blood ties.

The *Rou* is not an appropriate vehicle, however, to illustrate the politics of translation, for the simple reason that the largest part of it seems to be a compilation of history by Wace from sources unknown to us and from oral traditions. Wace's major sources, Dudo of Saint-Quentin's *De Gestis et Moribus Primorum Ducum Normannorum*, and Guillaume de Jumièges' *Gesta Normannorum Ducum*, only provide him with early Norman history: Dudo treats only of the first three dukes, and Guillaume's history concludes before 1066; a few paragraphs about the Norman Conquest and the death of William I were hastily added. It is difficult to tell what Wace is "translating" for the major part of his work (i.e., the part treating William the Conqueror and his sons), and much of his information is not contained in any other source that has survived.

Wace's *Roman de Brut*, on the other hand, is a reasonably faithful translation of the *Historia Regum Britanniae*. In addition to the Vulgate version, which faithfully represents the tradition of the work of Geoffrey of Monmouth, Wace made use of the *First Variant Version*, an anonymous text that scholars situate sometime between 1138 and 1150 and that is stylistically different from Geoffrey's *Historia*. In general the work is more moralistic, containing more frequent allusions to the Bible and to classical sources, and more laconic, omitting unpleasant details. Although it is shorter than Geoffrey's version, the *First Variant Version* contains details that occur in Wace's work but not in the Vulgate. Pierre Gallais therefore concluded that the author of the *First Variant Version* used Wace as a source (Gallais 1966). In contrast, David Rollo, Robert A. Caldwell, and Neil Wright (the editor of the *First Variant Version*) are all in agreement that it was Wace who followed the *Variant* faithfully. Rollo asserts, "Wace used the 'First Variant' as his base text" (Rollo 1998, 135, n. 5); Caldwell tells us that Wace "clearly used the Vulgate as well as the *Variant*, though probably not until he got to book VIII of the Latin text" (Caldwell 1956, 680). Wright agrees, saying that the *Brut* "represents a conflation (effected not without skill) of the Variant and vulgate texts" (Wright 1988, lviii-lix). The politics of translation can be clearly observed in Wace's *Brut*; as Caldwell notes, "Wace did not translate his primary source so much as he adapted it, used it as a point of departure, paraphrasing, expanding, and elaborating on it as seemed best to him" (Caldwell 1956, 678). In this essay I would like to present examples of Wace's extensive amplifications and comment on the personal opinions that are visible in these passages.

Wace's *Brut*, finished in 1155, scarcely twenty years after Geoffrey wrote his Latin history, was the first vernacular rendition of Arthurian material and enjoyed great popularity. While Geoffrey was writing for other clerics, Wace was writing for the Norman court. Jean Blacker-Knight, in her article "Transformations of a Theme: Depoliticization of the Arthurian World in the *Roman de Brut*" (Blacker-Knight 1988), observes the disappearance of the political message from the *Brut*.[3] It is clear, as Blacker-Knight claims, that Geoffrey had a sermon for his fellow Britons; he includes several long, chastising addresses to his countrymen at various intervals in his *Historia Regum Britanniae*, all of which are omitted in toto by Wace, who was not interested in showing how the loss of the island could be traced to the sins of its inhabitants. He was not obsessed by civil war, and he was not writing for other clerics. His audience was a new one: the Norman nobility, who wanted to be flattered and entertained. The age of chivalry was at hand, and Wace produced from Geoffrey's moralizing lecture a tale of courtliness, grandeur and amusement. Wace's work does, however, contain a subtle politicization, as David Rollo has shown in his discussion of Wace's original addition of the passage on the Round Table, at which the nobles sat as equals, united in their allegiance to Arthur:

> Wace delineates a system of royal control predicated on the nuclear court and an illusion of egalitarianism. His Table is both a facile compliment and an absolute constraint, at one and the same time symbolizing the grandeur of feudal magnates, and circumscribing their liberties. As soon as ennobled by this honorific peerage, the barons of the court Wace proposes effectively disappear as individuals: they may be valorous, chivalric and even courtly, but within *Brut* they function only as martial retainers for Arthur (Rollo 1998, 114).[4]

The details are Wace's own invention, and, as Rollo suggests, no doubt celebrate the end of Stephen's anarchy and Henry II's assertion of authority. Indeed, Wace's considerable amplification of the Arthurian part of the *Historia* shows a collapsing of history, with the figures of Arthur and Henry converging, as Rollo and others have pointed out.

But can all the changes made by Wace from his sources be chalked up to the wish to entertain a non-clerical, noble audience or to the wish to flatter Henry II? If we look at the *Brut* and the *Rou*, we see a steady pattern of moral and intellectual intrusion: A different kind of "politics of translation" takes place, one that inserts the personality, principles and prejudices of the translator into the tale. Wace was a churchman and a noble, and his emphasis on decent behavior toward one's blood kin comes across even more strongly than in Geoffrey's original (although Wace is much less prone to distribute blame). Wace's work is no lecture, but moralizing is not absent from it.

Virtually all critics have stressed Wace's tendency to make small shifts in chronology to enhance a story line, his willingness to add details not in his original or sometimes to suppress information given by Geoffrey that would detract from the credibility of his story (one thinks of his suppression of the prophecies of Merlin, for example).[5] The assumption is common that the reason for such changes is to tell a better story, to better entertain the courtly audience. But some of the changes resist this explanation. Let us look at a paragraph in the *Historia* and in the *First Variant Version* that Wace has considerably enlarged and altered. Arthur has been consolidating his possessions and putting down uprisings from the Scots. The Scots take refuge on the islands of Loch Lomond; Arthur besieges them and brings them to the point of starvation after fifteen days. They die in the thousands, Geoffrey tells us. The Scots surrender, and the aftermath is given by Geoffrey in one little paragraph:

> Cumque nulli prout reperiebatur parceret, convenerunt omnes episcopi miserande patrie cum omni clero sibi subdito reliquias sanctorum & ecclesiastica sacra nudis ferentes pedibus. misericordiam regis pro salute populi sui imploraturi. Qui mox ut presentiam regis nacti sunt. flexis genibus deprecati sunt eum ut pietatem super contrita gente haberet. Satis etenim periculi intulerat, nec erat opus perpaucos qui remanserant usque ad unum delere. Sineret illos portiunculam habere patrie. perpetue seruitutis iugum ultro gestaturos. Cumque regem in hunc modum rogassent. commouit eum pietas in lacrimas. sanctorumque virorum peticionibis adquiescens. veniam donauit (Griscom 1929, 442).[6]

Here is how Lewis Thorpe translates this passage—the passage that is all that Geoffrey has to say about Arthur's treatment of the defeated Scots:

> [He treated them with unparalleled severity, sparing no one who fell into his hands. As a result all the bishops of this pitiful country, with all the clergy under their command, their feet bare and in their hands the relics of their saints and the treasures of their churches, assembled to beg pity of the King for the relief of their people. The moment they came into the King's presence, they fell on their knees and besought him to have mercy on their sorrowing people. He had inflicted sufficient suffering on them, said the bishops, and there was no need for him to wipe out to the last man those few who had survived so far. He should allow them to have some small tract of land of their own, seeing that they were in any case going to bear the yoke of servitude. When they had petitioned the King in this way, their patriotism moved him to tears. Arthur gave in to the prayers presented by these men of religion and granted a pardon to their people (Thorpe, 219).]

The *First Variant Version* presents this vignette with the same economy, but adds the detail that the Scots remained steadfast in the Christian faith:

> Postea rediens ad stagnum quod dimiserat perseuerauit Scotos et Pictos infestare donec episcopi omnes miserande patrie cum omni clero suo reliquias sanctorum et cruces in manibus ferentes

conuenerunt atque regem nudis pedibus flexisque genibus adeuntes pro se populoque suo nimis afflicto misericordiam prestaret atque arma ab interfectione gentis misere contineret, adicientes se satis penas luisse pro Saxonum superbia quibus illi non consenserant nisi coacti: nunc permitteret eius generosa nobilitas portiunculam gentis sue que remanserat in Dei cultu perseuerare, seruitutis iugum perpetue sub eius dominio ferre, et uectigalia qualiacumque federatos reddere. Commotus ergo rex pietate super afflictos ueniam donauit atque expugnacionem eorum dimisit (Wright, 143).

[Then, returning to the lake which he had left, he continued to attack the Scots and the Picts when all the bishops of the wretched country, with the priests under their command, carrying relics of the saints and crosses, assembled and, barefoot and kneeling, begged the king for mercy from such suffering for themselves and their people and (asked) that he should cease hostilities against the suffering people, saying that they had been punished enough for the rule of the Saxons, to which they did not consent and in which they did not participate: now surely his generous nobility would allow that portion of his people who had remained in the Christian faith to continue to bear the yoke of servitude under his dominion and to pay tribute. Moved by the patriotism of the afflicted people, the King therefore granted mercy and lifted the siege.][7]

There is nothing negative about King Arthur in Geoffrey's account; quite the contrary: Arthur is touched by the patriotism of the Scots and grants them a pardon. Arthur's reputation is enhanced. The eloquent pleaders are "these men of religion," the churchmen of the country. We know from the preceding paragraph that Arthur starved the Scots out; we have also seen that he "spared no one." The rebels, after all, deserved their punishment. In the *First Variant Version*, we have some new details: the fact that the Scots persevered in their Christian faith ("que remanserat in Dei cultu"), and the offer to pay whatever tribute the king might require ("vectigalia...reddere") and no mention of a request for land from the king. Otherwise, the portrayal is the same. Arthur returns to the lake where the Scots had taken refuge, treats them with severity, is confronted by the bishops, barefoot and bearing relics, who plead for the nation; Arthur is asked for mercy (and land, in the Vulgate), and, moved, Arthur grants mercy.

Now let's see how Wace changes this episode. Out of the paragraph-long description in his Latin sources, he fashions a vivid picture of 61 lines. The vignette begins as did Geoffrey's paragraph:

Es vus evesques e abbez,
Muines e altres ordenez,
Cors sainz[8] e reliques portant,

Pur les Escoz merci querant.[9]

[Behold the bishops and abbots,
monks and other churchmen,
carrying relics,
begging for mercy for the Scots.]

The next line introduces an element totally absent in Geoffrey's
account, as well as in the *Variant*. Wace shows us the women of the
country, bearing the marks of grief (their faces scratched, their clothing
torn); not only are these women present, but the focus shifts to them. It
is they who are barefoot ("tutes nuz piez"). They appear to be speaking
to Arthur along with the churchmen; Wace simply says that "tuit"
speak:

Res vus lé dames des cuntrees,
Tutes nu piez, eschevelees,
Lur vesteüres decirees
E lur chieres esgratinees,
En lur braz lur enfanz petiz:
Od pluremenz e od granz criz
As piez Artur tuit s'umilent,
Plurent e braient, merci crient:
"Sire, merci!" ce dient tuit (9469-77).

[And there you see the ladies of the region,
All of them barefoot, with disheveled hair,
Their garments torn
And their faces scratched,
In their arms their little children:
With laments and loud cries
They all kneel humbly before Arthur,
Weep and wail, begging mercy:
"Sire, have mercy!" say all of them.]

But isn't this appearance of women and children in need just another
good example of Wace's transformation of Geoffrey's work into a
courtly tale? Do not the rules of chivalry single out women and children
as privileged recipients of a good knight's aid? Could this be simply a
case of Wace giving the audience a story in accord with their emerging
code of conduct?

It is unlikely that Wace went to so much trouble to expand this
episode so greatly just because he thought his audience would respond
to the new story. The frequency and evocative nature of scenes of
suffering (especially suffering innocents) in Wace's works would seem
to betray genuine concern on the author's part. As an additional

example of courtly attitudes toward women, we may cite Wace's depiction in the *Rou* of Robert Curthose, returning from the Holy Lands to find that his brother Henry has usurped his authority. Invading England, Robert besieges Winchester, only to abandon the siege when he learns that his sister-in-law, Henry's wife, is in residence, and she is pregnant:

> Mais l'on li dist que la reïgne, sa serorge, esteit en gesine, il dist que vilains[10] sereit qui dame en gesine assaldreit; vers Londres fist sa gent torner...[11]
>
> [But they told him that the queen, his sister-in-law, was pregnant, and he said that it would be a dishonorable man who would attack a pregnant woman; he turned his army toward London...]

Certainly, many of the nobles in attendance when the *Rou* was read would have had fathers who fought against Robert Curthose. Describing a chivalrous attitude on Robert's part would not be a ploy to please Wace's courtly audience. Wace's own preference for Robert comes through clearly in the *Rou*. He relates from oral tradition a tale of a garden in which the people of Caen decided to support Henry instead of Robert; the garden withered and the trees never bore leaves again (*Rou* III, 11297-11308). It is Wace's own sense of chivalry, and his own political sympathies, that come through in that work.

In our passage from the *Brut*, we can fairly see that Wace was asking himself questions about the noble King Arthur's conduct. He puts into the mouths of the Scottish women and churchmen eloquent accounts of the effects of the king's ruthlessness on an entire people:

> Pur quei as cest païs destruit?
> Aies merci des entrepris
> Que tu, sire, de faim ocis.
> Se tu nen as merci des peres,
> Veies ces enfanz e ces meres,
> Veies lur fiz, veies lur filles,
> Veies lur genz que tu eissilles!
> Les peres rend as petiz fiz,
> E as dames rend lur mariz;
> Rend a ces dames lur seinnurs
> E les freres rend as sururs! (*Brut*, 9478-88)
>
> [Why have you destroyed this country?
> Have mercy on these victims
> Which you, sire, are starving to death.
> If you do not feel pity for the fathers,
> Look at these children and these mothers,
> Look at their sons, look at their daughters,

Look at their people whom you are destroying!
Give back to the little boys their fathers,
And return to the ladies their husbands;
Return to these ladies their lords
And return brothers to sisters!]

The plight of the innocents is stressed by the repetition of the word "veies." As a rule, Wace elaborates on the results of war, famine and plague, providing chilling examples where Geoffrey coolly notes the events. In this passage we sense sympathy for underdogs, but also we see Wace's concern for kin. Blood ties were sacred to Wace, and we see (below) that he intensifies the horror of internecine strife—not because it damages the state (Geoffrey's lesson), but because it is immoral in the individual.

The next fifteen lines make a point ignored by Geoffrey: The Scots did not help the Saxons (Arthur's real foes, who had fled to Scotland) willingly but were helpless:

Assez avum espeneï
Que li Saissun passent par ci;
N'est giens par nostre volenté
Qu'il unt par cest païs passé.
Ço peise nus que par ci passent;
Mult nus damagent, mult nus lassent.
Si nus les avum herbergiez,
Tant nus unt il plus damagiez,
Noz chatels unt pris e mangiez
E en lur terres enveiez.
N'avium ki nus defendist
Ne ki cuntr'els nus guarantist.
E si nus les avum serviz,
Nus le feïmes a enviz.
La force ert lur, nus suffriun,
Ki nul succurs n'atendium (9489-9504).

[We have paid enough
For the Saxons' passing through here;
It was certainly not with our permission
That they passed through this country.
It grieves us that they came through here;
They greatly harmed and exhausted us.
If we harbored them,
They only harmed us more.
They took our animals and ate them
And drove them to their lands.
We had no one to defend us

(Or) who would protect us against them.
And if we served them,
We did it unwillingly.
The force was theirs (i.e., they had power over us),
(We) who expected no help.]

The *First Variant Version* gives Wace the statement that the Scots have suffered enough for the Saxon rule to which they did not consent and in which they did not participate. Wace elaborates considerably on this statement: The Scots were not abettors of the Saxons, but their victims. And if the Saxons profited from their flight through Scotland, it was not the wish of the Scots. They were twice victimized, once by the Saxons, and then by Arthur, the pursuer of the Saxons. If they provided any aid at all to the Saxons, it was under duress. Wace had an understanding of the complexities of warfare and rivalry, and he uses the "under duress" justification in the *Rou* as well. Before the Battle of Hastings, William sends messages to Harold Godwinson stressing the latter's perjury—remember the oath he took on a tub of relics? Wace is one of the few who tell us that William tricked Harold, hiding the relics under a cloth. Harold's shock when he is shown the relics only emphasizes his lack of intention to make such an oath (that William is the legitimate heir to England): "Heraut forments'espoënta / des reliques qu'il li mostra" [Harold was greatly frightened / by the relics that he [William] showed him] (*Rou* III, 5715-16). On the battlefield, Harold retorts to the charge of perjury:

> se jo onques rien li pramis
> por ma deliv(e)rance le fis,
> por me delivrer li jurai,
> quantqu'il me quist li otreiai;
> ne me deit estre reprové
> ker nel fis nïent de mon gré.
> La force ert soe, si cremeie,
> se sa volenté ne faiseie,
> que jo ja mais ne revertisse
> e que toz tens la remainsisse (*Rou* III, 6819-28).

[If I ever promised him anything
I did it for my deliverance,
to save myself I swore,
whatever he asked for, I granted it;
I should not be reproached for it now
because I did not do it of my own free will.
The force was his (i.e., he had power over me), and I was afraid,
if I didn't do what he wanted,

that I would never return (to England)
and that I would remain forever (in Normandy).]

Wace's portrayal of Harold Godwinson, the favorite villain of the Normans, was certainly not calculated to please his courtly audience. In fact, his impolitic portrayals of certain ancestors and enemies may have been a factor in Henry II's withdrawal of patronage. It seems clear that in the *Rou*, we see a historian striving to be fair—and we also see evidence of Wace's own principles. One should not perjure oneself, but neither should any leader force anyone into an oath. If the oath is not entered into willingly, it has no force. Such seems, at least, Harold's argument, reported by Wace. The justification of duress and helplessness is the same in these two instances, and the language is exactly the same as well: "La force ert lur," say the Scottish women and churchmen; "La force ert soe," says Harold.

First Wace shows us the vivid suffering of the innocents: the women and children (not mentioned by Geoffrey or the anonymous author of the *Variant*). Then he stresses the lack of choice on the part of the Scots and the fact that they suffered under the Saxons, only to be punished for that suffering by King Arthur. So far, Arthur doesn't look like the ideal ruler at all. But Wace's next addition makes him look even worse: Not only are the Scots victims, but they are Christian, just like Arthur and the Britons. Their oppressors, the Saxons, were pagans. Does it make sense that a Christian king would savagely (he "spared no one," remember) attack a Christian people in his pursuit of a pagan one? Once again, the Scottish women and churchmen make the point without equivocation:

Li Saissun esteient paien
E nus erium crestïen,
De tant nus unt il plus grevez
E plus laidement demenez.
Mal nus unt fait, tu nus faiz pis;
Ço ne t'iert mie enur ne pris,
D'ocire cels ki merci querent,
Ki par ces roches de faim muerent.
Vencu nus as, mais lai nus vivre;
Quel part que seit, terre nus livre!
Fai nus, se vuels, vivre en servage,
E nus e tut nostre lignage;
Aies merci des crestïens;
Nus tenum la lei que tu tiens.
Crestïenté iert abaissiede
Se ceste terre est eisselede,
E ja en est peri le plus (9505-9521).

[The Saxons were pagan
And we were Christian,
Because of that they hurt us more
And treated us more shamefully.
They harmed us, you harm us more;
You will never have honor or gain
From killing those who ask for mercy,
Who are dying of hunger on these rocks.
You have conquered us, but let us live;
Wherever it may be, give us land!
If you like, make us live in servitude,
Us and all of our lineage;
Have mercy on Christians;
We obey the law that you obey.
Christianity will be degraded
If this country is destroyed,
And already most have perished.]

Wace makes the point repeatedly in this passage: "The Saxons harmed us, you harm us more... / We obey the law that you obey,... / Christianity will be degraded." It might be naive to speak of the "compassion" of a twelfth-century author whom we know only through his works, but the fact remains that Wace's amplifications seem to indicate an acute awareness of human suffering.[12]

Some may see the episode of the Scots as an example of Arthur's unusual generosity; after all, he did pardon the Scots and leave them in peace. The passage in Wace's *Brut* ends thus:

Artur fu mult buens el desus;
De cel chaitif pople ot pitié
E des cors sainz e del clergié;
Vie e membre lur parduna,
Lur humages prist sis laissa (9522-26).

[Arthur was kind about all this;
He took pity on this captive people
(And was moved to pity by) the relics and the clergy;
He granted them life and limb,
He accepted their homage and then left them.]

If this episode is supposed to illustrate Arthur's kindness and generosity, it is not very effective. For one thing, Arthur's tears are absent. The tears are also absent in the *Variant*, but there Arthur is at least "commotus," and Wace says only that he is kind. The Latin sources stress the effect the patriotism of the Scots exerts on the king, but Wace omits that detail. Instead, Wace evokes much more moving scenes with the grieving widows and children.

Wace has an idea of the proper behavior of kings, just as he has an idea of proper individual conduct. Ironically, he puts these words into the mouth of the conqueror Arthur (protesting the Romans' threat to take Britain by force):

> Mais force n'est mie dreiture
> Ainz est orguil e desmesure.
> L'um ne tient mie ço a dreit
> Que l'um ad a force toleit (*Brut*, 10829-32).

> [But force is never justice,
> Rather it is pride and excess.
> One never holds justly that
> Which one has taken by force.]

In the *Rou*, Wace shows us William the Conqueror on his deathbed regretting his injustice in taking England by force. The same tale is found (in more detail) in Ordericus Vitalis' *Ecclesiastical History* and in William of Malmesbury's *Chronicle of the Kings of England* and is not original to Wace. In addition to the deathbed scene, he alludes to this moral problem in the scene where, following the battle, William sets up his tent and wants to have his evening meal among the corpses. His follower Walter Giffort protests, saying that not all the English may be dead, and it would be dangerous—"nos lor faison, ço dient, tort" [We are doing them a wrong, they say] (*Rou* III, 8906). Much of the *Rou* contains dialogue apparently invented by Wace, and some of this dialogue sheds light on his attitude toward responsible kingship. When Harold Godwinson's brother Gyrth suggests a scorched earth policy so that the Normans will not be able to forage, Harold is shocked. Burn the fields, kill the livestock, urges Gyrth (*Rou* III, 6927-38). Harold says that he will not do it, even if it might mean victory: "maisons ne viles nen ardra / ne ses homes ne robera, / ne lor aveir ne lor toldra" [he will not burn houses or cities / nor will he rob his people / nor take away from them their goods] (*Rou* III, 6942-44). A ruler's obligation is the welfare of his people. Harold's answer seems to have been invented by Wace, as it does not appear in any other source:

> "Comment," dist il, "dei jo grever
> la gent que jo dei governer?
> Destruire ne grever ne dei
> la gent que deit garir soz mei" (*Rou* III, 6945-48).

> ["How," he said, "could I harm
> the people I am supposed to govern?
> I must not destroy or harm

the people who are supposed to thrive under me."]

Although Wace says nothing about William's harsh suppression of revolt following the Battle of Hastings, surely he knew that this attitude of Harold's was in stark contrast to William's behavior. Needless to say, words like Harold's were guaranteed to offend the noble Norman courtly audience.

Despite his aristocratic origins, Wace seems to have felt much concern for "la menue gent." This is clear in his additions to the passage concerning the defeated Scots in the *Brut*, which is almost a companion piece to Harold's dilemma in the *Rou*. Arthur had already caused suffering to "la menue gent"—Harold decides to avoid it, although it may cause his defeat.

Sympathy for the losers in war and admiration for the losing captain can also be seen in the passage concerning Arthur's conquest of Gaul and his combat with the tribune Frollo. Geoffrey relates the combat in book ix, chapter 11 (Vulgate version). He tells us that Arthur's army is huge: all young men of military age flocking to his banner in Britain, and many of the Gauls themselves having been bribed to join his army. Wace gives us a picture of some 199 lines, and this picture reveals much more humanity than Geoffrey's. Wace says that many French have joined Arthur, either out of fear, or having been seduced by his beautiful words, or because of bribes and gifts, or just from wanting to be associated with Arthur. Arthur's army is too large to successfully oppose, and Frollo takes refuge in Paris, his people having stockpiled supplies. Geoffrey gives us one sentence about the people's plight after a one-month siege and Frollo's offer of single combat to decide the matter:

> Emenso deinde mense cum frollo gentem suam fame perire doluisset mandauit arturo ut ipsi soli duellium inissent & cui uictoria proueniret alterius regnum optineret (Griscom, 448).

Lewis Thorpe translates this sentence as follows:

> A whole month passed. Frollo grieved to see his people dying of hunger, and sent a message to Arthur to say that they should meet in single combat and that whichever was victorious should take the kingdom of the other (Thorpe, 224).

The *First Variant Version* has a lengthier description, but Wace's details of stockpiling are absent, as are the people's plea to Frollo to make peace and the people's wish that whichever side would put an end to the war might win. As we might expect, Wace elaborates on the concerns of the leader for his people and on their suffering:

A Paris fist la guarnisun
Porter, des viles d'envirun;
A Paris Artur atendra
E a Paris se defendra.
Tant de la gent ki vint fuitive,
Tant de la gent d'illuec naïve,
Mult fu d'umes la cité plainne.
Chescuns en sun endreit se peinne
De blé e de viande atraire
E des murs e des portes faire.
Artur sout que Frolles faiseit,
Ki a Paris se guarnisseit;
Emprés lui vint si l'esega,
Es burs entur se herberga;
L'eue e la terre fist guarder
Que viande n'i pout entrer.
La ville tindrent bien Franceis,
E Artur i sist prés d'un meis;
Grant pople aveit en la cité,
De viande orent tost chierté;
Tut le purchaz e tut l'atrait
Qu'en poi de tens aveient fait
Orent tost mangié e usé
Mult veïssiez pople afamé! (9961-9984)

[He had supplies brought to Paris
From surrounding cities;
In Paris he will await Arthur
And in Paris he will defend himself.
So many people fled there,
So many natives were already there,
The city was crowded with people.
Everyone exerted himself to
Bring grain and provisions
And to build walls and gates.
Arthur knew what Frollo was doing,
Who was provisioning himself in Paris;
He (Arthur) came after him and besieged him,
He put up his men in the surrounding castles;
He had the water and land guarded
So that provisions could not enter (the city),
Soon there was scarcity of food;
All the purchases and supplies
That had been amassed in a short time
Were now eaten and consumed;
There you would see a famished people!]

All of these details of the garrison are lacking in Geoffrey's account and in the *Variant*. Wace gives us a vivid image of the suffering of the inhabitants, and typically he takes care to mention the women and children (not mentioned either by Geoffrey or the author of the *Variant*):

> Poi unt vitaille, e grant gent sunt;
> Enfant e femes grant duel funt;
> Si la gent povre en fust creüe
> La cité fust bien tost rendue.
> Mult vunt criant: "Frolle, que faiz?
> Pur quei ne quers a Artur paiz?"
> Frolles vit le pople destreit
> Pur la vitaille ki falleit,
> Vit lé genz, ki de faim mureient,
> E vit que rendre se vuleient,
> Vit la cité mise a eissil.
> Mielz volt sun cors mettre en peril
> E en abandun murur
> Que plainement Paris guerpir (9985-9998).

> [They have little food, and there are many people;
> The children and women lament loudly;
> If the poor people had been listened to
> The city would have soon been surrendered.
> Many cry, "Frollo, what are you doing?
> Why do you not ask Arthur for peace?"
> Frollo saw the people distraught
> Because of the food, which was lacking,
> He saw the people who were dying of hunger,
> And he saw that they wanted to surrender,
> He saw the city being destroyed.
> He would rather put his own body in peril
> And die, exposing himself to danger,
> Than simply abandon Paris.]

The single combat takes place on an island outside the city, watched by the inhabitants. Geoffrey says that "conveniunt uterque in insulam que erat extra ciuitatem populo expectante quod de eis futurum erat" (Griscom, 449). In Thorpe's translation, "the two men met on an island outside the city, the populace gathering to see what would happen to them" (Thorpe, 224). As we might expect, Wace will not be so terse. He takes the opportunity to evoke the suffering of those who fear death and the defeat of their city:

> Dunc veïssiez pople fremir,
> Homes e femes fors eissir,

> Sur murs saillir e sur maisuns
> E reclamer Deu e sus nuns
> Que cil venque que pais lur tienge
> Si que mais guerre ne lur vienge.
> La gent Artur, de l'altre part,
> Sunt en escult e en esguart,
> E deprient le Rei de glorie
> Qu'il dunt a lur seinnur victorie (10019-10028).

> [Then you could see the people tremble,
> Men and women pour forth,
> Jump on walls and on top of houses
> And implore God and invoke his name,
> That whoever could provide peace would win
> So that war would never afflict them again.
> The people of Arthur, in contrast,
> Listen and watch closely,
> And pray the King of Glory
> To give the victory to their lord.]

Naturally Arthur kills Frollo, and the populace opens the city gates to surrender. Nevertheless, Wace adds a line absent from Geoffrey: "Frolles fu mult pruz e hardiz" [Frollo was courageous and daring (10069)]. Obviously, a leader concerned with the welfare of his people is admired by Wace.

Geoffrey gives us many pairs of warring brothers and emphasizes the evils of civil wars; the Britons brought upon themselves the loss of sovereignty over their island. Although Wace is unconcerned with who rules Britain, the sanctity of blood ties is stressed throughout both his major works. Tonuuenna, the mother of warring brothers, says to her son, the rebel Brennius: "Un sul frere as, cel deiz amer" [You have only one brother, you should love him] (*Brut*, 2803). The crime of Judon, who killed her surviving son Porreus, after he had killed his brother Ferreus, shocked Wace: "Fud mes mere si enragiee! / Deus! Ki vit mais si fait pecchié!" [Was there ever a mother so enraged! / God! Who has ever seen such a sin!] (*Brut*, 2174-5). Geoffrey is guilty of no such outbursts. When the good king Elidur hid his evil brother, Wace approves: "Deus! Ki vit mais tel pieté, / Tel amur, tel fraterneté!" [God! Who ever saw such piety, / such love, such brotherliness!] (*Brut*, 3523-4). Androgeüs helps his besieged uncle Cassibellanus and bases his behavior on the importance of kinship:

> Mais des que l'on pert sun parent
> N'i ad puis nul amendement.

Ne deit l'on pas haïr a mort
Sun parent pur un poi de tort;
Encore se püent acorder
E lur mesfait entr'amender (*Brut*, 4707-12).

[But as soon as one loses his relative
There is no amendment.
One should not hate
His relative for minor wrongdoing.
They may yet be reconciled
And their misdeed repaired.]

Androgeüs astounds Caesar with his loyalty to his uncle Cassibellanus, against whom he (Androgeüs) has been waging war:

Mis uncles est si me nurri;
Quant il quiert que jo le aï,
Sis huem sui, ne li puis faillir (*Brut*, 4801-3).

[He is my uncle and he raised me;
When he asks me to help him,
I am his man, and can not fail him.]

A few lines earlier, Androgeüs had indicated the same recognition that blood overrides political advantage: "Mis uncles est, ne li faldrai, / Neü li ai, or li valdrai" [He is my uncle, I will not fail him, / I have harmed him, now I will be of use to him] (*Brut*, 4765-6). Although Geoffrey relates the dispute between Androgeüs and his uncle, and Androgeüs' final plea to Caesar on his uncle's behalf, he never mentions blood ties at all. For Geoffrey, this is a case of dispute between rivals for power. For Wace, it is the blood kinship that matters.

The *Roman de Rou* also shows clearly Wace's respect for blood ties. Robert Curthose says to his brother, Henry I, who is taking his lands:

D'un pere et d'une mere fumes,
un pere e une mere eümes,
fraternité garder vos dei (III, 10679-81).

[We come from one father and one mother,
one father and one mother we had;
I must honor our fraternity.]

Of the strife between the sons of William the Conqueror, Wace says:

Grant fu la guerre e grant fu l'ire
—mais tot ne pois conter ne dire—
del rei Henri e de son frere,
d'un pere nez e d'une mere (*Rou* III, 11337-40).

> [Great was the war and great was the anger
> —but I can't tell everything—
> of King Henry and of his brother,
> of one father born and of one mother.]

In fact, Wace provides a similar passage elsewhere in the *Rou*—a passage that has no source; did Wace invent it to enhance the tragedy of the Norman civil war between Henry I and Robert Curthose? He shows the opposing armies crossing the forest of Alton,[13] fearing combat since every man had a relative on the other side:

> d'ambes dous parz out filz e peres,
> oncles, nevoz, cosins ou freres,
> nus nen osout avant aler
> por ses parenz qu'il crient tuer;
> nus ne velt ferir son cosin
> ne son parent ne son veisin (*Rou*, III, 10369-74).

> [On both sides there were sons and fathers,
> uncles, nephews, cousins and brothers,
> nobody dared to go forward
> because of his relatives he feared to kill;
> nobody wanted to strike his cousin
> or his relative or his neighbor.]

Even Henry and Robert felt uneasy:

> Dote li reis, dote li dus,
> mais jo ne sai qui dota plus,
> por ço dotoent e cremeient
> qu'a lor parenz se combatreient;
> d'ambes parz aloent dotant,
> nus d'els n'osout aler avant.
> Les barons ont aperceü,
> par els meïsmes ont seü
> que la chose alout malement
> que parent tuast son parent,
> cosin cosin e frere frere,
> parent parent e filz son pere (*Rou* III, 10381-92).

> [The king fears, the duke fears,
> but I don't know who feared the most,
> they feared and dreaded
> that they would combat their relatives;
> on both sides people went along, fearing,
> none of them dared to go forward.
> The barons realized
> and knew themselves
> that things would turn out badly

(if) relative killed relative,
cousin cousin and brother brother,
relative relative and son father.]

The nobles took it upon themselves to make peace between the brothers. Wace repeats one last time, "Ne deit mie son frere abatre" [One must never attack one's brother] (*Rou* III, 10421). We thus see that Geoffrey's concern for internecine strife is not absent from Wace's works; but while Geoffrey is concerned about the functioning of the realm, Wace appears to be concerned with the personal morality of such strife.

Wace's *Roman de Brut* may appear at first glance to be "depoliticized" because of the author's consistent omissions of Geoffrey's many chastising diatribes, blaming the Britons for their own demise. If we look at ways in which Wace changed the story he found, however, we see a translator infusing his work with his own personal morality, refracting the authority of his sources. Wace's compassion for the victims of war and his respect for kinship are only two of many more personal principles that determine modifications in the story he tells. Wace is less concerned with who wins than with how the struggle is carried on and who suffers from it. To say that Wace's code is Christian and aristocratic may seem meaningless—wasn't every writer in the European twelfth century Christian and aristocratic? We can nevertheless see conservative aristocratic principles coloring Wace's world view, and we can see a difference between the superficial "Christian" concerns of clerics who treat the history of religious houses and royal families, of investitures and endowments, those writers who see defeat as punishment for sin and who use historical events as fodder for sermons, and Wace, a man who depicts the human suffering of the common people and urges fidelity to family. Wace's source material is refracted through the prism of the translator's own views. The *Brut* is not really "depoliticized"—it is subtly "politicized" in a more general and universal way.

Notes

1. Wace's difficulties with his patron have aroused the most interest in critics. See Blacker-Knight (1984), Gouttebrouze (1991), the dissertation of Tomchak (1983), and Tyson (1979).
2. As the late Hans-Erich Keller pointed out, Gaston Paris' 1880 emendation of line 3225 of the third part of the *Rou* is universally accepted today. The previously meaningless

line, "de par sa mere fu sis aives" [he was his grandfather on the maternal side], was emended by Paris, who thought it should have been "de par ma mere fu mis aives" [he was my grandfather through my mother], which would then make Wace the grandson of Robert I's chamberlain, Toustain. The privileged information on Robert the Magnificent's death, on his request that Toustain take relics back to Normandy and deposit them in a certain monastery, etc.—information that is contained only in the *Rou*—is thus explained. Wace's noble origin would be in keeping with his general tendency to stress pride in birth. See Keller (1990) and Paris (1880).

3. See also Blacker's book, *The Faces of Time* (1994), in which she mentions Wace's "relative absence of political bias" in the *Brut* (34).

4. Unfortunately, no study has yet been undertaken of Wace's political views or his attitude toward authority other than literary. While we can all regret that Wace's *sirventeis* have not survived (they may have shed light on his political opinions), still it is possible to gather evidence (liberally sprinkled throughout the *Rou* and less prolifically in the *Brut*) of attitudes toward power and its uses.

5. In addition to Blacker, Gouttebrouze and Tyson, see d'Alessandro (1994), Durling (1989) and Houck (1941) for discussions of Wace's manipulating of Geoffrey's text.

6. The various versions of the *Historia Regum Britanniae* will be identified in the text by editor. Acton Griscom is the editor of the Vulgate version; Lewis Thorpe is the editor of the English translation of that version; and Neil Wright is the editor of the *First Variant Version*.

7. The translation from the Latin is my own.

8. "Cor sainz" can mean "Eucharist" or "relic," but in the present context it is surely just a synonym for "relique."

9. Lines 9465-9468 of Wace's *Roman de Brut*, part II, ed. Ivor Arnold (1940). Future quotations from this work will be identified in the text by line number. All translations from the Old French are my own.

10. Rupert Pickens has pointed out that Wace was one of the first authors to use "vilein" as an adjective rather than a noun. In this example, Robert is using the word to describe dishonorable behavior. See Pickens (1997, 165-200). See particularly pp. 177-182, which contain the section *Vasselage et vilenie*.

11. *Le Roman de Rou de Wace*, ed. A. J. Holden (1970-73), part III, lines 10337-10341. All quotations from the *Roman de Rou* will be taken from this edition and will be identified in the text by section of the poem and line number in parentheses. Note that Holden has not capitalized the first word in each line, as Ivor Arnold has done in the *Brut*. All translations from the *Rou* are my own.

12. At the beginning of the third part of the *Rou*, Wace vividly describes the reasons for a peasant revolt; as a conservative aristocrat, Wace did not think such rebellion appropriate, but nevertheless elaborates on all the woes the peasants endure, creating sympathy for the serfs. See *Rou* III, 815-958. A passage in the *Brut* describing a plague and its horrible destruction furnishes another example of Wace's concern for human suffering. Geoffrey contents himself with saying that there was a plague and many died, but Wace evokes a vivid image of people falling ill in the fields, going about their business; he describes gravediggers burying the dead and then falling dead themselves into the fresh grave. See *Brut*, lines 14673-14698. Wace found some details in the *First Variant Version*, but he adds others and uses his famous anaphora to digress on the leveling nature of death, dwelling on a "Dance of Death" image that would be common two centuries later (and which is absent in both his sources).

13. A. J. Holden notes that all the manuscripts of the *Rou* contain "une version

déformée de ce nom" but identifies the forest of "Altone," as Wace spells it, as the "bois d'Alton, au nord de Winchester" (*Rou* III, 245, note to line 10343 of part III of the poem).

Works Cited

Blacker, Jean. *The Faces of Time. Portrayal of the Past in Old French and Latin Historical Narrative of the Anglo-Norman Regnum.* Austin: University of Texas Press, 1994.

Blacker-Knight, Jean. "Transformations of a Theme: The Depoliticization of the Arthurian World in the *Roman de Brut*." In *The Arthurian Tradition: Essays in Convergence*, ed. Mary Flowers Braswell and John Bugge, 54-57. Tuscaloosa, Ala.: University of Alabama Press, 1988.

—. "Wace's Craft and His Audience: Historical Truth, Bias, and Patronage in the *Roman de Rou*." *Romance Quarterly* 31 (1984): 355-362.

Caldwell, Robert A. "Wace's *Roman de Brut* and the *Variant Version* of Geoffrey of Monmouth's Quentin. *De Moribus et Actis Primorum Normanniae Ducum*. Ed. Jules *Historia Regum Britanniae*." *Speculum* 31.4 (Oct. 1956): 675-682.

D'Alessandro, Domenico. "*Historia Regum Britanniae* et *Roman de Brut*: une comparaison formelle." *Medioevo romanzo* 19.1-2 (April 1994): 37-52.

Dudo of Saint-Quentin. *De Moribus et Actis Primorum Normanniae Ducum*. Ed. Jules Lair. Caen: Le Blanc-Hardel, 1865.

Durling, Nancy Vine. "Translation and Innovation in the *Roman de Brut*." In *Medieval Translators and Their Craft*, ed. Jeanette Beer, 9-39. Kalamazoo, Mich.: Medieval Institute Publications, 1989.

Gallais, Pierre. "La Variant Version de l'*Historia Regum Britanniae* et le *Brut* de Wace." *Romania* 87.1 (1966): 1-32.

Geoffrey of Monmouth. The *Historia Regum Britanniae of Geoffrey of Monmouth*. Ed. Acton Griscom. London: Longmans, Green and Co., 1929.

—. *The History of the Kings of Britain*. Trans. Lewis Thorpe. London: Penguin Books, 1966.

—. The *Historia Regum Britanniae* of Geoffrey of Monmouth II: *The First Variant Version*. Ed. Neil Wright. Cambridge: D. S. Brewer, 1988.

Gouttebrouze, Jean-Guy. "Pourquoi congédier un historiographe, Henry II Plantagenêt et Wace (1155-1174)." *Romania* 112 (1991): 289-311.

Houck, Margaret. *Sources of the Roman de Brut of Wace*. Berkeley: University of California Press, 1941.

Keller, Hans-Erich. "The Intellectual Journey of Wace." In *The Medieval Text: Methods and Hermeneutics*, ed. William C. McDonald, 185-207. Detroit: Fifteenth-Century Symposium, 1990.

Ordericus Vitalis. *The Ecclesiastical History of Orderic Vitalis*. Ed. and trans. Marjorie Chibnall. 6 vols. Oxford: Oxford University Press, 1968.

Paris, Gaston. "Maistre Wace's *Roman de Rou et des ducs de Normandie*." *Romania* 9 (1880): 592-614.

Pickens, Rupert. "Vasselage épique et courtoisie romanesque dans le *Roman de Brut*." *De l'Aventure épique à l'aventure romanesque: Mélanges offerts à André de*

Mandach. Ed. Jacques Chocheyras, 165-200. Bern: Peter Lang, 1997.

Rollo, David. *Historical Fabrication, Ethnic Fable and French Romance in Twelfth-Century England*. Nicholasville, Ky.: French Forum Publishers, 1998.

Tomchak, Laurie Scott. "Wace's Work: Patronage, Repetition and Translation in the *Roman de Rou*." Dissertation, University of California, Irvine, 1983.

Tyson, Diana B. "Patronage of French Vernacular History Writers in the Twelfth and Thirteenth Centuries." *Romania* 100.2 (1979): 180-222.

Wace. *Le Roman de Brut de Wace*. Ed. Ivor Arnold. 2 vols. Paris: Société des anciens textes français, 1938-1940.

—. *Le Roman de Rou de Wace*. Ed. A. J. Holden. 3 vols. Paris: Editions A & J Picard, 1970-1973.

William of Jumièges. *Gesta Normannorum Ducum*. Ed. Jean Marx. Paris: Auguste Picard, 1914.

William of Malmesbury. *William of Malmesbury's Chronicle of the Kings of England*. Trans. J. A. Giles. London: Henry G. Bohn, 1847.

The *Pro Ligario*: *Volgarizzamento* as a Means of Profit

Cristiana Fordyce
Boston College

In 1267, the illustrious citizen Brunetto Latini was allowed to return to victorious Guelf Florence after six years of exile in France. The notary and chancellor, who had served the city until the defeat of his party, had continued his commitment to the city abroad by assisting rich Florentine merchants residing in France. Providing support to the mercantile class, the primary function of most lawyers, meant for Brunetto the backing of the commune not only economically, but politically. Before and after his exile, Brunetto was to Florence what Coluccio Salutati would be a century later: a rhetorician who made the art of letter-writing the most powerful weapon for the defense of the city.

Brunetto conceived rhetoric as a tool of persuasion, as an art that could not just convince the mind, but conquer the will.[1] He found the model for this kind of rhetoric in the classics, especially in Aristotle and Cicero, as his entire production aspired to educate his fellow citizens to a rhetoric of *utilitas*. Giovanni Villani, Florentine historiographer of the fourteenth century, noted how Brunetto Latini was "a worldly man, ...the...master in refining the Florentine and in teaching them how to speak well, and how to guide and rule...." (Wicksteed 1906, 312-13). Villani's comment highlights how Brunetto had actually accomplished his goal by revealing to his fellow citizens the secrets of a rhetoric capable of leading to an end. Essential to the civic and political life of the city, the *ars rhetorica* offered for Brunetto the solution to the problems of the city as well as of the individual.

Brunetto was aware that the practical knowledge of the merchants needed the support of eloquence since, as Cicero advised, eloquence and knowledge had to be joined in the same end for the resolution of a specific problem.[2] Moreover, eloquence appeared to Brunetto to be of paramount importance in a society that lived by the labors of its tongues and that had stemmed from a profit economy based on the art of persuasion. Brunetto, who had made his living from the power of rhetoric, was fully aware of the new supremacy of the word. In the *Tesoretto*, he advised his fellow citizens to speak properly and after having evaluated the circumstances, because:

> Ché non ritorna mai
> La parola ch'è detta
> Sì come la saetta
> Che vae e non ritorna (Latini 1981, vv. 1604-9).

But rhetorical ability could save one from any situation, since: "Chi ha la lingua adorna / poco gli basta" (Latini 1981, vv. 1610-11).

The word, like merchandise, had come to occupy a fundamental place in each aspect of the mercantile society, possessing no other value than what the individual was capable of negotiating for it. The word had become the means of estimation of every aspect of life. From the marketplace to the university, from good reputation to *vituperium*, the word had redefined means and ends. The new sin of the city was committed by means of language, as the word became the vehicle of defamation and *vituperium*, destroyers of that public image by now essential to any citizen of the new city.[3]

Dino Compagni, in the canzone *Pregio*, advised the Florentine bourgeoisie to care for their reputation by acknowledging the importance of common opinion and public estimation. Both in the *Pregio* and in his *Chronicle*, Dino revealed how the world of the individual and the world of the community, the world of the city and of its citizens, had become totally interwoven, forced into a continuous negotiation—a quest for agreement on the definition of the individual price.[4]

Sensitive to the importance of appearance and image, Brunetto constantly advised his audience to be aware of milieu and to cultivate *buona usanza*, the common approval, which would return in honor and public appreciation. *Troppa sicuranza*, which Brunetto associated with excessive self-confidence, on the other hand, was to be avoided, as it could damage one's reputation.

> Ché troppa sicuranza
> Fa contra buona usanza:
> Sì ch' anzi che t'amendi
> N'avrai danno e disonore.
> Però che a tutte l'ore
> Ti tieni a buona usanza,
> Però ch'ella t'avanza
> In pregio e in onore (Latini 1968, 13).[5]

The new kind of life and activities that awaited the mercantile class required not a rhetoric of elegance, but of *utilitas*, an art that could preserve good name, assure gain, make alliances and fortify individual will into a common want. With this idea of *utile* Brunetto translated his authors and, in Cicero's case, he used modern profit as the criterion to substitute for the classical *elegantia*. The practical message of Cicero's *De Inventione* did not escape Brunetto, who, in commenting on one of the master's passages, glossed: "Compagno è quelli che per alcuno patto so congiunge con un altro se sono fermi per eloquentia poi divengono fermissimi" (Latini 1968, 13). He demonstrated an absolute belief in a "performative" rhetoric, a rhetoric whose language does not describe or decorate, but deliver a true action (Austin 1961, 222-24).

Like Villani, Brunetto considered himself the educator of the new ruling class of Florence, his intellectual prowess committed to his audience in a clear, "ready to use" message.

> Farò mio detto piano
> Che pur un solo grano
> Non fie che tu non sacce
> Ma vo'...
> Che tutto lo'ntende (Latini 1981, vv. 401-5).

The request of a clear *ars dictandi* had been presented to Brunetto by the same merchant audience, who claimed effectiveness and clarity. To notaries such as *ser* Brunetto, the Florentine Dino Compagni would, in fact, recommend:

> Se buon pregio vole avere Notaro
> in leal fama procacci sé vivere
> Ed in chiaro rogare e' n bello scrivere (Compagni 1889, 221).

The new virtue that Brunetto proposed, especially through the lesson of Cicero, was the ability to master the art of eloquence, indispensable tool for the citizen of the commune seeking *bona fama*, the essential virtue to assure profit, and a relevant position on the political stage of the commune. Yet Brunetto was aware that if the ancient authors were an essential inspiration for the activities of his fellow bourgeois class, they did not need to represent a model of slavish imitation. If, on the one hand, for example, he proclaimed that Cicero was for him "sichura colonna sicchome fontana che non è istagna" (Bolton Holloway 1993, 259), on the other, he did not hesitate to point out the limits of the ancient master's teaching for the present times. In the *Rettorica*, a translation from the Ciceronian *De Inventione*, Brunetto was inspired by the most genuine mercantile spirit. As intermediary between the offer of his ancient masters and the demand of his bourgeois audience, Brunetto felt compelled to deliver to the latter exactly what it needed, tempering the original text when necessary. In the *Rettorica*, Brunetto stands up with his *auctoritas*, as the treatise is transformed into a sort of debate. Brunetto is more than a commentator as his voice becomes so strong to often overpower Cicero's own voice:

> Ma in perciò che Tulio non dimostrò che sia rettorica ne' quale è il suo artefice, si vuole lo sponitore per piú chiarire l'opera dicere l'uno e l'altro... (Latini 1968, 4).

Brunetto, with his intense experience with the merchants and the chancery, knew that the *scienza di dettare* was as important as *la scienza del dire* and, with the intention to update the classic teaching to the needs of the thirteenth-century audience of the commune, he did not hesitate to integrate Cicero's lesson. Determined to gain the most benefit from the lesson of the ancient author, he placed his voice side by side with his master's without awe or hesitation, aware of the importance of his enterprise:

> Rettorica è scienza di due maniere: una la quale insegna dire, e di questa tratta Tulio nel suo libro; l'altra insegna di dettare, e di questa...ne tratta lo sponitore (Latini 1968, 3).

From the classics, Brunetto intended to deliver to his audience not elegance of style, but utility of message. His effort of translation was for a public that needed the ancient authors but was without the linguistic means to engage them. In the *Tesoretto*, Brunetto offers the vernacularization as a means against obscurity and as a promise of clarity:

> Ti parlerò per prosa...
> Parlandoti in volgare,
> che tu indenda e apare (Latini 1981, vv. 420-6).

Far from a linguistic exercise, translating represented for the Florentine rhetorician a contribution to the sake of the commune. In all the vernacular texts, in fact, the civic commitment of the translator is highlighted by a constant overlapping of the contemporary reality to the historical one. For example, Brunetto updates the Ciceronian terms with the equivalent of his communal life. He translates *legatus* as *ambasciatore*, *patria* as *contrada*, and *respublica* as *comune*; Brunetto's adaptations clearly show the prioritization of reality over textual accuracy (Segre 1991, 60). The reason is to be found in that Ciceronian *utilitas*, as the Florentine master never failed to underline the paramount importance of the practical implementation of the message. In the epilogue of his translation of the Ciceronian oration *Pro Ligario*, for example, Brunetto writes to Manetto, the addressee:

Ora io caro amicho assai satisfacto alle tue preghiere ma conviene che tu sii studioso leggitore ma via piú bene d'intendere perciò ch'elle ragioni sono molte et sono forti et soctili ma piú l'userai e piú t'avranno savere (Bolton Holloway 1993, 260).

Brunetto admired his models, but without submission to substance or form. When Brunetto translated Aristotle's *Ethics*, for example, he cared not just to update the lexicon, but bent the very essence of the message. He did not hesitate to reverse the Aristotelian order of the perfect form of government. Where Aristotle states that democracy should be condemned in favor of monarchy, Brunetto, loyal more to his civic commitment than to literary text, remarks that the political organization of the commune is above all forms of government (Bolton Holloway 1993, 8; 223).

If Brunetto stole the secrets of rhetoric and the concept of *utile* from Cicero, in Aristotle's *Ethics* he discovered new emphasis upon the active role of the mind; a secular dimension of an individual *voluntas* cooperating with the common good.[6] In translating for his city Brunetto followed the example of his master Cicero not only in message, but in inspiration. Cicero considered "putting Greek Philosophy into Latin as a service to his country when political circumstances prevent him from serving it more directly" (Cicero 1991, 1). In the same way Brunetto began his activity of translation while in exile, at the time he attended the compilation of the *Tresor*.

In the *Pro Ligario*, one of the three Ciceronian orations translated around the time of the *Rettorica*,[7] Brunetto certainly demonstrates to be inspired by the principle of *utilitas* of this latter work and by the desire to prove how rhetoric could be a means of control of the individual destiny.

The translation shows a strong faith in the power of the vernacular, a secure hand and an exceptional linguistic independence (Segre 1959, 132). Following his ancient master, who, despite the admiration for his Greek models, "argues at length against those who despise Latin Literature in comparison with Greek" (Cicero 1991, 1), Brunetto seems to use the *Pro Ligario* as proof of the strength of his native language. He follows precisely the Latin model when it seems to evoke the rhythm of the vernacular, but does not hesitate to shorten long sentences in more conceited structures when necessary.

The ancient text, by touching upon issues such as good name, civic rehabilitation and common good, was very appealing to the Florentine mercantile audience, who lived in a world in which profit stemmed directly from reputation. The *Pro Ligario* was certainly an important text for the demonstration of persuasive rhetoric, as the oration is a harangue in which Cicero pleads for the life and reputation of his friend and ex-political ally Ligario. Once a supporter of Pompey, Ligario chooses not to return to Rome after the civil war. Accused of treason, the Senate seeks from Caesar perpetual exile for Ligario and possibly the death penalty. The challenge that awaits Cicero is the fight, with the weapons of rhetoric, against the uncertain outcome of his friend's future.

Provided with almost no evidence of Ligario's innocence, the orator plays his harangue in two moments. In the first, emphasizing the contingency of fickle events, Cicero highlights the good will of the defendant, proving that Ligario had never intended to betray Caesar. In the second, he appeals to Caesar's clemency, claiming that mercy is what earned the dictator his good name and the utmost respect among Roman citizens.

The oration seems to be a powerful application of the teaching of the *De Inventione*. Brunetto, political exile and *advogado*, found affinity in this oration with the author and an excellent example of how rhetoric can attempt to control *mala fortuna*. But Brunetto was not a passive interpreter of the Roman author even in this passionate text. The vernacularization of the *Pro Ligario* is not fully "Ciceronian": The voice of the translator and his rhetoric intervene in the most powerful passages to strengthen the persuasive discourse by making abundant use of syntactic explanations, interpolations and explanatory relative sentences. For example:

> Quinto Ligario fue in Africa contro a te e contro al tuo onore (Latini 1959, 170). [Q. Ligarium in Africa fuisse.]

> Ma ritorno a me che fui in quelle medesime arme (Latini 1959, 174). [Ad me revertar.Isdem in armis fui.]

> Fa dunque di costui quello che hai fatto nuovamente del nobilissimo e nominatissimo Marcello...il quale tu hai restituito e perdonato del tutto (Latini 1959, 184). [Fac igitur quod de homine nobilissimo et clarissimo fecisti nuper in curia.]

From the above examples, it is evident that Brunetto was not only trying to clarify the text, but emphasize the focal points of the petition, namely honor, reputation and *vituperium*. If on the one hand, the Italian does not appear as elegant and sharp as its model, on the other hand, Brunetto's text is undoubtedly tailored to an audience sensitive to issues of public image and common estimation.

Fama, we should recall, was particularly important to the

merchant because it was essential to his trade. It was a merchant's job to guarantee with his own credibility the merchandise of the supplier to the client. *Fama* for the merchant was synonymous with profit. The merchant's *fama* and credibility were based on his good name, which was difficult to establish because, like the merchandise, it was based not on intrinsic value, but on price, which was relative and determined by the marketplace.

Brunetto's efforts in the *Pro Ligario* were meant to update Cicero's message to his audience's needs and teach his fellow citizens the secrets for the acquisition of this uncertain, but indispensable, common consent. It was illustrative, to this end, to translate the verb *existimes* with the market lexicon *prezze*:

> Pensa la miseria loro e quella di Broco; ch'io so bene quanto tu il prezze (Latini 1959, 182). [Animadverte horum omnium maestitiam...huius T. Brocchi de quo non dubito quid existimes.]

The new Italian text had to reflect the anxiety of the merchants in a simplified, fluid language. If Cicero presents Ligario's desire to return to his family in Rome as proof of political loyalty, Brunetto's translation, stressing burning desire and will, seems to suggest the image of merchants forced by their business to long periods of time in faraway, foreign markets, longing for their home. The elegant, but somewhat rigid, indefinite moods of the Latin models effectively render the spirit of the intention, but they seem to pale in comparison to the image of a boat that unfolds the sails toward home, as the absolute ablatives and gerunds are opened to the "personalized" mode of the indicative.[8]

> Onde saputa di ciò la novella...perciò che Ligario aveva drizzato l'animo a casa e desiderava tornare dai suoi; ne' non sofferia di lasciarsi implicare da nessuna bisogna (Latini 1959, 175).
>
> [Quo audito...cum ligarius domum spectans, ad suos redire cupiens, nullo se implicari negotio passus est.]

Brunetto is entirely focused on his communal milieu; *contrada* is such a powerful pressing reality to be more than appropriate to translate the Latin *patria*. Interestingly, the translator opts for this choice in a passage where Cicero accuses Ligario's adversaries of maliciously denying a recall from exile, a burning topic for the citizens of Florence, and especially for Brunetto, who had been himself banned from the city.

> E io so bene Teverone, che la tua intenzione è di non procacciare altro se non che Ligario non sia in Roma...ne' dimori nella contrada (Latini 1959, 175).
>
> [Nam quid agis aliud? Ut Romae ne sit,...ne sit in patria.]

Brunetto's translation is concerned, clearly, with the *utilitas* of the master text. His choice over *elegantia* is done with a full awareness of the richness and sophistication of the model. In the dedicatory of the *Pro Ligario*, Brunetto acknowledges:

> Piacque al valoroso tuo cuore,...che la orazione che fece Marco tullio...io la dovessi volgaricare...la fatica è grande...per lo dectato che è alto, et in latino, e forte (Bolton Holloway 1993, 259).

The utility of the message overrules any concern. Brunetto has no hesitation, the translation must be in *comune parlare* as, for example, in the case of: "e così Ligario che schiferebbe..." (Latini 1959, 172). [Itaque Ligarius, qui...fugeret.]

The challenge of the translation consists in rendering the same power of the original so that the message is not lost. Brunetto succeeds both in the comprehension of the original text as well as in achieving an effective, explanatory translation.

Cicero's defense was articulated in the demonstration that Ligario's misfortune was caused by contingency, not by an ill intention to betray Caesar. Brunetto, comprehending Cicero's strategy, elects temporality as the core of his work. Temporality is stressed to an even higher degree in the translation than in the original text. Beginning with the prologue of the oration, we have signals of the importance of time, both explicitly admitted by the translator and rhetorically rendered in the text. Brunetto introduces Manetto, his wealthy banker friend of the Florentine community in exile in France, to the destiny of Ligario and requests that his friend pay attention to the specific contingencies of the events:

> Voglio adunque che or te sia noto che Marco tullio allora consolo di roma fue da la parte di Pompeo. Et fu cacciato...Ma quando tullio fe' questa oratione, egli era tornato in roma, perché Julio cesare aveva mandato per lui... (Bolton Holloway 1993, 260).

The circumstances that lead to the event are more important than the event itself. The trial, the oration, even Ligario are secondary elements. The subjunctive of "che ti sia noto" prepares Manetto for the parts that will require him to be a *studioso leggitore*. The first two perfect verbs are joined paratactically and prepare the background for the real event, introduced hypotactically by *quando*. In this sentence the perfect is not the same as the previous ones: The "quando fe' questa orazione era tornato a Roma" makes clear that this perfect *fe* must be read with the value of a present tense. The accurate and sophisticated hypotactical web that Brunetto weaves in his introduction does not fail to catch Cicero's spirit. The translator intentionally emphasizes the pride of the pardoned orator, choosing to privilege the artist over the historical image who, in truth, had undoubtedly pleaded Caesar for mercy and forgiveness. Brunetto instead chooses to offer to the reader the image of a strong and powerful senator back from exile and to his glory for the sole decision of Caesar: "perché Julio aveva mandato per lui." Brunetto is evidently interested in showing the free spirit of the republican Cicero, who loved Rome but did not bend to the tyrant. The sentence, caught between the ambiguity of an explicative and a causal, is all that Brunetto is willing to reveal about the historic reality of Cicero's life.

The prologue intends to guide the reader to the core of the translation: The will and desire of Ligario have always been with Caesar. While the events have led Caesar and the Senate to question Ligario's integrity, this is due to uncontrollable, unfavorable circumstances: Ligario is the victim of overwhelming events.

In the passage where Cicero stresses Ligario's desire to return to Rome, Brunetto makes sure not only to accentuate and expand Ligario's want, but uses the Latin sentences for a full display of the chain reaction of circumstances. He transforms the absolute ablative into a consequential *onde* and expands lexically with the noun *novella* with the purpose of strengthening the sense of causality. In addition, the imperfect and the simple past render not just the events, but the feelings of Ligario, pivotal to the demonstration of his good will. Cicero, in fact, had based his defense on the proof that his ill-fated friend was kept in the province of Africa if not by force, at least against his will. Brunetto, accordingly, resorts to a careful manipulation of tenses to express Ligario's impatience and resignation. The translator proceeds, changing rhythm and punctuation:

> Dunque la sua andata [in Africa] non dee affendere l'animo tuo? Certo no; e la rimasa? Meno. Perciò che l'andata fue senza rea volontade, e la rimasa fue con onesta necessitade (Latini 1959, 172).

> [Profectio certe animum tuum non debet offendere; num igitur remansio? Multo minus. Nam profectio voluntatem habuit non turpem, remansio necessitatem etiam honestatem.]

Ligario's accusation was based on the fact that he remained in Africa, a province hostile to Caesar and loyal to Pompey. Thus, Cicero founded the defense on the demonstration that Ligario's stay, being determined by unforeseeable circumstances such as the civil war, could not be considered as a sign of treason against Rome. In his defense the

Roman orator separates the two periods of Ligario's service, namely when he was sent as ambassador to Africa and when he was elected governor of the province, from the third incriminating one, when the defendant resolved to stay in Africa after Pompey's defeat. In this instance, the translator succeeds in constructing a defense stronger than the Roman master's by equating the three moments of Ligario's service in Africa, hence "melting" the suspicious third moment into the previous, clearly innocent, ones. Brunetto immediately announces his new tripartite temporal structure, as he is eager to tie the loose end of that third time left "uncovered" by Cicero:

> Dunque sono questi tre tempi senza peccato: uno, quand'elli andò nell'ambasceria, il secondo quando elli fu fatto signore del paese; il terzo quando elli rimase in Africa dopo la venuta di P. Varo... (Latini 1959, 172).

> [Ergo haec duo tempora carent crimine; unum cum est legatus profectus, alterum cum a provincia praepositus Africa est. Tertium tempus quod post adventum Vari in restit.]

The rhetoric shown by Brunetto, if not elegant, certainly passionate, points to much more than a literary exercise. The three orations that Brunetto chose to translate were all political in character and vibrant with regard to the civil commitment to the city. They were lessons of rhetoric and lessons of life for the communal citizens of Florence. The rhetorical intensity displayed in the *Pro Ligario* was generated by his civic passion and personal experience. The content of the oration came from a topic dear to Brunetto, a man who had known the bitterness of exile and who loved his city. Especially in the passage that deals with Cicero's own engagement in the political scene, we observe in Brunetto a particularly explicit, "involved" translator. In his version of the *Pro Ligario*, not only two people are involved, Cicero and Ligario, but three: Brunetto is with them.

> E io so bene Teverone, che la tua intenzione è di non procacciare altro se non che Ligario non sia in Roma, ch'elli stai fuori di suo albergo ch'elli non si possa raunare con li suoi cari fratelli, ne' meco...e ch'elli non viva con noi,...ne' dimori nella contrada (Latini 1959, 175).

> [Nam quid agis aliud? Ut Romae ne sit, ut domo careat, ne cum optimis fratribus,...ne nobiscum vivat,...ne sit in patria.]

The intensity of Brunetto's translation in this passage appears to betray personal feelings, as the addition of "ne' mecum" seems to suggest. This passage, which as we noted above shows the updated lexicon of Brunetto's day, betrays concepts of liberality, forgiveness, civil community and family. Another example is offered in the passage where Ligario's brothers and their loyalty are used in the proof of loyalty to Caesar. The image has the structure of a synecdoche. If the other two brothers, who are in Rome and loyal to Caesar, are united and pray for the salvation of this third one left in Africa, and if it is true that Caesar trusts these two and that they trust Ligario, then Caesar must consider the third brother innocent as well. In fact, it is not admissible that this one is stained with a crime against not just Caesar, but at this point against his own brothers who are faithful to Caesar. The conclusion of such argumentation is crucial to the defense and rhetorically powerful:

> O tu riterrai tre Ligari in Roma o tre ne distruggeri se ti piace colui di cacciare in bando (Latini 1959, 182).

> [aut tres ligarii retinendi in civitate sunt aut tres ex civitate exterminandi.]

In both the aforementioned passages, Brunetto innovates with explicative forms: a relative sentence in the first case and a dubitative in the second. Brunetto also avoids the use of indefinite modes, preferring the definite ones, the active form of the verb, and the hypotactic subordination in passages that are crucial to the proof of Ligario's innocence: *aveva drizzato, desiderava tornare, non sofferia, o tu ne distruggerai.* The sentences are knotted in a hypotactic system of cause-effect as in a chain reaction where no event stands by itself but is determined by and determinant to others. This can be noted even at the level of lexicon in the last analyzed passage; in the verb *distruggerai,* Brunetto does not hesitate to place civil and biological death on the same level.

The translator does not alter the Latin text for pure linguistic experimentation. The message that inspires it is the only guideline for Brunetto. In the following passage, it is quite evident that he is aware which parts needed to be bent for emphasis.

> Che dirò dei fratelli di Ligario? ...chi non sa che gli animi di questi frati sono sí conspirati e gittati in una forma di un solo volere e di una fratellasca agguaglianza? ...Appare dunque di voluntate tutti furono teco (Latini 1959, 182).

> [Qui est, qui horum consensus conspiratem et paene conflatum in hac prope aequalitate fraterna noverit.... Voluntate igitur omnes tecum fuerunt.]

If the second part is a faithful translation, the first is modified by the translator. Preferring the personalization of the sentence, Brunetto assimilates the structure of the second part to the first. In his elaboration, *conspirati e gittati in un solo volere* stresses the power of individual will and the intention to unify diversified wants in one aspiration for the common good of Ligario and the Roman republic.

Brunetto's sensibility to the community of men is both Ciceronian and Aristotelian as he marks his translation with attention to and care for the individual as member of the *humana societas*. When urging Caesar to pardon Ligarius, Cicero stressed that the condemnation of a member of the community would damage the entire city. Brunetto powerfully underlines these moments as, for example: "Non pensare, Cesare che qui si tratti pur di una persona" (Latini 1959, 182). [Noli, Caesar putare de unius capite nos agere.] The passage is interesting both philologically and politically, summarizing the ethical ideal that inspired the entire work of Brunetto. The word *persona*, even if fails to render the sophistication of the original, powerfully succeeds in interpreting the message and, as in the previous passage, draws attention to the individual.

The human experience was an essential focus for Brunetto. Throughout his life he was passionate about the concerns, needs and aspirations of his fellow citizens, the men who, with their commerce and gains, had brought prosperity and new intellectual stimulation to the commune. It was these men who were striving to become *persone*, the agents of change, the actors in their own drama, to whom Brunetto addressed his civic and literary enterprise. Brunetto intended to open his knowledge and experience to those who needed them with his translations:

Ben conoscho che'l bene
Assai val meno, chi'l tene
Del tutto in se' celato
Che chuel ch'è palesato (Latini 1981, vv. 93-6).

Committed to the commune as chancellor, and to the bourgeoisie as a Guelf, Brunetto knew that the prowess of Florence was in the hands of the mercantile class, at once the author and offspring of the profit economy. The support to this class signified the support for their activities and the skills necessary to foster their gains for the good of Florence.

Even if not a merchant, Brunetto, educated by constant contact with the mercantile class and the communal political organization, felt the need to offer a rhetoric of action to those who were wise enough to understand and implement it. Rhetoric had become the occasion to challenge and control the outcome of *fortuna*. Through Brunetto, the new powerful citizen of Florence learned to be in the race for power: "colui che vince e non colui che perde."

Notes

1. "...l'essenziale è persuadere, cioè scuotere l'animo perché l'auditore agisca secondo la convinzione che gli è stata trasmessa...la persuasione aggiunge qualcosa alla convinzione, nel senso che si impadronisce più. Totalmente dell'essere." See Perelman (1979, 57, 59).
2. Rhetoric, for Brunetto, must always aim to a specific target: "Rettorica è scienza di bene dire sopra la causa proposta, cioè la quale noi sapremo ornatamente dire" (Latini 1968, 4). And
   Intendo che eloquenzia congiunta con ragione d'animo,
   cioè con sapienza, piú e agevolmente ae potuto...as hedificare cittadi...fare fermissime compagnie et a novare amicizie... (Latini 1968, 11-13).
3. Casagrande (1987). See Introduction.
4. Compagni (1889, Book II); Compagni (1889, 214-224).
5. Brunetto does not recommend *buona usanza* for pure conformism. He would not hesitate to praise a conventionally unacceptable behavior if it could help to gain the benefits of honor and reputation. In the *Tesoretto*, Brunetto condemns the game of dice, but not when playing becomes necessary to uphold honor with friends and lords. See Latini (vv. 1426-1440).
6. In the *Ethics*, Brunetto translates a passage as follows:
   ciascuna arte ha un suo finale intendimento, lo quale drizza le sue operazioni. Adunque l'arte civile...è sovrana di tutte le altre arti. E la retorica è anche nobile, imperciò ch'ella ordina tutte l'altre che si contengono sotto di lei.... Adunque il bene che si seguita di queste scienze, sí è il bene dell'uomo (Bolton Holloway 1993, 431).
7. Brunetto also translated Cicero's *Pro Lege Deiotaro* and *Pro Marcello*. See *Le tre orazioni* (1832).
8. The notion "fortuna maris" appeared for the first time with Brunetto: "Au tens d'inver, quand les tempestes et les orribles fortunes suelent sordre parmi la mer" and would become a well-established topos of mercantile literature throughout the fourteenth century (Bec 1967, 302).

Works Cited

Austin, John L. *Philosophical Papers*. Oxford: Clarendon Press, 1961.
Baldwin, Charles S. *Medieval Rhetoric and Poetic*. New York: The Macmillan Company, 1928.
Bec, Christian. *Les marchands écrivains*. Paris: La Haye, 1967.
Bolton Holloway, Julia. *Twice-told Tales. Brunetto Latino and Dante Alighieri*. New York: Peter Lang, 1993.
Casagrande, Carla. *I peccati della lingua: disciplina etica della parola nella cultura medievale*. Roma: Istituto della Enciclopedia italiana, 1987.
Compagni, Dino. *La cronica di Dino Compagni delle cose occorrenti ne' tempi suoi e La canzone morale del Pregio, dello stesso autore*. A cura di Isidoro Del Lungo. Firenze: Successori Le Monnier, 1889.

Compagni, Dino. "La canzone morale del Pregio." In *La cronica di Dino Compagni delle Cose Occorrenti ne' Tempi Suoi e La Canzone Morale del Pregio, dello stesso autore.* A cura di Isidoro Del Lungo. Firenze: Successori Le Monnier, 1889.

Latini, Brunetto. *Il Tesoretto (The Little Treasure).* Ed. and trans. Julia Bolton Holloway. New York and London: Garland Publishing, Inc., 1981.

—. *La Rettorica Testo critico di Francesco Maggini.* Prefazione di Cesare Segre. Firenze: Le Monnier, 1968.

—. "Volgarizzamento dell'orazione *Pro Ligario* a cura di C. Segre." In *La Prosa del Duecento.* A cura di Cesare Segre e Mario Marti, 171-84. Milano–Napoli: Ricciardi Editore, 1959.

Le Goff, Jacques. *Time, Work, & Culture in the Middle Ages.* Trans. Arthur Goldhammer. Chicago: The University of Chicago Press, 1980.

Marti, Mario. "Verso la nuova coscienza umanistica." *Le Origini e il Duecento. Storia della letteratura italiana.* Torino: Garzanti, 1965, 1987.

Merouille, P. Carolus, S. J., ed. *M. T. Ciceronis Orationes Quaedm Selectae cum Interpretatione et Notis.* 280-92. Philadelphia: Thomas, Desilver Co., 1836.

Perelman, Chaïm Olbrechts and Lucie Tyteca. *Retorica e Filosofia.* Ed. and trans. F. Semerari. Bari: De Donato, 1979.

Rezzi, L. M., ed. *Le tre orazioni di M. T. Cicerone. Etc., volgarizzate da Brunetto Latini.* Milan, 1832.

Segre, Cesare. *Lingua, Stile e Società.* Milano: Feltrinelli, 1991.

—. *La Prosa del Duecento.* A cura di Cesare Segre e Mario Marti. Milan and Naples: Ricciardi Editore, 1959.

Sharples, R. W., ed. *Cicero: On Fate (De Fato) & Boethius: The Consolation of Philosophy (Philosophiae Consolationis) IV.5-7, V.* Warminster: Aris & Phillips Ltd., 1991.

Villani, Giovanni. *Croniche di Giovanni, Matteo e Filippo Villani, secondo le migliori stampe, e corredate di note filologiche e storiche.* Milano: Ufficio Generale Commissioni ed Annunzi, 1857-58.

Wicksteed, P. H., ed. *Villani's Chronicle.* Trans. R. E. Selfe. London: Constalde and Co., 1906.

Jean Froissart's *Chroniques*: *Translatio* and the Impossible Apprenticeship of Neutrality

Zrinka Stahuljak
Boston University

In his *Chroniques*, Jean Froissart (1337-1409) records the history of his time, the Hundred Years War between France and England in which the ruling Valois and Plantagenet dynasties disputed their respective hereditary rights to the French royal throne.[1] The French king Charles IV, the son of Philippe IV le Bel, died without a successor in 1328. While Edward III, the English king, was excluded because he was Philippe le Bel's grandson by his mother Isabelle, Philippe le Bel's nephew, Philippe VI of Valois, was crowned because his inherited right to the throne could be justified through the male bloodline.[2] In 1337, the year of Froissart's birth, Edward III's challenge to Philippe VI's right of succession to the French throne initiated the Hundred Years War.

Critics agree that in transmitting this conflict, Froissart assumed a neutral tone as well as a position of impartiality toward the warring parties (Ainsworth 1990; Brownlee 2000; Dembowski 1983). It is the goal of this paper to deepen the inquiry into the question of Froissart's historiographic neutrality. Since "the concept of *translatio* (transference)…is basic for medieval historical theory" (Curtius 1973, 29) as well as for the recording and the transmission of historical events, I propose to examine the status of neutrality of the historian as a self-appointed translator of the war in the different meanings that medieval historiography traditionally assigns to the notion of translation: narrative translation of "ordonner," linguistic translation and especially the topos of *translatio imperii*. I will focus on four edited versions of the Prologue to Book I of Froissart's *Chroniques* and on the episode known as "Voyage en Béarn" to the court of Gaston de Foix, count of Foix and Béarn, in Book III.[3]

According to Bernard Guenée, since the 1300s the historian has been a tool of political propaganda and of legitimation of new dynasties, and thus, by definition, partial (Guenée 1980, 332-336). During the Hundred Years War, the need for histories devoted to establishing "le bon droit de la dynastie des Valois, en face des prétentions des Plantagenets et des Lancastres" and to showing that "[l]es provinces comme la Normandie et la Guyenne, revendiquées par les Anglais, faisaient partie intégrante du royaume" is particularly strong (Bossuat 1958, 188).[4] Historians write national histories and "la matière de France est depuis le XIIe siècle la forme privilégiée de l'histoire, celle qui intéresse le plus large public" (Beaune 1985a, 332). On the other side, "generations of Plantagenet...kings [accept] the Arthurian legend as at worst a convenient historical fiction to support their claim for a sovereign England, independent of the French crown...Edward [III] promoted the idea of himself as a new Arthur" (Keiser 1973, 37). Using forged documents and popular propaganda, royal genealogies are promoted as national history in both France and England.[5]

Unlike his contemporaries who write in order to legitimize either the Valois or the Plantagenet dynasty competing for the French throne, Froissart positions himself as a mediator, as a translator, between the two kingdoms and their two rulers. As a historian, Froissart's position is unique in that he is not writing an "official" chronicle (Barber 1981, 24) or a national history. He is using neither written documents nor the royal archives of France to compose the *Chroniques* (Tucoo-Chala 1981, 124; Ciurea 1970, 279). To explain Froissart's stance of neutrality in the conflict, biographical reasons may be invoked. An indefatigable traveler, Froissart feels as a citizen of the world:

> Voirs est que je...ay...frequenté plusieurs nobles et grans seigneurs, tant en France comme en Angleterre, en Escoce et en autres pais et ay eu congnoissance d'eulx (ms. A, SHF 2:210).

> [J]e avoie esté en moult de cours de roys, de ducs, de princes, de contes et de haultes dames (SHF 12:78).

Froissart is at home in both England and France, whose aristocracies share a common transnational, universal culture, formed through marriages and ties of kinship, since the Norman conquest. As a young man, he spent eight years (1361-1369) at Edward III's court:

> [D]e ma jeunesse je avoie esté nourry en la court et hostel du noble roy Edouard...et de la noble royne Phelippe sa femme, et entre leurs enfans et les barons d'Angleterre qui, pour ce temps, y vivoient et demouroient (L 15:140).

Already fascinated with the ideal of chivalry, he found "a new Arthur" in the king. But what attenuates his predilection for the chivalrous ideals of the English royal court is Froissart's sense of belonging to his country of origin: Hainault. In 1346 John of Beaumont, the count of Hainault, deserted to the French side. In line with the politics of Hainault, Froissart declares himself to be French: "[Conte de Foeis] me receupt moult liement, pour la cause de ce que j'estoie Franchois" (SHF 12:75).[6] Thus Froissart is personally split between two disparate allegiances, to which a position of neutrality is a particularly well-suited response: He claims to be merely "recording" the events, which are "notablement registré...par juste enquête" (A 1:1),[7] "douquel costes" (A 1:1), "de quel pays et nation que il soient" (R 35).

In order to maintain this position of neutrality in his historiographic work, Froissart adopts several strategies. First, under the patronage of Edward's wife, Philippa, of the Hainault house, Froissart shifts from verse to prose, distancing himself from the use of rime, which is inadequate in the transmission of truth.[8] Originally, Froissart had begun a chronicle in verse to which he refers in the Prologue to Book I:

> [S]i emprins je assez hardiment...à dittier et à rimer les guerres dessus dites et porter en Angleterre le livre tout compilé, si comme je fis (ms. A, SHF 2:210).

But "cest livre," the chronicle in verse that he brought to Philippa, "n'est mie examiné ne ordonné si justement que telle chose le requiert. Car fais d'armes...doivent estre donnez et loyaument departis..." (ms. A, SHF 2:210), is something that cannot be achieved in verse form, because:

> [L]eurs rimmez et leurs canchons controuvées [de pluiseur gongleour et enchanteour] n'attaindent en riens la vraie matère (SHF 2:265, qtd. in Ainsworth 1990, 46, reference incorrect).[9]

Secondly, he abandons the use of written sources in exchange for oral testimonies. The subsequent prose manuscript versions of the Prologue to Book I attest to the progressive reliance on oral testimonies. Since the roots of the conflict predate his birth, in Book I Froissart relies heavily on the *Chronique* of his predecessor Jean le Bel. In the first two manuscripts, Amiens and SHF, he acknowledges his debt to Jean le Bel's *Chronique*: "Voirs est que messires Jehans li Biaus...en fist et cronisa à son tamps aucune cose à se plaisance; et j'ai ce livre hystoriiet et augmenté à le mienne..." (SHF 2:1). But in the last manuscript of Rome, he acknowledges only the use of oral testimonies (R 35). Oral testimonies that he collected from eyewitnesses also form the core of Book III. In its Prologue, Froissart states that in the earldom, "comté," of Foix and Béarn he was informed by

> chevaliers et escuiers...de la greigneur partie des fais d'armes qui estoient avenues en Espaigne, en Portingal, en Arragon, en Navarre, en Engletere, en Escoce et ens es frontieres et limitacions de la Langue d'och (SHF 12:78-9).

Providing as many testimonies as possible, rather than relying on one written narrative, can only support neutrality—the more all-inclusive the narrative is, the more impartial it is. In order to "moy acquitter envers tous, ainsi que drois est" (ms. A, SHF 2:210), "ne m'en vueille pas passer que je n'esclarcisse *tout* le fait ou cas...*tout* au long de la matiere" (SHF 13:222, qtd. in Guenée 1981, 279) (my emphasis). These numerous accounts are given orally, in person, "sans que je y envoiasse autre personne que moy" (SHF 12:2). If "truthfulness seems to be linked to oral narration," as Kevin Brownlee has pointed out (Brownlee 2000, 69), it is because the testimonies are given directly to the historian whose presence legitimizes them: "[L]a vraie information que je ay eu" (R 35). The very orality and variety of testimonies that Froissart collected found the truthfulness of the historiographic text. Thus in the earlier manuscript of Amiens, the responsibility to be truthful was placed exclusively on the witness, "tels gens sont juste imquisiteur et raporteur des besoingnes et...pour leur honeur il n'en oseroient mentir" (A 1:1). But in the later SHF and Rome manuscripts, Froissart inscribes his presence in the collective "on" to further guarantee the faithfulness of his report: "[N]ullement on n'en doit mentir" (R 35).

Reliance on oral testimonies, however, obliges the historian to distinguish between the protagonist, who is interviewing witnesses and the author, who is putting them in writing.[10] In order to support his neutrality, Froissart creates a narrative with a double perspective by splitting his "je" into the "je" of the author, "je Jehans Froissars," the one who takes it upon himself to "metre en prose et ordonner...la vraie information," which the "je" of the protagonist, the traveler, collected earlier, "que je ay eu des vaillans honmes, chevalies et esquiers" (R 35).[11] Thus Froissart-author has to assume responsibility only for the translation of testimonies into narrative, for their "ordonnance" (SHF 2:210). He claims not to have altered the testimonies he collected:

> Et devés savoir que je ai ce livre croniset et historiiet, ditté et ordonné apriés et sus la relation faite des dessus dis, a mon loial pooir...

and he neutralizes his own voice:

...sans faire fait ne porter partie ne coulourer non plus l'un que l'autre (R 35).

For Froissart, preserving the multiplicity of voices in their original form guarantees that whatever bias the witnesses may have, that bias is not Froissart's own.[12] Even if the witnesses are distorting the events, Froissart-author is not.

Finally, this narrative translation could not exist without another aspect of historiographic translation: linguistic translation. Froissart interviewed witnesses who related the events of the war in languages other than French, as well as witnesses who spoke French but whose native language was not French. Yet Froissart, the author, does not guarantee the faithfulness of his linguistic translation. His neutrality is upheld precisely by avoiding the issue of language. His silence on the issue mutes the fact that the multiplicity of voices is rendered in only one language, French. Granted, French, the language that Froissart spoke and wrote in, was the universal language of aristocracy and that worked to his advantage.[13] At the English royal court, as Philippa's *clerc*, he wrote in French: "Phelippe de Haynnau...à laquelle en ma jeunesse je fus clerc et la servoie de beaulx dittieers et traitiés amoureux" (L 14:2). His fame, perpetuated precisely through this common language, preceded him in his travels: "Lequel conte de Foeis, si trestost comme il me vey...me dist...en bon françois que bien il me congnoissoit, et si ne m'avoit oncques veu mais pluseurs fois avoit bien oy parler de moy" (SHF 12:3). The count of Foix, Gaston, addresses Froissart in the French language, that is in Froissart's language and not "en son gascon" (SHF 12:76). Thus, despite the fact that Froissart has left the borders of the French kingdom, he is still "at home" at the court of Gaston de Foix. In its capacity of being a universal language, French has the ability to create a sense of being at home wherever Froissart is. The very comfort of being at home everywhere in the world precludes any need to question that universality.

On the other hand, French was no longer just a universal language; it was also becoming a marker of belonging. As is generally recognized, during the Hundred Years War, France and England began to irrevocably break away from their common background and inch toward separate national identities. These national identities were not formed in the modern sense of nation identifying itself with one language, one culture and one history, but in the sense of the division of the universal pan-European world into separate kingdoms and the *prise de conscience* of their difference. Living in the permanent state of war, the population gradually organized itself into a cohesive and integral body in order to better defend itself. As a result, the first signs of national sentiment, of belonging to a larger community, "le pays commun, *communis patria*"[14] appeared along with signs of local, provincial belonging, "le pays où [le citoyen] était né, *patria sua* ou *propria*"(Guenée 1981, 158).[15] The conflicting interests that the two sides had in the French throne and territory slowly disintegrated what used to be one shared Anglo-French culture and transformed it into two cultures in political opposition (Vale 1996, 9-47). Elsewhere, other parties in the conflict started to identify themselves against each other. For instance, in the war between the Spanish and the Portuguese, a side conflict of the Hundred Years War: Despite the fact that the French and the Spanish were fighting together against the English and the Portuguese, they nevertheless maintained their distinctive French-ness or Spanish-ness. "[C]hevaliers et escuiers, Gascons, Bourgoingnons, François, Pikars et Bretons"(SHF 12:145) fought on the Spanish side, yet "de quelle nation que ils fussent puisque ilz n'estoient point des Espaignolz et que ilz estoient *estrangiers*, on les tenoit et nommoit François" (SHF 12:155; my emphasis).[16] Thus increasingly, Froissart finds himself in situations where to be French is to be seen as a foreigner, "estrangier." The French language may still be a universal means of communication, but Froissart is viewed as "other" because his native language is French. At the same time, the fact that witnesses translate into French from their native language allows Froissart to name them as others, as "foreigners": "Car là sont et retournent moult volentiers tous chevaliers et escuiers *estrangiers*" (SHF 12:2) (my emphasis).

In the midst of this ongoing conflict, Froissart is thus confronted with the disintegration of the universal world in which the perception of foreignness/otherness is less and less compensated for by transnational, commonly shared values. Rather, this perception of otherness increasingly contributes to the splintering of the universal world along particularized national values and interests.[17] It is to this feeling of a loss of unity, cultural and linguistic, that Froissart's silence on the issue of linguistic translation can be attributed.[18]

In writing the *Chroniques*, Froissart used various strategies to establish his neutrality. But it is with yet another device of historiographic translation that Froissart attempts both to support his neutrality and to overcome the splintering of the world: He uses the transnational topos of *translatio*, appearing in the Prologue to Book I. In the manuscript of Amiens, Froissart uses the idea of chivalric prowess, "proeche" (A 1:1), but he does not frame it within the topos of *translatio*. It is the Prologues to Book I in two later manuscripts, SHF and Rome, that contain *translatio*, or the transfer, of prowess.[19] I would like to suggest that Froissart introduces only at a later point in his writing the historiographic topos of *translatio imperii* in order to reinforce his claims to neutrality in the face of growing national divisions. The character of *translatio imperii* is universal, not national, because it signifies "the transference of dominion from one empire to another" (Curtius 1973, 29). The inherent transnationalism of this concept, due to its mutability "sailli[r] d'un pays en aultre" (SHF 2:5) as well as its groundedness in an outside authority of "les anciiennes escriptures" (SHF 2:5) and of "livres anciiens" (R 37), allows Froissart to neutrally observe the movement of prowess "d'un roiaulme en aultre" (R 37).

In his rewriting of the topos of *translatio imperii* in the Prologue to Book I, Froissart gives a privileged place to the notion of "proece." In this he follows the changes that medieval historiographic writing underwent from early to late Middle Ages. At the end of the Middle Ages, the historical concept of *translatio imperii* is no longer applicable, as the imperial power is no longer central to this transfer since European nations lost the title of Emperor to the Germans in the twelfth century.[20] Thus, "[c]hevalerie est une forme de l'Empire mieux adaptée au cas du royaume" (Beaune 1985b, 406). In keeping with the values of the feudal society, "[c]hevalerie...représente [l']idéal de la prouesse" (Jongkees 1967).[21] In the vernacular, then, chivalric prowess is a translation of the erudite transnational concept of *translatio imperii*.

Critics have been inclined to judge Froissart's use of the ideal of prowess as outdated, because of the disparity between this ideal and the brutal realities of the Hundred Years War (Ainsworth 1990, 70-85; Huizinga 1959).[22] To the contrary, I believe that in choosing the topos of *translatio* of prowess, Froissart maintains the currency of his *Chroniques* precisely because *translatio*, a transference of dominion from one kingdom to another, bears direct relevance to the Hundred Years War and the transfer of the French royal throne. Indeed, there is evidence that Froissart was acutely aware of the nationalization of the conflict. The temporal progression in manuscripts testifies to his awareness. In the manuscript of Amiens, the conflict is still presented as feudal, "entre le roy de Franche et le roy d'Engleterre" (A 1:2). Later, Froissart replaces it with "entre les Englès et les Français" (SHF 2:7), to finally understand it, in the Rome manuscript, as a conflict between two kingdoms, "entre France et Engleterre" (R 39). Froissart, instead of using the topos of *translatio* as an ideal, uses it to remain neutral and yet topical, a mediator-translator between the two countries. The transnationalism of this concept allows him at the same time not to engage in the conflict, unlike his contemporaries who used *translatio* to establish dominance of one nation over another.[23] In that light, Froissart's glorification of his *Chroniques* as being like no other history, "nulle hystore" (SHF 2:2), is justified. His history, unlike any other, inspires "jones bacelers" to seek advancement, "se avancier" (SHF 2:2-3) in the name of a universal ideal of "proèce," rather than in the name of a national kingdom. To the "nationalism" of national histories and propaganda, Froissart opposes a universal concept.[24]

According to Froissart, prowess is the only vehicle for the legitimate transfer of patrimony. When the legitimate son inherits the title from the father, he also inherits the duty to be worthy of his heritage, in other words, to be at least as "preu" as his father was:

> Or doient donc tout jone gentil homme...avoir ardant desir d'acquerre le fait et le renommée de proèce, par quoi il soient mis et compté ou nombre des preus, et regarder et considerer comment leur predicesseur, dont il tiennent [leurs] hyretages...sont honnouré et recommendé par leurs biens fais (SHF 2:2-3).

Prowess is the condition of possibility for inheritance, which the birthright alone cannot guarantee. Precisely because prowess is thus conflated with birthright, the heritage can go to the legitimate as well as to the illegitimate heir, a bastard, exclusively on the basis of their prowess. That a cowardly bastard is called a "batard non dispensé" (SHF 12:153) suggests the possible existence of a "batard dispensé." Thus a knight, advising the bastard-king of Portugal, explains that "au parfait de l'eritaige vous ne povez venir fors que par bataille" (SHF 12:141). Only the prowess of a bastard validates the transmission of the title to him: "[V]ous verés et trouverés en ce livre...comment plusieur chevalier et escuier se sont fait et avanciet, plus par leur proèce que par leur linage" (SHF 2:3). But by the same token, a lack of prowess can cost a legitimate heir a title inheritable by birthright. Thus, for Froissart, the hereditary right from father to son, in other words, the male bloodline, is invalid until legitimized by prowess.

Surprisingly, it is precisely the legitimization of inheritance by prowess that includes the female bloodline in the distribution of heritage. In all versions of Book I, Froissart very clearly points out that the exclusion of the grandson of Philippe IV le Bel, Edward III, because his inheritance came to him through the female line, was the cause of the war:

> Li .XII. per et li baron de France...voloient dire—et maintenir encorrez voellent—que li royaummez de Franche est bien si nobles que il ne doit mie aller à fumele ne par consequense à fil de fumelle

de par sa mere venant là où sa mere n'a ne ne puet avoir point de droit (A 1:6).[25]

According to Froissart, the transmission of "le royaumme, l'iretaige de France et le courounne dou royaumme de France" deviated and the Hundred Years War started: "Ensi ala li dis royaummes *hors de la droite lignie*...de quoy grant gueres en sont nees et venues et grans destructions de gens et de pays où royaumme de France et ailleurs" (A 1:6) (my emphasis).[26] Froissart considers the exclusion of the female bloodline a perversion of hereditary rights, "hors de la droite lignie," because the succession to the French throne should not have been determined without prowess, who is the mother and the final authority to all heirs: "Proece" is "mère materièle et lumière des gentilz hommes" (SHF 2:2). Thus Froissart, through the topos of *translatio*, again increases the currency of the *Chroniques*, in that he problematizes through "proece" the very stake of the Franco-English conflict: the validity of the transfer of the French royal throne through the male bloodline only.

The exclusion of the female bloodline decreased the pool of candidates for the French throne, and thus the French king was not chosen from the company of the most "preus." This led to the misfortune of the French kingdom, which is now "desconfi" (A 2:2). By reintroducing the female bloodline into the pool of heirs from which the French king should have been selected, Froissart objects to the bias of the decision that made Philippe of Valois king of France. The biased decision of "[l]i .XII. per et li baron de France" (A 1:6) is in opposition to his transnationalism. Even though Froissart does not mention it, he probably was aware of the fact that Philippe of Valois was given preference over Edward III because he was French, "pur ceo qu'il estoit nee du realme" ("Scalachronica," qtd. in Guenée 1981, 161) and because he spoke French, "parce que nous comprenions sa langue" (Jean Gerson, qtd. in Beaune 1985b, 401).[27] However, Froissart's objection to the exclusion of Edward III, whose "querelle fu debatue et point longement soustenue" (R 175), is not an indication of his own political preference. Froissart maintains the transnational point of view, as each king, whether French or English, a descendant of a male or female line, must through prowess merit his inherited right to the throne:

> Homs, qui voels venir a vaillance par Proece, considere conment on asciet a table dou roi, de duch et de conte le preu, et on met arriere le couwart pr̥eceus, *ja soit il de plus hault linage*. (R 39) (my emphasis).[28]

Froissart thus focuses on the *translatio* of prowess as the only standard of arbitration in the conflict because it is transnational and genealogically inclusive.

Translatio of prowess allows him to remain neutral, to avoid any explicit commitment to either the French or the English side in the conflict of *translatio imperii*. Since prowess legitimizes the transfer of title, Froissart bypasses the genealogy of birthright. Prowess alone will determine who is the legitimate heir to the French throne. Because the conflict is still ongoing, Froissart's only duty is to faithfully and neutrally "record" the exploits of prowess, "de quel pais et nation que il soeint" (R 35), and to patiently outwait the war. Froissart's neutrality as a historian is thus portrayed as necessary because prowess, and not Froissart, will ultimately determine the outcome.

Froissart also posits an analogy between chivalric prowess in the war and his own narrative prowess of "ordonner." Whenever he glorifies prowess, he both explicitly and implicitly glorifies his own historiographic endeavor. In describing "le preu," Froissart uses such terms as "cesti qui mist ceste cevaucie ou ceste armée sus, et qui ordonna ceste bataille si facticement" (SHF 2:4). He also talks about "le preu" and the physical endurance necessary to carry out the tasks (SHF 2:3) "en grant painne, en sueur, en labeur, en soing, en villier, en travillier jour et nuit sans sejour" (SHF 2:4). Likewise, Froissart the historian is the one "qui ce livre mist sus," with "mout de paine et de traveil" and "le labeur de ma teste et...l'exil de mon corps" (A 1:1). In Book III, Froissart says that he "ne voloie mie sejourner de non poursuivir [s]a matiere..." (SHF 12:2) and so he sets out to the court of Gaston de Foix. The image of Froissart wandering in search of adventures to exemplify his own narrative prowess matches the wandering of prowess:

> Proeche ne voelt point sejourner a l'ostel, mais errer et travillier et querre partout ens es pais prochains et lontains les armes et les aventures (R 36).

In Book IV, he draws an explicit comparison with the knight:

> Car ainsi comme le gentil chevallier ou escuier qui ayme les armes, en persévérant et continuant, il s'i nourrist et parfait, ainsi en labourant et ouvrant sur ceste matière je me habilite et délite (L 14:3).

Thus Froissart celebrates *translatio* of prowess not only thematically, but also structurally with his own work: The performance of a neutral historiographic writing is upheld as a feat of prowess. If Froissart's neutral writing is "preu," the text then participates in the *translatio* of prowess, since the exploits of the "preu" or of "le vaillant honme" are worthy of transmission to posterity:

> Premierement, le vaillant honme travellent lors corps en armes pour conquerir la glore et renonmee de che monde; li peuples parole recorde, et devise de lors estas; auquns clers escripsent et registrent lors oevres et baceleries, par quoi elles soient mies et couchies en memores perpetueles (R 37).

Since the feats of "le vaillant honme" are kept in collective "memores" through the books, the text that is transmitting them is, in turn, made part and parcel of the transmission of *translatio studii* into the future that it itself enables:

> Je sui seurs que...ce sera à yaus matère et exemples de yaus encoragier en bien faisant...(SHF 2:3), [c]ar bien sçay que ou temps advenir, quant je seray mort et pourry, ceste haulte et noble hystoire sera en grant cours (SHF 12:2).

The desire to fulfill his own *translatio studii*, "je sui seurs," "bien sçay," motivates the focus on the *translatio* of prowess as a way of remaining neutral and thus as a way of being "preu" and worthy of transmission.

As we saw, Froissart seeks to maintain a position of neutrality on different levels of his historiographic endeavor. However, these claims of neutral, impartial "translation" of the conflict are jeopardized in several different ways. Narrative translation of "ordonner" is from the outset most obviously compromised because of the relation between writing and memory. Froissart's guarantee that "touteffois je mis bien en memoire tout le compte que il m'avoit dit, ainsi comme il appert" (SHF 12:181) is not as credible once we find out that he wrote down the words of witnesses after the fact of hearing their testimony, sometimes not even the same day: "[T]outes très bien les retenoie, et si tost que aux hostelz...descendu estoie, je les escripsoie, fust de soir ou de matin, pour avoir en tou[t] temps advenir mieulx la memoire" (SHF 12:65).

Furthermore, Froissart also fails to remain neutral both linguistically and in the transmission of *translatio imperii* (and therefore of *translatio studii*). His neutrality is first called into question by the fact that his *Chroniques* is written in French, the language of only one of the warring parties. Although the English use it to communicate with the French, French is not their primary language: "[N]'estoient pas si enclins, ne usés de l'entendre et concepvoir sur la fourme et manière que les François bailloient" (L 15:114). The French language can be said to be privileged in the *Chroniques* by being repeatedly singled out among the variety of languages spoken. Whenever French is spoken, Froissart underlines its usage and remarks on its quality, while he routinely neglects to mention the use of other languages. Thus, for instance, he praises Gaston de Foix for the quality of his French:

> Lequel conte de Foeis...me dist en riant en bon françois que bien il me congnoissoit." (SHF 12:3); [T]rop volontiers en parloit à moy, non pas en son gascon, mais en bon et bel françois" (SHF 12:76).

Froissart remarks on the fluency and elegance of Gaston de Foix's French not once, but twice. On the one hand, Gaston de Foix's "bon et bel françois" refers to the quality of his spoken French, to its esthetic accomplishment.[29] I believe, however, that it also refers to a certain ideology of the French language, as a language that is inherently "bon et bel": "On attribue dès le XIIIe siècle au *français* des qualités d'harmonie et de beauté, qui sont aussi celles de la *France*" (Beaune 1985b, 398) (my emphasis). To speak French with the elegance of Gaston de Foix brings out the beauty proper to the French language. So when Froissart claims that he wants to "esclarcir par bel langaige" the historical "matière" that he collected, he makes French appear as the only language up to par "to clarify" and "to exemplify," "pour rengroissier...et pour exemplier" (SHF 12:3). Yet this apparent superiority of French over other languages is unavoidable for Froissart. He is faced with the transformation of French from a universal to a national language, and his writing in what is increasingly a national language appears to prioritize it. Unintentionally and unavoidably, the very fact that the war is translated into French endangers the neutrality of the historiographic narrative. In the growing nationalization of the conflict, the use of French may be seen as a kind of victory of French over English, as the language into which historiographic prowess can best be translated. Since *translatio imperii* is traditionally linked to *translatio studii,* the linguistic victory of French over English in the field of *translatio studii* may, in turn, be seen as an involuntary and yet inescapable indication of the outcome of the military conflict.

The difficulty, if not the impossibility, of remaining neutral also manifests itself in Froissart's rewriting of the genealogy of prowess. He is unable to decide where it ends, precisely because he is awaiting the end of the conflict that only prowess can determine. Therefore, in the manuscript of the SHF edition, he outlines a double genealogy of prowess. One genealogical line is the line of

> les neuf preus qui passèrent route par leur proèce, les douze chevaliers compagnons qui gardèrent le pas contre Salehadin et se

poissance, les douze pers de France qui demorèrent en Raincevaus…(SHF 2:5).

The second genealogical line retraces the *translatio* of prowess from its beginnings, first in the "royaume de Caldée" "après le deliuve et que Noés et se generation eurent repeuplé le monde," through "Jherusalem," "Perse," "Grèce," "Troie" et "Romme" (SHF 2:5-6). From Rome

> proèce…s'en vint demorer et regner en France, par le fait premierement dou roy Pepin et dou roy Charle, son fil, qui fu rois de France et d'Alemagne et emperères de Romme, et par les autres nobles rois ensievant. Apriès, a regné proèce un grant tamps en Engleterre, par le fait dou roy Edowart et dou prince de Galles, son fil…(SHF 2:6).

Froissart writes, then, two versions of *translatio*, one ending in France and the other in England *via* France. In so doing, he splits the *translatio imperii* into two different types. The split of *translatio* betrays Froissart's awareness of the disintegration of the universal world. Namely, the first genealogical line is transnational: "les neuf preus" are of different nations and religions,[30] and "les douze chevaliers compagnons" is a reference to the multinational group of knights in the Third Crusade. Only "les douze pers de France qui demorèrent en Raincevaus" is "nationally" identified, even though this identification remains ambiguous since Froissart recognizes Charlemagne, further in the text, as "rois de France et d'Alemagne et emperères de Romme." Froissart, however, still assigns a place where the transnational line ends, and, at his insistence, it ends in France with "les douze pers de *France*" (my emphasis). To this transnational genealogy of prowess, Froissart opposes a "national" genealogical line, retracing its steps from kingdom to kingdom, from "le royaume de Caldée" to England. The "national" genealogy ends not in France, but in England "par le fait dou roy Edowart et dou prince de Galles." Froissart attempts to preserve his neutrality by splitting *translatio* between transnational and national. But this split manages only to reiterate the conflict. In order to avoid taking sides, Froissart is forced to write a text where the very notion of *translatio* is divided and made to fight against itself. The discord between France and England is now waged between the two genealogical lines of a split *translatio imperii*. If to remain neutral means not to participate in the conflict, then Froissart has failed to the extent that his text stages a textual conflict. Indeed, the conflict has contaminated the text that wanted to avoid it.

To further complicate the matter, Froissart continues to develop the national genealogical line: "Or, ne sai je mies se proèce voet encores cheminer oultre Engleterre ou reculer le chemin que elle a fait" (SHF 2:6). At first, it appears that Froissart favors England. But a more careful reading reveals that in spite of an explicit mention of England, prowess is still in *translatio*: It will either continue beyond, "oultre Engleterre," and thus presumably to a country where it has never been before or it will "reculer le chemin" and thus presumably come back to France.[31] With the possibility that prowess could go "oultre Engleterre," Froissart suggests that prowess could avoid the alternative of *either* France *or* England and end up in some third country that would be *neither* France *nor* England. If the definition of neutrality is "to take neither side," then Froissart attempts to neutralize prowess, to disengage it from the conflict by suggesting a third alternative site that would be neither of the two explicitly proposed. The substitution of a neither/nor alternative for a conflictual either/or does not, however, resolve the textual conflict; it merely displaces it to an unknown place. Neither does this last sentence, "Or, ne sai je mies se proèce voet encores cheminer oultre Engleterre ou reculer le chemin que elle a fait," resolve the genealogical split: The either/or alternative (either beyond England or back to France) restages the conflict in two distinct lines, in two distinct alternatives of *translatio imperii*.

The later manuscript of Rome apparently cancels this split of *translatio*, which the SHF manuscript staged, and presents only one genealogical line ending in England:

> Apriès elle vint demorer en France par le fait dou grant Carlemainne, qui fu rois de France et d'Alemagne, et empereur de Ronme. Apriès a resgné Proece un temps en Engleterre par le fait dou roi Edouwart.... Or ne sçai pas se elle voelt encores aler plus avant ou retourner..." (R 38).

Nevertheless, even this unique line does not cancel Froissart's neutrality. First, through the use of the verb "resgner" in the past tense we are again "oultre Engleterre." So if England *was* but no longer *is* the site of prowess, and if only in the future prowess will "aler plus avant ou retourner," the question becomes: Where is prowess now at the time of the conflict?[32] Furthermore, Froissart reiterates the lack of a definable site, even more poignantly than in the manuscript of the SHF edition. While there he repeated "Engleterre" twice ("[a]priès a regné proèce un grant tamps en Engleterre"; "[o]r ne sai je mies se proèce voet encores cheminer oultre Engleterre"), here Froissart punctuates the present unavailability of the site of prowess by refraining from explicitly naming any site, "[o]r ne sçai pas se elle voelt encores aler plus avant ou retourner...," not even the last one known in the past (that is England). Conditioned by the ongoing character of the conflict, the *translatio* of prowess remains unresolved and is thus suspended with no place to call its own.

Froissart, however, manages to find a geographical site where prowess in its non-resolution, in its temporal suspension, can reside. This place is the earldom of Foix and Béarn. Gaston de Foix, the count of Foix and Béarn, adopted a successful politics of neutrality in the conflict, which led to the acquisition of the sovereignty of Foix and Béarn, which the earldom maintained until 1620 (Tucoo-Chala 1961):

> [I]l ne courrouceroit point volontiers [le roy de France ou le roy d'Engleterre], et trop bien de leur guerre il s'est sceu dissimuler jusques à ores, car onques ne s'arma de l'une partie ne de l'autre, et est bien de l'un et de l'autre... (SHF 12:46).

We read the very marks of neutrality in the neither/nor construction "une ne de l'autre" as well as in one and the other "un et autre." These two constructions highlight the fact that Foix and Béarn is the embodiment of this third place where prowess could reside precisely because it manages to have good relationships with France *and* England, and yet to be *neither* on the French *nor* on the English side. As for Gaston de Foix, the political leader of this third site, he is both the embodiment of neutral politics and of "proece." His political neutrality does not detract from his political stature. Gaston, according to Froissart, equals the rank or prestige of the French and English kings: "[I]l est aujourd'uy le plus saige prince qui vive et...nulz hauls sires, telz que le roy de France ou le roy d'Engleterre, courceroit le plus envis" (SHF 12:46).[33] Gaston's prowess is explicitly upheld as "vaillance" (SHF 12:78). It seems that Froissart heralds Gaston as the embodiment of prowess because he is the neutral body par excellence, the embodiment of both the temporal and spatial suspension of prowess.

Because he is both "preu" and neutral, and even "preu" because neutral, Gaston de Foix can be said to function as Froissart's political alter ego. His political neutrality and the prowess attached to it parallel the neutrality and prowess of Froissart's own historiography. Furthermore, Gaston's court is the site of encounter for various parties involved on opposite sides of the conflict (SHF 12:2). Froissart's work, likewise, provides a forum for conflicting views (SHF 12:238). The similarity between Froissart and Gaston de Foix accounts for the special fondness with which Froissart singles out his court ("je ne fus oncques en nulle qui mieulx me pleust"), among many other courts "de roys, de ducs, de princes, de contes et de haultes dames" that he has known (SHF 12:78). Gaston's court is a neutral and glorious metaphorical representation of the gloriously neutral corpus of the *Chroniques*, as well as of the glorious, neutral body of the historian who provides ideologically diverse testimonies.

But the very figure that embodies the prowess of neutrality also subverts it. Gaston, the embodiment of neutrality and prowess, both conflated in this one body, indeed displays some rather untraditional qualities of prowess. He neither fought in the Hundred Years War nor staged chivalric tournaments (Tucoo-Chala 1976, 29-31)[34] and in order to maintain his neutrality, he had to refrain from engaging in any conflict whatsoever.[35] We end up with this paradox, this logical conflict: The one who is the most "preu" of all is the one who does not ever fight to prove that he is "preu." At the same time, Gaston, like Froissart, considers only a "preu" to be worthy of succeeding him: "'[L]e visconte de Chastelbon est son cousin germain et son hiretier.' 'Et aux armées est-il vaillant homme?' 'Certes nennil...et pour tant ne le peut amer le conte de Foeis" (SHF 12:71). If Gaston can only love a "preu" who is "aux armées ...vaillant homme," he ends up loving that which he himself cannot be: a fighting "preu." In the figure of Gaston, prowess subverts itself; it is made to fight against its own definition. It becomes that which by definition it can never be, that is, a lack of prowess. The conflation of prowess with neutrality ultimately subverts prowess and, with it, the very notion that Froissart has used to ground and neutralize his own historiographic work.

Notes

I would like to thank my dissertation advisor, Claire Nouvet, for her guidance, editing and encouragement in the preparation of this article. I thank Kevin Brownlee for reading an early version of the article and for providing me with insightful comments.

1. In 1340, Edward III assumed the title of king of France, as would all the future English kings (Vale 1996, 6).
2. This was the end of the Capetian dynasty and the beginning of the Valois dynasty. The question of succession through the female bloodline had never before posed itself, and the lack of precedents, that is, women who would have inherited the French throne in the past, determined therefore that women should not inherit in the future either. On the invocation of "lex salica" used to justify the exclusion of the female line, see Beaune (1985b, 357-92) and Déprez (1975, 27-37).
3. For the manuscripts edited by George T. Diller, I use the following abbreviations: For the manuscript of Amiens, I use "A" followed by the volume and page number, and for the manuscript of Rome, I use "R" followed only by the page number (the manuscript is edited in one volume). For the manuscripts in the edition of La Société de l'histoire de France (manuscripts A and B), I use the abbreviation "SHF" followed by the volume and page number; for the manuscript A available in the "Variantes" of the SHF edition, I use (ms. A, SHF) followed by the volume and page number. For the edition by Kervyn Lettenhove, I use the abbreviation "L" followed by the volume and page number. The Amiens and the Rome manuscripts

contain only Book I of the *Chroniques*, whereas manuscripts A and B in the SHF and Lettenhove editions contain all four books of Froissart's *Chroniques*.

4.   Bossuat is, in particular, referring to the *Chroniques de Saint-Denis*, *L'Abrégé de Guillaume de Nangis*, and *Chronique dite de Mont Saint-Michel*. For instance, Charles V, king of France (1364-1380) was particularly active in establishing the right of the Valois dynasty to the French throne: "Dans son long exposé, Charles V voulait simplement prouver que, depuis Charlemagne, la Guyenne faisait partie du royaume de France et que ses ducs, qu'il fussent ou non rois d'Angleterre, devaient hommage au roi de France" (Guenée 1980, 336). See also Beaune (1985a; 1985b, 405-9).

5.   "L'interminable conflit franco-anglais obligea lui aussi les adversaires, et surtout les Français, à un intense effort de propagande. Pour l'alimenter, les juristes forgeaient de nombreux arguments, mais on en demandait aussi beaucoup à l'histoire" (Guenée 1980, 335). "Pesants traités, épopées, pamphlets, mais plus encore lettres patentes adressées par le roi à ses bonnes villes et lues par les hérauts aux marchés et aux carrefours, chansons et poèmes débités par des jongleurs dont les officiers du roi surveillent les propos, sermons coupant processions, prières publiques et messes solennelles, provoqués par le pouvoir qui en inspire les thèmes, voilà les moyens qu'utilise la royauté à partir du XIVe siècle pour faire pénétrer en profondeur les idées nées autour d'elle" (Guenée 1981, 162).

6.   Froissart's understanding of chivalry as a universal concept would have already prevented him from championing the English cause exclusively.

7.   The expression "notablement régistré" appears in three manuscripts: SHF ms. B, Amiens and Rome.

8.   Elsewhere, Froissart is acutely aware of the influence that various patrons exert: "On ne dye pas que je aye la noble hystoire corrompu par la faveur que je aye eu au conte guy de Blois, qui le me fist faire et qui bien m'en a paié tant que je m'en contempte.... Nennil vrayement! Car je n'en vueil parler fors que de la verité et aler parmy le trenchant, sans coulourer l'un ne l'autre. Et aussi le gentil sire et conte, qui l'istoire me fist mettre sus et ediffier, ne le voulsist point que je la feisse autrement que vraye" (SHF 13:223-4, qtd. in Ainsworth 1990, 47, 123).

9.   For a conclusive debate about the existence of a manuscript in verse and the referent of "cest livre," see Ainsworth (1990, 32-50).

10.   "Lorsqu'un historien entendait raconter des événements trop récents pour déjà disposer d'une source écrite, il ne pouvait mettre ses phrases dans les phrases de personne. Il était contraint d'être auteur" (Guenée 1980, 214).

11.   "[T]he authority of Froissart-author resides in his artful control of language and narrative structure. The authority of Froissart-character, on the other hand, resides in his artless, spontaneous manner of getting hold of historically significant information through the oral examination of witnesses" (Brownlee 2000, 66). Ainsworth (1990, 140-171), Dembowski (1983) and Zink (1980) also talk about this split "je" and an ever-growing autonomy of Froissart as author.

12.   "Ainsi, l'aspect surprenant et en même temps la véracité de la narration sont mis en évidence par sa répartition entre ces voix diverses, par les reprises, les croisements, les rencontres des différents points de vue qui l'exposent, s'en étonnent, la confirment, se résolvent à l'inexplicable, hasardent des hypothèses..." (Zink 1980, 76).

13.   "[T]he *lingua franca* of clerical diplomats was Latin...The *lingua franca* of courtly discourse, imaginative literature, and record-keeping was French" (Vale 1996, 43).

For a broad overview of the use of written French in England, see Suggett (1946). For a summary of the international success of French, see Beaune (1985b, 395-416).

14. Even if it can be counterargued that the inhabitants of the kingdom of France did not share a common nationality and a common language, since Philip-Augustus (1180-1223), the French kings strove to consolidate the integrity of the kingdom (Spiegel 1993, 11-54).

15. By birth Froissart belongs to "la conté de Haynnau et...la ville de Valenciennes, dont je suy de nation" (SHF 12:70), "en mon pays et en ma nation" (SHF 12:115), but he also has a sense of France as *communis patria*: "[J]'estoie Franchois" (SHF 12:75).

16. It is important to mention that the manuscript of Book III dates from after 1389, in other words, well into the Hundred Years War, when the effects of disintegration of the universal world would already have been visible.

17. Froissart's disappointment during his return visit to England in 1395, after twenty-seven years of absence, could also be attributed to the loss of universalism. See Medeiros (1992).

18. Keeney feels that the perception of foreignness began as early as the end of the thirteenth century: "Dislike of real foreigners, as distinguished from the foreigner from the next village, was stimulated by the prominence of aliens in the entourage of Henry III and by the long series of foreign wars beginning in the reign of Edward I" (Keeney 1947, 536).

19. There is little agreement on the date of composition of the Amiens manuscript. However, I am inclined to agree with the most recent argument of George T. Diller, who places the date between 1377 and 1382 (Diller 1991). See J. J. N. Palmer (1981) for an earlier argument in favor of a later date of composition, 1385 to 1391. The manuscript B of the SHF edition was composed in or after 1391. General consensus has been reached on the dating of the Rome manuscript after 1399.

20. The Hohenstaufen dynasty first acquired the title in 1137. See Beaune (1985b, 405-409), Folz (1969) and Jongkees (1967, 50). Therefore, Froissart concentrates on *translatio* of royal power from kingdom to kingdom: "Or ai eu pluisseurs fois grant imagination sus l'estat et afaire de proece, et penset et imaginet conment et ou elle a tenu ses termes, et venu d'un *roiaulme* en aultre" (R 37) (my emphasis).

21. "La Chevalerie et la Clergie [*translatio studii*], qui représentent le double idéal de la prouesse et de la sagesse, ce sont avec et après la Foi [*fides, sacerdotium*] les éléments constitutifs de la civilisation" (Jongkees 1967, 42). "*Translatio studii* (transferral of learning from Athens or Rome to Paris)" was later coordinated with *translatio imperii* (Curtius 1973, 29).

22. I believe that the reason for the contradiction between the realities of the Hundred Years War and the ideals of chivalry is due to the transnational concept of chivalry, which is at odds with the growing nationalization of the kingdoms at war.

23. "Le vieux mythe [des origines troyennes] fortement remanié entre 1200 et 1500 répondait toujours à de multiples fonctions: garant du prestige, de la cohésion, de l'unité ethnique de la nation, il servait aussi non seulement de défense dans les guerres anglaises. . . mais d'argument fondamental face à la papauté et à l'empire. Il justifiait, en outre, pas mal d'aventures extérieures" (Beaune 1985a, 332).

24. McRobbie gives an example of how in the Hundred Years War the ideal of prowess transcends the national in the crowning of "the *French* knight, Eustache de Ribemont,...by Edward III himself as the outstanding combatant of *either* side at Calais" (McRobbie 1971, 17) (my emphasis).

25. "Siques apriès le mort du darrain roy Carle, li .XII. per et li baron de France
donnerent le courounne à leur avis et ne le donnerent point à le sereur qui estoit
roine d'Engleterre par tant qu'il voloient dire—et maintenir encorrez voellent—que
li royaummez de Franche est bien si nobles que il ne doit mie aller à fumele ne par
consequense à fil de fumelle de par sa mere venant là où sa mere n'a ne ne puet
avoir point de droit. Siques par ces raisons li .XII. per et li baron de France
donnerent de leur certain acord le royaumme, l'iretaige de France et le courounne
dou royaumme de France absoluement em plain palais à Paris à monsigneur
Phelippe de Vallois, fils jadis à Monseigneur Carle de Vallois frere germain à ce
biau roy Phelippe et en hosterent le roy d'Engleterre et son fil qui estoit hoir marlez
et estoit filz de la sereur le darrain roy Carlon" (A 1:6).
    There has been an ongoing debate among historians of the Hundred Years War,
as well as among literary critics, about the causes of this conflict. Some argue that it
was, from the start, national (Beaune 1985b; Déprez 1975; Guenée 1981), others
that it was feudal, that is, a conflict between a vassal and a suzerain over the duchy
of Gascony (Vale 1996).
26. Froissart even goes as far as blaming the perversion of genealogy for "les guerres,
les pestilenses et tribulations...ens ou roiaulme de France" (R 46).
27. According to Déprez, already in the thirteenth century, abbé Suger thought that "la
France et l'Angleterre étaient deux Etats qui devaient vivre indépendants, et il
n'était pas plus juste et naturel que les Français fussent soumis aux Anglais que les
Anglais aux Français" (Déprez 1975, 34, note 2).
    Culturally the English and the French courts were closely related. Politically,
however, even before the outbreak of the Hundred Years War, the English kings had
a sense of distinction from the French, a sense of an Englishness threatened by the
French. Thus both Edward I and Edward II called for a defense of the English
language against the invading French (Keeney 1947, 545), and Henry III refused
Louis IX's advice to take foreigners for advisors (Guenée 1981, 161). Edward III, in
order to motivate his army, used the mottoes in English (Vale 1982, 47; 76). On the
efforts of the English to emancipate themselves from the French, see Beaune
(1985b, 415).
28. "The concept of translatio...implies that the transference of dominion from one
empire to another is the result of a sinful misuse of that dominion" (Curtius 1973,
29). For Froissart, the lack of prowess is sinful. Thus he is able to explain the
deposition of the English kings, Edward II and Richard II, who were dethroned
because they were not "preus" enough. See Ainsworth (1990, 205-15; 254-302).
29. Kevin Brownlee argues that "bon et bel" alludes to stylistic and artistic virtuosity
(2000, 68). See also Ainsworth (1990, 141).
30. Three pagans: Hector, Ceasar, Alexander; three Jews: Joshua, David, Judas
Maccabeus; and three Christians: Arthur, Charlemagne and Godfrey of Bouillon, are
grouped together (Huizinga 1949, 72-3).
31. What the text of the SHF manuscripts leaves unclear is the question of whether in
between France and England, prowess resided in some other kingdom:
"Proèce...s'en vint demorer et regner en France, par le fait...dou roy Charle...qui fu
rois de France et d'Alemagne et emperères de Romme, et par les autres nobles rois
ensievant. Apriès, a regné proèce un grant tamps en Engleterre": (SHF 2:6). It is the
mention of "les autres nobles rois ensievant" who appear without a specific
belonging to a place that creates the confusion. The later manuscript of Rome
clarifies the fact that there is no other kingdom where prowess might have resided
while moving from France to England, but that the passage between the two

kingdoms was direct: "Apriès elle vint demorer en France par le fait dou grant Carlemainne, qui fu rois de France et d'Alemagne, et empereur de Ronme. Apriès a resgné Proece un temps en Engleterre par le fait dou roi Edouwart…" (R 38).

32. Since prowess is not in the past, present or future, the question is what kind of time is the time of the conflict.

33. In "Dit dou Florin," in reference to Gaston, Froissart says (vv. 310-324):
J'ay moult esté et hault et bas
Ou monde, et veü des estas,
Mes, excepté le roy de France
Et l'autre que je vi d'enfance,
Edouwart, le roy d'Engleterre,
Je n'ai veü en nulle terre
Estat qui se puist ressambler
A celui dont je puis parler,
Se ce n'est Berri et Bourgogne.

34. Tucoo-Chala also points out that Gaston was an accomplished hunter. In his youth, Gaston went on a crusade to Prussia, during which he rescued the wife of the future Charles V (Tucoo-Chala 1976).

35. Both Peter Ainsworth (1972) and Kevin Brownlee (2000) argue that Gaston's description is a traditional device of panegyric for the patron, evidently a rather curious one.

Works Cited

Ainsworth, Peter. "Style direct et peinture des personnages chez Froissart." *Romania* 372, 4 (1972): 498-522.

—. *Jean Froissart and the Fabric of History. Truth, Myth and Fiction in the Chroniques*. Oxford: Clarendon Press, 1990.

Barber, Richard. "Jean Froissart and Edward the Black Prince." In *Froissart: Historian*. Ed. J. J. N. Palmer. Suffolk, Va.: The Boydell Press, 1981.

Beaune, Colette. "L'Utilisation politique du mythe des origines troyennes." *Lectures médievales de Virgile. Actes du Colloque organisé par l'Ecole française de Rome, 25-28 octobre 1982*, 331-55. Rome: Ecole française de Rome, 1985a.

—. *Naissance de la nation France*. Paris: Gallimard, 1985b.

Bossuat, A. "Les Origines Troyennes: Leur rôle dans la littérature historique au XVe siècle." *Annales de Normandie* 8, 1 (1958): 187-197.

Brownlee, Kevin. "Mimesis, Authority, and Murder: Jean Froissart's Voyage en Béarn." *"Translatio studii." Essays by His Students in Honor of Karl D. Uitti on His Sixty-Fifth Birthday*, ed. R. Blumenfeld-Kosinski et al., 65-85. Amsterdam: Rodopi, 2000.

Ciurea, D. "Jean Froissart et la société franco-anglaise du XIVe siècle." *Le Moyen Age* 76, 2 (1970): 275-84.

Curtius, Ernst. *European Literature and the Latin Middle Ages*. Trans. Willard R. Trask. Princeton: Princeton University Press, 1973.

Dembowski, Peter F. *Jean Froissart and his Méliador. Context, Craft, and Sense*. Lexington, Ky.: French Forum Publishers, 1983.

Déprez, Eugène. *Les Préliminaires de la Guerre de Cent Ans. La Papauté, La France et L'Angleterre (1328-1342)*. Genève: Slatkine, Megariotis Reprints, 1975.

Diller, George T. "Introduction." *Chroniques*. Livre I. Le manuscrit d'Amiens. Ed. George T. Diller. Genève: Droz, 1991.

—. "Froissart: Patrons and Texts." In *Froissart: Historian*, ed. J. J. N. Palmer, 145-60. Suffolk, Va.: The Boydell Press, 1981.

Folz, Robert. *The Concept of Empire in Western Europe from the Fifth to the Fourteenth Century*. Trans. Sheila Ann Ogilvie. London: Edward Arnold, 1969.

Froissart, Jean. *Chroniques*. Tome premier, Iere partie. Ed. Siméon Luce. Paris: Société de l'histoire de France, 1869.

—. *Chroniques*. Tome douzième. Ed. Léon Mirot. Paris: Honoré Champion, 1931.

—. *Chroniques*. Début du premier livre. Manuscrit de Rome. Ed. George T. Diller. Genève: Droz, 1972.

—. "Dit dou florin." *Dits et Débats*. Ed. Anthime Fourrier. Genève: Droz, 1979.

—. *Chroniques*. Livre I. Le manuscrit d'Amiens. Ed. George T. Diller. Genève: Droz, 1991.

Guenée, Bernard. *Histoire et culture historique dans l'Occident médiéval*. Paris: Aubier Montaigne, 1980.

—. *Politique et histoire au Moyen Age. Recueil d'articles sur l'histoire politique et l'historiographie mediévale (1956-1981)*. Paris: Publications de la Sorbonne, 1981.

Huizinga, Johan. *The Waning of the Middle Ages*. New York, London and Toronto: Anchor Books, 1949.

—. *Men and Ideas*. New York: Meridian Books, Inc., 1959.

Jongkees, A. G. "*Translatio Studii*: les avatars d'un thème médiéval." In *Miscellanea Mediaevalia in memoriam Jan Frederik Niermeyer*, 41-52. Groningen, The Netherlands: J. B. Walters, 1967.

Keeney, Barnaby C. "Military Service and the Development of Nationalism in England, 1272-1327." *Speculum* 22 (1947): 534-49.

Keiser, George R. "Edward III and the Alliterative Morte Arthure." *Speculum* 48, 1 (1973): 37-51.

McRobbie, Kenneth. "The Concept of Advancement in the Fourteenth Century in the *Chroniques* of Jean Froissart." *Canadian Journal of History* 6, 1 (1971): 1-19.

Medeiros, M. T. de. "Voyage et lieux de mémoire. Le retour de Froissart en Angleterre." *Le Moyen Age* 98, 3-4 (1992): 419-28.

Menache, Sophia. "Mythe et symbolisme au début de la Guerre de Cent Ans. Vers une conscience nationale." *Le Moyen Age* 98, 1 (1983): 85-98.

Palmer, J. J. N. "Book I (1325-1378) and its Sources." In *Froissart: Historian*, ed. J. J. N. Palmer, 7-24. Suffolk, Va.: The Boydell Press, 1981.

Spiegel, Gabrielle. *Romancing the Past: The Rise of Vernacular Prose Historiography in Thirteenth-Century France*. Berkeley; Los Angeles; London: University of California Press, 1993.

Suggett, Helen. "The Use of French in England in the Later Middle Ages." *Transactions of the Royal Historical Society* 28 (1946): 61-83.

Tucoo-Chala, Pierre. *La Vicomté de Béarn et le problème de sa souveraineté des origines à 1620*. Bordeaux: Bière Imprimeur, 1961.

—. *Gaston Fébus: un grand prince d'Occident au XIV siècle*. Pau, France: Editions Marrimpouey Jeune, 1976.

—. "Froissart dans le Midi Pyrénéen." In *Froissart: Historian*, ed. J. J. N. Palmer, 118-31. Suffolk, Va.: The Boydell Press, 1981.

Vale, Juliet. *Edward III and Chivalry. Chivalric society and its context 1270-1350.* Suffolk, Va.: The Boydell Press, 1982.
Vale, Malcolm. *The Origins of the Hundred Years War. The Angevin Legacy 1250-1340.* Oxford: Clarendon Press, 1996.
Zink, Michel. "Froissart et la nuit du chasseur." *Poétique* 41 (1980): 60-77.

Translation, Censorship, Authorship and the Lost Work of Reginald Pecock

Andrew Taylor
University of Ottawa

On the fourth of December, 1457, a crowd of twenty thousand gathered at Saint Paul's Cross in London to hear Reginald Pecock, bishop of Chichester, recant his errors.

> ...I confess and acknowledge that I have beforetime, presuming of mine own natural wit, and preferring the judgment of natural reason before the New and Old Testaments, and the authority and determination of our mother Holy Church, have holden, feeled, and taught otherwise than the Holy Roman and Universal Church teacheth, preacheth and observeth; and over (besides) this...I have made, written, and taken out and published many and divers perilous and pernicious doctrines, bookes, works, and writings, containing in them heresies and errors contrary to the faith catholic and determination of Holy Church.[1]

At this point, according to the surviving document, Pecock switched to Latin and listed his seven theological errors, the last of which was "that anyone may rightly understand the literal sense of Holy Scripture, nor is anyone required for the sake of salvation to hold to any other sense." (Item, bene licebit unicuique Scripturam Sanctam in sensu litterali intelligere, nec teneretur aliquis de necessitate salutis alicui alteri sensui inhaerere.) Resuming in English, he exhorted the crowd not to "give faith or credence to my said pernicious doctrines, heresies, and errors; neither my said books keep, hold, or read in any wise" but to "bring all such books, works, and writings as suspect of heresy...unto my said lord of Canterbury or to his commissaries or deputies." Then Pecock surrendered to the executioner fourteen volumes of his works that they might be consigned to the flames, thus demonstrating his obedience to the Church and saving his life.

Pecock's recantation says nothing directly about translation, either of the Bible or of other religious texts, nor is the topic of biblical translation mentioned more than a handful of times in his entire surviving corpus. Yet it is translation, above all biblical translation, that lies at the heart of Pecock's project, at the heart of the Lollard project that Pecock was trying to combat and at the heart of the Church's condemnation of both. Pecock's misfortunes testify to the political tensions surrounding the question of religious translation in late medieval England—arguably the most controversial religious, cultural and political issue in the land from the late fourteenth century until the Reformation. In turn, these tensions, and the censorship they provoked, also helped to strengthen Pecock's sense of authorial identity, leading him to draw together his written works into a coherent body in a way no writer in English had before him.

The issue of translating the Bible was charged in England in part because English had only begun to acquire the status of a national written language. French Bibles had been available for centuries, and their use had gradually spread with the spread of literacy. An English Bible, on the other hand, was a novelty, and a novelty with a clear political agenda. Since aristocrats and the upper gentry already had access to Bibles in French, translating the Bible into English was an overtly populist move.[2] Indeed, it could be seen as a triple threat, to ecclesiastical hierarchy, to theological orthodoxy and to political stability. The Lollards, a loose affiliation of religious reformers, combined demands for biblical translation with a savage critique of ecclesiastical powers and central doctrines, notably that of the Sacrament (Hudson 1978, 24-29). Lollard preaching was regarded by some as a factor in the Rising of 1381 (Saul 1997, 300). When in 1409 Archbishop Arundel issued a set of constitutions directed against the Lollards that placed severe restrictions on preaching and specifically forbade any written translation of Scripture into English, he was attempting to suppress a threat to the authority of both the Church and the Lancastrian regime.[3] The Lollard uprising of 1413-14 further reinforced the association between the demand for an English Bible and more general political radicalism, so that the call for wider translation of almost any religious text came to be seen as a threat to political stability. By this point, as Anne Hudson puts it, the "conviction that vernacular scriptures were legitimate...could be sufficient to bring the arrested person to the stake" (Hudson 1989, 125). Indeed, unless one belonged to the gentle classes, simply owning an English book was regarded as prima facie evidence of Lollardy. In this charged political context, Pecock's efforts to encourage the laity to read for themselves must have seemed to many of his contemporaries dangerously misguided.

Pecock's abjuration brought to an end a project that had engaged him for at least thirteen years, during which time he had first been master of Whitington College in London, then bishop of St. Asaph, and finally bishop of Chichester. Although Pecock does not appear to have had any substantial family connections, he had somehow managed to become a favorite of Prince Henry and of other parties at court, and it was this that led to his promotion.[4] In keeping with his prominence in the capital, Pecock was an enthusiastic polemicist and began to assume the task of defending the Church against its critics. In 1447, for example, he preached a controversial sermon at Saint Paul's Cross on the reasons bishops might legitimately avoid preaching. It is worth noting that Pecock, despite his enthusiasm for religious debate, was not a fully trained theologian. He had his Master of Arts and Bachelor of Divinity from Oxford, but that was all; the Doctorate of Divinity he eventually received was purely honorary. This did not prevent Pecock from writing at length on theological questions, and, more dangerously still, writing on them in English.

Starting in 1443 Pecock began to bring out a series of interconnected manuals of religious instruction, beginning with the long systematic work, the *Reule of Crysten Religioun*, which was followed by the lost work, the *Afore Crier*, a short introductory manual, the *Donet*, and its more elaborate continuation, the *Folewer*.[5] Pecock saw these works as part of a unified and comprehensive system for popular theological instruction, and he linked them by repeated cross-references. In the *Reule of Crysten Religioun*, for example, Pecock claims to be offering "right sufficient and right cleere knowing of God and of us self" of a kind that cannot easily be acquired from sermons, and adds that the material in the *Reule* should be supplemented with "the othere bookis to this present book perteynyngly knytte to and annexid—whiche ben and schulen be the *Afore Crier* to this book and to his purtenauncis, the *Donet* or key of this book, the *Filling of the IV Tables*, the *Book of Divyne Office*, and the *Encheridion*, and othere mo bookis of whom mensioun is maad in the said book clepid the *Afore Crier*" (9). Pecock's other works are filled with similar cross-references; the *Donet* alone contains sixty-four references to the *Reule* and fourteen to the *Folewer*. From these references, it is possible to construct a reasonably complete listing of Pecock's works even though only six actually survived—none in more than one manuscript. Not only do we know what Pecock wrote, but we can often trace the stages in the publication of each treatise from private circulation (which Pecock claimed was without his consent) to official publication; and to those works he actually completed, we can add a list of those that were promised as "forthcoming." In the *Folewer*, for example, he asks his reader to "Holde thei her pacience unto tyme thei heere of the *Book of Feith*" (70)—a work he had almost completed.

Considered individually, Pecock's works are not that impressive; while dangerously heterodox in a few passages, for the most part they are conventional and, frankly, dull. Pecock writes like a lawyer, never using one word where three will do. He never attains the spiritual poetry of the late medieval English mystics such as Richard Rolle, and much of what he offers is a laborious treatment of catechetical material or rather ponderous anti-Lollard polemic. For the greater part, his treatises are predictable and safe. Nor is it easy to cast Pecock as a zealous reformer, since much of what he writes, especially his *Repressor*, is a defense of religious abuses such as episcopal absenteeism or such obvious pieces of hypocrisy as the Franciscan practice of counting money with a stick as a way of preserving their vow of poverty. To some of his detractors, Pecock's rationalization of these abuses is in keeping with his abjuration, both showing that he was no sincere reformer but merely a misguided opportunist, a man who tried to advance his career by justifying ecclesiastical corruption and got tangled up in factional politics, allowing his inflated sense of his own abilities to draw him into theological quarrels whose complexities were beyond him.

But if his individual writings are often weakly conformist, his overall project is both monumental and radical. Graded according to difficulty, his works would take an English reader from elementary catechetical points to questions of considerable theological complexity. His interlinked English treatises might well be considered the last great attempt to create a vernacular theology in England before Tyndale's Bible in the 1520s.[6] They are not translations or paraphrases of specific texts so much as a translation and popularization of a whole field of professional discourse. In this respect, Pecock follows in the footsteps of John Wycliffe, who had argued in the 1380s for conducting theological discussion in English. In keeping with such a project, Pecock has a remarkable optimism in the capacity of human reason to understand religious discussion and Scripture.[7] As is so often the case with others, his politics are rooted in his view of human nature. Pecock believes that the average layperson can become a righteous, possibly even sophisticated, reader and can deal with central doctrinal matters, if not with such vexed theological questions as the nature of the Trinity. When in the *Reule* he comes to this particular question, one that is both subtle and perilous, he switches into Latin (88). But such signs of caution are rare. For the most part, Pecock's confidence in what laypeople might be expected to read and understand runs strong. In the *Repressor*, for example, he expresses the hope of one day writing a short primer on logic, since

> miche good wolde come forth if a schort compendiose logik were devisyd for al the comoun peple in her modiris langage; and certis to men of court, leernyng the Kingis lawe of Ynglond in these daies, thilk now seid schort compendiose logik were ful preciose (1: 9).

Here Pecock implies that laypeople might be expected to follow a regular course of study, just as he does in the *Reule*, when he notes that one of the advantages of dealing with difficult religious matters in a book is that the laypeople may read the works repeatedly and seek advice in how to interpret them (21). He even argues that it is good for lay readers to struggle with theological texts they cannot quite grasp, since this will teach them to respect the learning of clerics:

> ...it may be expedient and profitable that summe of tho bookis whiche ben to be maad in lay tunge, and to be delyverid to lay men, be so hard that thei be not lightly and esili undirstonde of the wittiest lay men which shulen rede and studie and lerne therinne; forwhi therbi summe and many lay men mowe be tamyd and repressid and chastisid fro pride and fro presumpcioun (*Folewer* 7-8).

Similarly, Pecock notes in the *Reule* that by struggling to cope with the harder material, his readers will "be quyckened, scharpid, provokid, and effectualy up lifted to come higher into witt and undirstonding" (22).

Pecock's sense of his pastoral mission extended to all laypeople, but he was not really writing for plowmen. He claims that his abbreviated version of the *Donet*, the *Poor Man's Mirror*, was so short "that welnigh ech poor persoon maye bi sum meene get coost to have it as his owne" (*Donet* 226), but poor laypeople were more likely to benefit from an improvement in preaching, also one of Pecock's major concerns. One of the groups of readers he did have in mind was composed of the poorer clerics and parish priests with little Latin but regular preaching duties. In addressing this group, Pecock was following a well-established tradition going back to the Fourth Lateran Council, which made the educational needs of the lower clergy an episcopal responsibility. Pecock gives a better sense of the kind of lay readership he normally had in mind, however, when he notes in the *Reule* that laypeople regularly deal with business and legal questions that are as hard as any questions in theology:

> ...lay peple muste needis and shulen be drive forto conceive herder and derker trouthis with harder and derker evidencis in plees of lond, in plees of dette and of trespace, in rekenyngis to be maad of receivers and rent gaderers in the account of an audit, yhe in bargeyns made of greet marchaundis and in rekenyngis making thereupon, as a man schal soone wit if he take homlynes with mercers of London (93-94).

Pecock had close connections with London mercers. He understood their spiritual needs, and they provided him with a strong sense of a potential readership. Literate and prosperous members of the urban merchant class, many of them with a strong personal devotional practice, were likely to be harshly critical of unsophisticated or ill-educated clerics and to seek religious fulfilment elsewhere. Many of them harbored sympathies for the Lollards, whose central demand was for an English Bible and whom, not inappropriately, he calls "Bible men."[8]

The urgency of Pecock's mission and its connection to the question of biblical translation emerge most clearly in Pecock's *Repressor*, his long defense of the customs and privileges of the Church against Lollard criticism. For Pecock, the Lollards represented a serious intellectual and political movement, one that could not simply be dismissed. While the *Repressor* is a justification of the Church against all its moral critics, it is the Lollards who most concern Pecock, and the first thing he does, before he begins his defense of Church practices, is to attack Lollard fundamentalism. Pecock accuses the Lollards of three specific errors. The first error is believing that no ordinance is to be considered authoritative unless it is grounded in the Old or New Testament. The second error is believing that every Christian man or woman who is meek in spirit can find the true understanding of Scripture and that "the more meke he or sche be, the sooner he or sche schal com into the verry trewe and dew undirstonding of it, which in Holi Scripture he or sche redith or studieth" (1: 6). The third error is believing that once this truth is found in Scripture, the reader should ignore any arguments advanced by clerics, and "bowe awey her heering, her reeding, and her undirstonding fro al resonyng and fro al arguying or provyng which eny clerk can or wole or mai make bi eny maner evydence of resoun or of Scripture" (1:7).

Pecock, in contrast, stresses that properly guided reason can advance to proper understanding. This properly guided reason makes use of syllogistic logic and the intellectual apparatus of biblical exegesis—here Pecock is deliberately rejecting Lollard fundamentalism and justifying the intellectual apparatus of the Church:

> If substanciali leerned clerkis in logik and in moral philosophie and in dyvynyte, and ripeli exercisid ther yn, weren not and schulden not be forto wiseli and dewli geve trewe undirstondingis and exposiciouns to textis of Holi Scripture: or ellis, though suche clerkis ben, and the lay parti wolen not attende to the doctrine, whiche tho clerkis mowe and wolen (bi proof of sufficient and open evydence) mynystre to the lay parti; but the lay parti wolen attende and truste to her owne wittis, and wolen lene to textis of the Bible oonli, Y dare wel seie so many dyverse opinions schulden rise in lay mennys wittis bi occasioun of textis in Holy Scripture about mennys moral conversacioun, that al the world schulde be cumbrid therwith and men schulden accorde to gidere in keping her service to God as doggis doon in a market, whanne ech of them terith otheris coot... (*Repressor* 1: 85-86).

Clerics, using their logical training, can make the crucial distinctions that allow for correct interpretation of Scripture. Without this institutionally sanctioned commentary, and the canonical texts it relies on, every man will advance his own interpretation, however wild, and the result will be social chaos. This is what Pecock is determined to combat.

So far Pecock seems to be on safe ground, and it is difficult to see why his writings were so controversial. In particular, the seventh error attributed to Pecock, that anyone can understand the literal sense of Scripture, seems a gross injustice, since this is effectively the very position Pecock rejects as the Lollard error of believing that anyone who is sufficiently meek can understand Scripture. But although the council may have exaggerated or misrepresented Pecock's position on some matters, the charges brought against him were not entirely trumped up. In rejecting Lollard fundamentalism, Pecock stresses the authority of sanctioned commentary and of the Fathers, as was proper, but he stresses far more the power of reasoning, the "doom of reason" as he calls it.

> But Y wold se that oure Bible men whiche holden hem so wise bi the Bible aloone, yhe, bi the New Testament aloon, couthen bi her Bible aloon knowe whiche feith is a lawe to man and whcih feith is not a lawe to man, and thanne he dide a maistire passing his power. Wherbi and bi many othere pointis of Goddis lawe and service to man, whiche mowe not be knowen bi oonli the Bible but by doom of resoun and moral philosophi ... the Bible men mowe take good marke that myche nede schullen alle tho have to the help of weel leerned clerkis (*Repressor* 1: 37).

Rejecting the alleged Lollard position that meekness of spirit is enough to understand Scripture, Pecock insists on the need to use reason. The lay reader is expected to follow a logical argument and read studiously but not to move beyond his or her ability, leaving harder questions to the more fully trained intelligence of the clergy. If the Lollards, as Pecock represents them, put their trust in the spiritual condition of the reader, Pecock puts his in the reader's brains.

Pecock certainly had full confidence in his own powers of reasoning, so much so that his intellectual independence apparently raised concerns quite early in his career. In the *Folewer* he addresses these concerns directly:

> Now schal ye seie what I have herde seid of me: "This man seith and techith mych thing, but he seith al of him silf and of his owne heed, fforwhi he alleggith not for him alwey Hooli Scripture or sume doctours" ...[but] if the writer of Hooli Scripture or a doctoure seie and write a thing which he hath not but out of resoun and for resoun, and for that he leernyd it oonli of resoun, whi schulde not resoun be alleggid for thilk thing and trouth more and rather than the writer of thilk process of scripture annd more and rather than the doctoure? [After all] ech doctoure writynge eny book of divinitye takith al that he writeth bi doom of resoun (8-9).

This leads to a dangerous conclusion: that in matters other than those of faith, reason takes *precedence* over the writings of the Fathers and even over Scripture itself. In the *Reule*, Pecock distinguishes between those truths that may not be known by natural reason and are therefore known by faith alone and those we can know by reason. The first he reveres:

> But certis this excellent reverence wol Y not geve to Holy Scripture above alle othere writyngis of men for the tretynge or techyng or declaracioun of eny article or of eny trouthe in natural lawe of kynde or in moral lawe of kynde of which mencioun and remembrance is maad in Holy Scripture (10).

In the *Repressor* he expands on this position, arguing that religious truths predate the New Testament:

> Certis treuthis of lawe of kind which Crist and his Apostlis schewiden forth to the peple were bifore in the grete see of lawe of kinde in mannis soule eer Crist or his Apostlis were born into this leef (1: 30).

Pecock then advances a perilous analogy to a clerk who goes into a library to study a matter of faith in the Bible before delivering his opinion on it in a public sermon at Saint Paul's Cross or in a letter to a friend. Just as the authority for any statement the clerk might make would lie in the Bible or other books in the library, rather than in what he said publicly, so

> alle the trouthis of lawe of kinde whiche Crist and hise Apostlis taughten and wroten weren before her teching and writing, and weren writen bifore in thilk solempnest inward book or inward writing of resounis doom passing alle outwarde bookis in profite to men for to serve God (1: 31).

Pecock is advancing what is, at the very least, a dangerously broad claim for the powers of reason. Admittedly, he limits the claim to matters of "lawe of kind," i.e., to matters of general knowledge as opposed to fundamental articles of faith, but even given that restriction his position is not orthodox. Pecock goes so far as to envisage situations in which reason might *correct* Scripture in matters of kind, as opposed to simply elucidating Scripture or clarifying apparent contradictions within it:

> And if eny semyng discorde be bitwixte the wordis writen in the outward book of Holi Scripture and the doom of resoun, write in mannis soule and herte, the wordis so writen withoutforth oughten to be expowned and to be interpretid and brought for to accorde with the doom of resoun in thilk mater; and the doom of resoun oughte not forto be expowned, glosid, interpretid, and broughte for to accorde with the seid outward writing in Holi Scripture of the Bible or oughwhere ellis out of the Bible (*Repressor* 1: 25-26).

Pecock's method of composition, which involves extensive self-reference and self-paraphrase but relatively few references to other authorities or to

Scripture, provides concrete illustration of this dangerous independence. His confidence in human reason at the expense of authority, even the authority of Scripture, provides at least partial justification for the objection raised at the council that he had preferred "the judgment of natural reason before the Old or New Testament" and "vilipended and rejected the authority of the old doctors" (Pecock 1860, 1: xxxvii drawing on Gascoigne).

Pecock's remarks were all the more dangerous because he placed no clear social limits on this "doom of reason." The "doom of reason" is not confined to the clergy or to any social caste in particular; it is open to both laymen and laywomen, according to their varying intellectual capacities. Furthermore, all people, no matter what their occupation or level of intellectual preparation, have the moral responsibility to use their capacity to its fullest. This means not just using it on lesser matters, such as property disputes, but on fundamental questions of morality. Pecock's writings conjure up a vision of a society in which the educated merchants and gentlefolk would devote a good part of their lives to religious reading and religious debate.

In this respect, Pecock ran headlong against the conservative orthodoxy of his day. The English Bible was not seen as especially threatening as long as its readership was closely socially circumscribed. Even after the Wycliffite Bible had been officially condemned, it continued to circulate among respectable gentlefolk and aristocrats without apparently causing anyone much concern. Some of the known owners of the Wycliffite Bible may have been closet Lollards, but Henry VI, who owned a copy, certainly was not (Krochalis 1988). Popular access to the Bible, on the other hand, provoked intense anxiety. The chronicler Henry Knighton, for example, writing in about 1390, believed that Wycliffe's translation had opened the floodgates and that "that which formerly belonged to those clergy who were sufficiently learned and intelligent, was made available to any lay person, even women, who knew how to read." (1889-95, 2:152). Knighton greatly exaggerated the availability of English Bibles, but his words do illustrate the common official attitude to the specter of universal Bible-reading. Pecock's proposal to make basic theological and religious treatises available in English would inevitably raise similar anxieties.

Ironically, in his support for lay reading Pecock is not that far from the Lollards themselves. He shares their strong optimism in the capabilities of the average lay reader, and the principle, which can be traced back to Wycliffe, that theological discussion can and should take place in English. He advocates a strongly independent reading practice that encompasses a broad range of moral and theological questions, and he objects not to people reading the Bible for themselves (a topic on which he is largely silent) but to their reading it without proper guidance:

> This what Y have now seid of and to Bible men Y have not seid undir this entent and meenyng, as that Y schulde feel to be unleeful laymen forto reede in the Bible and forto studie and leerne ther yn, with help and counseil of wise and weel leerned clerkis and with licence of her governour the bischop; but forto rebuke and adaunte the presumpcioun of tho lay persoones, which weenen bi her inreding in the Bible forto come into mroe kunnyng than thei or alle the men in erthe—clerkis and othere—mowe come to, bi the Bible oonli without moral philosophie and lawe of kinde in doom of wel disposid resoun, Y have seid of and to the Bible men what is now seid (*Repressor* 1: 37).

Pecock is even closer to some Lollard thinking than it first appears. On the one hand, the Lollard fundamentalism Pecock attacks is arguably something of a straw man. Some Lollards may have harbored a populist resentment of all forms of organized learning and maintained that meekness was all that was really needed, but this was certainly not the view of all Lollards, least of all the educated and privileged London merchants with whom Pecock often came in contact. On the other hand, the rational examination of Scripture that Pecock advocates is much like that advocated by Wycliffe or the author of the General Prologue to the Wycliffite Bible, which draws on the work of Saint Augustine, especially his *De doctrina christiana*, and on the tradition of commentary in the *Glossa ordinaria* to establish basic exegetical guidelines (Forshall and Madden 1850, esp. 1: ch. 12). Neither Pecock nor the author of the General Prologue to the Wycliffite Bible would go so far as to claim that anyone can understand the literal sense of Scripture, at least not without adding important qualifications. Pecock certainly insists that any reader of religious texts should exercise due diligence and due humility, seeking clerical guidance as needed. Given such qualifications, however, both Pecock and the author of the General Prologue agree on the possibility of a diligent lay reader getting it right often enough to be worth the risk. The crucial difference is that Pecock applies this argument explicitly only to his own works and not to the Bible. But it is easy to extrapolate. The council that condemned Pecock for maintaining that anyone could understand *Scripture* could well have argued that this was the clear implication of Pecock's writings, even if he conscientiously avoided stating it directly.

Pecock's efforts to write for the laity were matched by his efforts to encourage book production, and here, too, he came into contact with men of Lollard sympathies. Wendy Scase has traced out one of the networks through religious books circulated in London and has shown that Pecock collaborated with London merchants and with those in the London book trade in a number of schemes designed to provide poor secular clerics with access to religious texts (1992). As a young rector, Pecock was one of the clerics who assisted in distributing the books of Richard Whittington (the famous Dick Whittington, "thrice Lord Mayor of London town"), who died in 1423, and of John Carpenter, Common Clerk of London. Whittington's will established a library at the Guildhall for the benefit of poor clerics. When Carpenter, who had acted as Whittington's executor, made his own will, he arranged for Pecock and another rector to select some of his books for the Guildhall, "for the profit of the students there, and those discoursing to the common people," but he also added a curious provision, that no inventory of his books be made. Scase notes:

> By means of this extraordinary arrangement, Carpenter seems to have calculated to arrange for the disposal of his books in a way that would benefit his soul and the new city library, and to evade—with the collaboration of the two city rectors Pecock and Lichfield—the intervention of the ecclesiastical authorities, into whose hands, perhaps, or just to whose notice, simply, he did not wish his books to pass (1992, 269).

Pecock was also closely connected at this time to one John Colop, a member of his London parish and a business associate of Carpenter's, who had connections in the book trade. Colop assisted in the distribution of Whittington's estate, and in his own will he provided money for the copying of a common-profit book, a compendium of religious texts that was to be loaned out to a poor cleric as long as he had need of it and then passed on to another, all in exchange for prayers. Like the Guildhall library, the common-profit books were a means of getting books into the hands of the poor secular clergy. What is alarming, however, is that Colop's common-profit book, Cambridge University Library MS Ff.vi.31, contains several Lollard texts such as the *Holy Prophet David Seith* (edited by Deanesley 1920, 445-56; discussion in Wogan-Browne et al. 1999, 149-56). Pecock, then, was part of a network of Londoners committed to broadening religious education through reading, even if this involved circumventing the ecclesiastical authorities. He was collaborating with men who, if not Lollards, had strong Lollard sympathies. This does not mean that Pecock was a closet Lollard, but he did share many of the Lollards' central assumptions, and it seems entirely credible that he would have met with Lollard leaders for regular discussion, as he claims:

> I have spoke oft tyme, and bi long leiser, with the wittiest and kunnyngist men of thilk seid sort, contrarie to the chirche, and which han be holde as dukis amonge hem, and which han lovede me for that Y wolde pacientli heere her evydencis, and her motyves without

exprobracioun (*Book of Faith*, 202).

However sincerely Pecock may have feared and disapproved of the Lollard movement, he was, in some areas, dangerously close to being a fellow traveler.

Pecock's decision to write in English must be seen as a political act. Ostensibly Pecock's works serve as a defense of the institutional Church that laypeople could read, but the full scope of the project goes far beyond this. In defiance of Arundel's constitutions, Pecock created a monumental body of religious discussion in English. The six surviving English works alone, to say nothing of the twenty or more that have perished, are enough to provide a plentiful supply of reading material, a lifetime's worth by the standards of a period when a dozen books would still be considered a large personal library. The real force of this huge project is to provide a less perilous alternative to the English Bible. Pecock's works would allow lay readers to tax their wits and participate in their religion with engaged intelligence, moving upward from simple articles of faith to more complex issues of theology, all without turning to the Bible directly.

Yet Pecock nowhere says this; he defends his use of English on several occasions, and at considerable length, but only on the grounds that it makes his polemic more widely accessible. In the *Reule*, for example, he justifies his use of English as a means of attacking two kinds of Lollards, those who scorn all works except the English Bible, and those who scorn all works except the English Bible and a few works of their own:

> If eny man wole aske and wite whi this present book and the bookis to hym perteynyng Y make in the commoun peplis langage, hereto Y answere that this present book, and alle othere bookis to him longing maad in the comoun peplis lanage, ben so maad principali forto adaunte, rebuke, drive doun, and converte the fonnednes and the presumpcioun of ij soortis of peple. On is of hem whiche holden hem silf so stifly and so singulerly, fooli, and oonli to the uce of the Bible in her modris langage, and namely to therof the Newe Testament, that thei trowen, seien, and holden bothe pryveli and as fer openly as they daren, alle othere bookis writun or in Latyn or in the comoun peplis langage to be writun into waast, and not oonly into waast but into the marryng and cumbring of Cristen mennes wittis fro the sufficient and necessarie leernyng which thei myghten and oughten have bi studie aloone in the Bible or oonly therof in the New Testament (*Reule* 17).

Here, as elsewhere, Pecock presents his own work as a means of correcting widespread Lollard error and justifying the Church's intellectual apparatus by making it more accessible, but goes no further.

Pecock would not be the only example of a writer who dealt with the question of the English Bible, but did so only by implication. An earlier example is *The Dialogue between the Lord and the Clerk*, which John Trevisa offered as a preface to his 1387 translation of Ranulph Higden's *Polychronicon*. The *Dialogue* pits the Lord, who may express some of the sympathies of Trevisa's noble patrons for translation, against the Cleric, who initially opposes any translation from Latin but is gradually persuaded of its benefits. The Lord's arguments parallel many advanced by the Lollards. He points out, for example, that if there really were no need for translations, then the Fathers, who translated Scripture out of Hebrew into Greek, and Jerome, when he translated it from Greek into Latin, would have been wasting their time (Babington and Lumby 1865-86, lines 61 ff.; see also Wogan-Browne et al. 1999, 130-31). It is difficult to imagine that anyone could seriously have worried about the dangers of translating the *Polychronicon*, an innocuous encyclopedia composed by a Benedictine monk of unimpeachable orthodoxy. But the debate between the Lord and the Clerk concerns the legitimacy of translation in general, and thus the far more charged issue of the translation of Scripture. In its support for lay education and the production of books for a lay readership, it hints at the ambitious project of the Lollards, and Anne Hudson goes so far as to label Trevisa's position "vernacular Wycliffism" (1988, 394-8).[9] If Trevisa felt the need to employ such indirection in the 1380s, then it is scarcely surprising that writers in the wake of Arundel's constitutions would do so. As Nicholas Watson argues, by the early fifteenth century "all but the most pragmatic religious writing could come to be seen…as dangerous" and Arundel's constitutions created "an atmosphere in which self-censorship was assumed to be both for the common good and (for one's own safety) prudent" (1995, 825, 831). If we accept Watson's account, then religious writing in the century following Arundel's constitutions is structured around that which it cannot say. Even someone as rashly independent on theological matters as Pecock leaves charged silences and crucial ambiguities at the heart of his works.

Like Trevisa's *Dialogue*, Pecock's works resolutely avoid the questions that most concern them. When Pecock discusses the right interpretation of Scripture the one question he never addresses is the most important question of all, what language Scripture is to be in. He touches on the issue only once in the *Repressor*, for example, and then only to offer a logical analogy. Pecock points out that the same argument that the Lollards use against pilgrimage, namely that it is not explicitly mentioned in the New Testament, could also be used against biblical translation (which is not explicitly mentioned there either). But in this argument, whether translation is a good thing is not to the purpose and Pecock reveals nothing of his own position. Elsewhere, Pecock is equally ambiguous.

When Pecock speaks of allowing lay reading of the Bible provided it is done under clerical supervision and with the license of the bishop, for example, it is not clear whether this would necessarily involve an *English* Bible, in which case the restrictions would have been almost impossible to monitor or would be limited to those laypeople who could read a French Bible or piece their way through a Latin Bible with the help of a personal chaplain. Pecock calls the Lollards "Bible men," a recognition of their central demand, but he neither explicitly condemns nor explicitly rejects this demand. He never makes it clear whether he supports or opposes biblical translation or whether his own work should be seen as an alternative to lay Bible reading or as a propaedeutic to it. Some have gone so far as to see Pecock as a promoter of biblical translation (Brockwell 1985, 153), and this seems to have been the judgment of the council when they accused him of his seventh error. There were even rumors circulating that Pecock was engaged in translating the Bible himself, and the Scriptural quotations in his works suggest that he knew the Wycliffite Later Version.[10] But if Pecock in his heart hoped for a day when English Bible reading would be accepted, he never came out and said so in any of his surviving works.

There is one possible point where Pecock may have tackled the question directly, a passage in the *Donet*, but all that remains is a fragment, for the chapter has been almost entirely excised from the single surviving manuscript:

> ...fro presumpcion and schulen be so clerid in her witt that her reding thanne in the Englishe Bible schal not hurte hem nor eny othir man (172).

Presumably Pecock is arguing against the presumption of the Lollards that the reading of the Bible can do no harm, but his own position, or that of the person who removed the quire, remains an open question. It seems symbolic of Pecock's career that on this central question, the key to his entire project, he was so often silent and that one of the few passages dealing with the question should have been removed from his book.

Pecock's accusers maintained the same charged silence. Apparently some of the temporal lords assembled at Westminster complained that Pecock "had written...on profound subjects in the English language" (Babington citing the Council of October in Pecock 1860, 1: xxxvi), thus setting in motion the investigation, but the Archbishop's court was more discreet. Pecock was accused not of breaking Arundel's constitutions, nor of aiding the Lollards, nor of supporting biblical translation, but of heresy, and his use of English was never mentioned in charges that were laid against him.

Pecock is largely forgotten, and only a few of his works survive, yet ironically he went further than any other late medieval English writer in his efforts to unite his works into a unified corpus and control its publication. For all his theological extravagance, Pecock was acutely conscious of ecclesiastical strictures on writing; he took great pains to ensure that his work was approved by ecclesiastical authorities and protested against the inaccurate or premature copies that he claimed had been made against his desire. Just as he linked his works together in his prefaces, he provided important qualifications about their meaning that he wanted understood "bifore the fynal uttryng and publischyng of eny of my bookis, English or Latyn" (*Folewer* 5). In the *Donet* he insists that "it is not myn entent forto holde, defende, or favoure, in this book, or in eny othire bi me writun, or to be writun, in Latyn or in the comoun peplis lanage, enye erroure or heresie or eny conclusioun which schulde be agens the feith or the lawe of oure lord god"(3). He insists in the opening pages of the *Folewer* that his positions are subject to correction and advanced only as part of logical arguments, rather than as absolute truths, so that such phrases as "I prove" or "I show" are not to be understood absolutely (5-6).

This anxiety forced Pecock to conceive his work in new ways. Of course, he is by no means the first writer in English to try to control the circulation of his works and their accuracy. Siân Echard argues that John Gower's Latin glosses show an effort to control the scribal presentation of his text (1998). Chaucer's address to his scribe, Adam Scriveyn, who allegedly mangles Chaucer's texts, is well known. But no other writer in English before Pecock took such elaborate measures to unite his work as a whole, laying out the connections among the various parts and ranking them according to difficulty for the benefit of a diverse readership. The pressures of ecclesiastical censorship helped Pecock to conceive of his work not as a continual series of tellings or retellings, or as a compilation of the works of others, or as one stage in an ongoing tradition, but as a clearly delineated corpus of material for which he was solely responsible. This corpus reflected his intention, and it was this intention that should be judged. An error or heresy, Pecock argues, is "not the ynke writen, neither the voice spokun, but it is the meenyng or the undirstondyng of the writer or speker signified bi thilk ynke writen or voice spokun" (*Donet* 4). To judge this authorial intention one must consider the entire corpus, with due regard for the author's explanations, justifications and directions, and if this is still not sufficient, Pecock adds, "recours may be had to my persoon forto aske of me, while Y am in this liife." (*Donet* 4-5). The entire body of his work and the single author are linked as one; the author provides the ultimate meaning for the corpus with which he is publicly identified once the work is "published," a term that in Pecock begins to acquire something of its subsequent meaning not merely as a presentation to a wider audience, but as a definitive setting of a text.

Pecock offers an early illustration of Foucault's famous maxim that "texts, books, and discourses really begin to have authors...to the extent that authors become subject to punishment" (1979, 148). Pecock's recognition that his work would be subject to harsh scrutiny and that he had to assume responsibility for it drove him to construct his work as a unified and interconnected corpus to a far higher degree than any previous English writer. As Pecock says in the *Reule*:

> ...I made my coors for book to book that ech of them myghte helpe the other to be maad, and that ech schulde accorde with other, and leene to other, and be joyned and knytt to other, right as chaumbris, parlouris and manye housis of offices answeren and cleeven to the chief hall for to make of alle oif hem so togidere palcid and knytt oon formal, oon semely, beuteful, eisful, and confortable habitacioun (22).

Perhaps we might even say that by Foucault's definition, Reginald Pecock was the first English author.

Notes

1. The story is recounted by Churchill Babington in his edition of *The Repressor* (Pecock 1860, 1: xlvi ff. Pecock's Latin recantation is preserved in Lambeth Wharton MS 577, p. 25, headed "Reginaldi Peccok episcopi Cicesterensis abjuratio in foro judicali."
2. French books continued to be used in England among the upper classes during the fifteenth century (Meale 1989, 207-09). Some prosperous laypeople even read the Bible in Latin. Huntington, San Marino, MS EL 9 H9, for example, originally copied in the thirteenth century, appears by the fifteenth century to have been owned by London merchants. On folio 384v, the following names appear: "henricus byntun, Thomas Unbrege, Iohannis stokys of fordenyche gentylman of decoler, Iohannes Frouike of londun marchate of debanker." The names of the merchants, which appear on the flyleaf, are all written in the same hand, raising the possibility that the book may have been jointly owned.
3. The text is in *Concilia Magnae Britanniae et Hiberniae* (Wilkins 1737, 3: 314-19). The far-reaching effects of the constitutions are discussed by Nicholas Watson (1995). Malcolm Lambert offers a good introduction to the tensions surrounding biblical translation during this period (1992, 225-27; 238-42; 255-56).
4. Babington, in his edition (Pecock 1860), provides a good account of the early sources for Pecock's life, notably the fifteenth-century *Theological Dictionary* of Thomas Gascoigne. There are several biographies, including the recent study by Wendy Scase (1996).
5. None of Pecock's works as yet exists in more than a single edition. For all quotations from Pecock's works, I have substituted "th" for thorn, "g" or "gh" for yogh, and "u" for "v" or vice versa, in accordance with modern usage. I have also made some

alterations to the punctuation and capitalization in these editions, which is, in any case, editorial.

6.   I owe this suggestion to Nicholas Watson.

7.   Pecock's commitment to the powers of reason has been assessed variously as reflecting his philosophical convictions, his sense of pastoral duty, his misguided ecclesiastical careerism, or the overenthusiasm of a theological amateur. Everett Emerson goes so far as to claim Pecock as "an almost unique thinker, one who was able to be at the same time an almost completely orthodox Christian and a philosophic rationalist with a regard for reason not to be found in any other mediaeval thinker" (1956, 235-36). This attitude is also characteristic of Pecock's legal thought (Doe 1990, 61-62; Landman 1999, 108).

8.   The best introduction to the social makeup of the London merchant class remains that of Sylvia Thrupp (1948). The Lollard presence in East Anglia and in wool towns such as Coventry was strong and is well recorded in early fifteenth-century heresy trials and has been the subject of a recent study by Shannon McSheffrey (1995), but our knowledge of Lollards, or those with Lollard sympathies, in London remains sketchy. The most telling evidence is the survival of a large number of copies of the New Testament or the four Gospels, which show a high degree of standardization (and may therefore have emanated from an organized scriptorium) and appear to be of London provenance. Anne Hudson assesses this evidence (1989, 125-42).

9.   While it is now no longer believed that Trevisa participated in the Wycliffite translation, he may well have known those, such as Nicholas Hereford, who did (Fowler 1960, 1995).

10.   J. L. Morison discusses this rumor (Pecock 1909, 44). On Pecock's knowledge of the Lollard Bible, see Charles Wager (1984).

Works Cited

Brockwell, Charles W., Jr. *Bishop Reginald Pecock and the Lancastrian Church: Securing the Foundations of Cultural Authority*. Lewiston, N. Y.: Edwin Mellen, 1985.

Deanesley, Margaret. *The Lollard Bible and Other Medieval Biblical Versions*. Cambridge: Cambridge University Press, 1920.

Doe, Norman. *Fundamental Authority in Late Medieval Law*. Cambridge: Cambridge University Press, 1990.

Echard, Siân. "With Carmen's Help: Latin Authorities in Gower's Confessio Amantis." *Studies in Philology* 95 (1998): 1-40.

Emerson, Everett H. "Reginald Pecock: Christian Rationalist." *Speculum* 31 (1956): 235-42.

Forshall, J. and F. Madden, eds. *The Holy Bible...Made from the Latin Vulgate by John Wycliffe and His Followers*. 4 vols. Oxford: Oxford University Press, 1850.

Foucault, Michel. "What is an Author?" In *Textual Strategies: Perspectives in Post-Structuralist Criticism*, ed. and trans. Josué V. Harari, 141-60. Ithaca: Cornell University Press, 1979.

Fowler, David C. "John Trevisa and the English Bible." *Modern Philology* 58 (1960): 81-98.

—. *The Life and Times of John Trevisa, Medieval Scholar*. Seattle: University of Washington Press, 1995.

Gascoigne, Thomas. *Loci e Libro Veritatum. Passages Selected from Gascoigne's*

Theological Dictionary Illustrating the Condition of Church and State, 1403-1458. Ed. James E. Thorold Rogers. Oxford: Clarendon Press, 1881.

Griffiths, Jeremy and Derek Pearsall, eds. *Book Production and Publishing in Britain, 1375-1475.* Cambridge: Cambridge University Press, 1989.

Hudson, Anne. "Lollard Book Production." In Griffiths and Pearsall 1989. Pp. 125-42.

—. *The Premature Reformation: Wycliffite Texts and Lollard History.* Oxford: Clarendon Press, 1988.

—, ed. *English Wycliffite Writings.* Cambridge: Cambridge University Press, 1978.

Knighton, Henry. *Chronicon Henrici Knighton; vel, Cnitthon, monachi leycestrensis.* Ed. Joseph Rawson Lumby. Rolls Series 92. London: Eyre and Spottiswoode, 1889-95.

Krochalis, Jeanne. "The Books and Reading of Henry V and His Circle." *Chaucer Review* 23 (1988): 50-77.

Lambert, Malcolm. *Medieval Heresy: Popular Movements from the Gregorian Reform to the Reformation,* 2nd ed. Oxford: Blackwell, 1992.

Landman, James H. " 'The Doom of Resoun': Accommodating Lay Interpretation in Late Medieval England." *Medieval Crime and Social Control,* ed. Barbara A. Hanawalt and David Wallace, 90-123. Minneapolis: University of Minnesota Press, 1999.

McSheffrey, Shannon. *Gender and Heresy: Women and Men in Lollard Communities, 1420-1530.* Philadelphia: University of Pennsylvania Press, 1995.

Meale, Carol. "Patrons, Buyers and Owners: Book Production and Social Status." In Griffiths and Pearsall 1989. Pp. 201-38.

Pecock, Reginald. *Reginald Pecock's Book of Faith: A Fifteenth Century Theological Tractate.* Ed. J. L. Morison. Glasgow: James Maclehouse and Sons, 1909.

—. *The Donet by Reginald Pecock...collated with the Poore Mennis Myrrour.* Ed. Elsie Vaughan Hitchcock. Early English Text Society 156. London: Oxford University Press, 1921.

—. *The Folewer to the Donet.* Ed. Elsie Vaughan Hitchcock. Early English Text Society 164. London: Oxford University Press, 1924.

—. *The Repressor of Over Much Blaming of the Clergy.* Ed. Churchill Babington. Rolls Series 19. 2 vols. London: Longman, Green, Longman, and Roberts, 1860.

—. *The Reule of Crysten Religioun.* Ed. William Cabell Greet. Early English Text Society 171. London: Oxford University Press, 1927.

Saul, Nigel. *Richard II.* New Haven, Ct.: Yale University Press, 1997.

Scase, Wendy. "Reginald Pecock." *Authors of the Middle Ages,* vol. 3. Ed. M. C. Seymour. Aldershot, England; Brookfield, Vt.: Variorum, 1996.

—. "Reginald Pecock, John Carpenter and John Colop's 'Common-Profit' Books: Aspects of Book Ownership and Circulation in Fifteenth-Century London." *Medium Aevum* 61 (1992): 261-74.

Thrupp, Sylvia L. *The Merchant Class of Medieval London (1300-1500).* Chicago: University of Chicago Press, 1948.

Wager, Charles H. A. "Pecock's 'Repressor' and the Wyclif Bible," *Modern Language Notes* 9 (1984): 97-99.

Watson, Nicholas. "Censorship and Cultural Change in Late-Medieval England: Vernacular Theology, the Oxford Translation Debate, and Arundel's Constitutions of 1409." *Speculum* 70 (1995): 822-64.

Wilkins, David, ed. *Concilia Magnae Britanniae et Hiberniae, a Synodo Verolamiensi A.D. CCCCXLIV. ad Londinensem A.D. MDCCXVII, accedunt Constitutiones et alia ad Historiam Ecclesiae Anglicanae spectantia.* 4 vols. London: Gosling, 1737.

Wogan-Browne, J., et al., eds. *The Idea of the Vernacular: An Anthology of Middle English Literary Theory.* University Park, Pa.: Pennsylvania State University Press, 1999.

Leo Africanus, Translated and Betrayed

Oumelbanine Zhiri
University of California, San Diego

An important body of knowledge, devoted to the need to re-situate historically the perception of different races and peoples, is already constituted and is constantly growing. In particular, many feel the necessity to concentrate on the vision that Europe presented and is still presenting of Africa, with as much precision as has been given to the study of the circumstances of the discovery of America. Such a research would help renew and prolong the reflection on the relation to the other. All these concerns call for increasing attention to the work of the sixteenth-century geographer Leo Africanus.

Among the numerous works that transformed the geographical knowledge of the European Renaissance, one is worthy of special notice; it is a collection of geographical texts and of travel narratives that came to play an important role in the history of European geography. Its first volume was published in 1550 and was soon followed by five others. This collection presented the reader with an image of the world based on travels and explorations that renewed the European knowledge of the earth. Entitled *Navigazioni e Viaggi*, the endeavor was coordinated by Giovanni Battista Ramusio, a high-ranking civil servant of the Republic of Venice. The numerous re-editions attest to the great success of this monumental work.

The first text of this first volume was to become very famous in and of itself and was translated and published separately in French, Latin, English and Dutch. It was authored by Leo Africanus, under the title *Della Descrizione dell'Africa e delle* cose *notabili che quivi sono*. The author's real name was Hasan Ibn Muhammad al-Wazzan al-Fasi. He was born in Granada around 1489 and left the country for Morocco after the fall of the last Muslim kingdom on the Iberian Peninsula, in 1492. He received a good education, focussing particularly on law and theology, as was traditional in Islamic countries. He also acquired an extensive knowledge of the literary, historiographical and geographical traditions in the Arabic language. As we will see, the circumstances with which he has been faced led him to write in Europe a text showing that he was a very well-read man. His career started quite early, when he entered the service of the Wattasid Sultan Muhammad the Portuguese.[1] His function as an ambassador gave him the opportunity to travel across Morocco, the Maghreb and Egypt. Other trips, perhaps taken for commercial reasons, led him to the sub-Saharan countries of West Africa. In 1518, during one of his journeys, the ship bringing Hasan back from Egypt to Morocco was boarded by Sicilian pirates, who offered him as a present to Pope Leo X. Hasan al-Wazzan converted to Christianity and received through baptism the names of his protector, Joannes Leo de Medici. Little is known about his stay in Italy, but an important day must be noted: March 10, 1526, when he completed the writing of the text that Ramusio was to publish in 1550 in *Navigazioni e Viaggi*.

His work is of great historical importance. Thanks to his cultural background, his career as a diplomat and the traveling it entailed, Leo was in a good position to provide his European readers with a particularly detailed description of a great part of Africa, especially its northern countries. His work was considerably at odds with the European writings on Africa and soon became the modern reference by which Europeans renewed the description of that continent. To be convinced, all one needs to do is to compare what had been written in Europe about Africa before the publication of the *Descrizione* (Boemus 1536; Münster 1544); the studies published after knowledge of Leo's work had profoundly changed European discourse on Africa. From the cosmographers and the cartographers of the sixteenth century (André Thevet, François de Belleforest, Gerard de Jode, Gerard Mercator, Luis del Marmol Carvajal) to the geographers and the travelers of the nineteenth century (Walckenaer, Renou, Barth), up to the historians who today see it as a document of great value on sixteenth-century Maghreb and West Africa, the work of Leo has been an essential source of information on a large part of the continent. Equally important is his influence on the consideration given to the African continent in European culture as well as in many texts. Until then, Africa had been relegated to a marginal position in the world and in history. This dismissal became less prevalent after the publication of Leo's work. It was not simply quoted by geographers and historians; it was also quoted in all kinds of different texts. This is a fact of prime importance. References to Leo's work can be found in philosophical, political and literary texts, some of them quite famous and influential, such as *The Anatomy of Melancholy* by Robert Burton*, De Subtilitate* by Cardano, the *Novelle* by Matteo Bandello or Jean Bodin's *Republique*. Thanks to Leo, modern Africa became part of Europe's cultural horizon.

However, in spite of the considerable number of texts using or studying his work, much remains to be done to better grasp its importance; new approaches and new questions make this work indispensable. More precisely, many questions remain unanswered about the text itself. The extent of the problem became clear when, in 1931, Angela Codazzi found a manuscript of the work of Leo Africanus belonging to the Vittorio Emanuele Collection of the Biblioteca Nazionale of Rome, where it remains today. The text was written in beautiful calligraphy, which reveals the penmanship of a professional identified by Dietrich Rauchenberger as Elie, a Maronite monk who copied a number of manuscripts belonging to the Oriental collection of the Vatican Library. This text was certainly dictated by Leo to the Arab-speaking copyist. As Rauchenberger concluded, it is that text that Ramusio used, or a version very close to it (1995).

The importance of this manuscript and its study is made clear by the fact that its discovery allows us to evaluate the role played by the editor in the preparation of a text for printing. The differences between the text of the manuscript and that of the published version are considerable. Many of these differences can be attributed to the desire to present a readable text to its audience. The manuscript is indeed written in an extremely faulty Italian highly tinged with Latin; in Alexis Epaulard's words, "[...]il est écrit dans un tel jargon que, même pour des contemporains, Ramusio a jugé bon d'en faire une véritable transposition en langue correcte" (1980, VI). Even when only the changes in grammar and, more importantly, vocabulary, are taken into account, one has to conclude that, considering the extent of the work accomplished, Ramusio's intervention deserves to be seen as a true translation and not a mere revision. It is clear that Ramusio's intent was not simply to correct the language and rewrite the sentences in order to make them more readily comprehensible. It is impossible, however, in this analysis to study all of Ramusio's interventions, for the omissions, modifications and additions he made concern every one of the 470 sheets of the manuscript. These modifications do not correspond to a unique concern; they call for a detailed study to help us better understand Ramusio's reasoning and his frame of mind as he rewrote and edited the manuscript.

Let us look at some of the most important of Ramusio's modifications. First of all, the manuscript has no title. In titling the work *Description of Africa*, Ramusio chose a standard title carried by many geographical works of the time. Another difference is obvious and affects every page of the text: Other than slashes (/) before and after numbers and, more rarely, marking the articulations of a sentence, the manuscript contains no punctuation. Ramusio punctuated the text to make it easier to read. As for organization, the manuscript is divided into chapters and books, some of which do not seem to be intended to belong to the same whole. Indeed, the last book, devoted to the description of the rivers, minerals, animals and plants of Africa, appears to have been conceived as a separate work. Ramusio did not accept this division as it was, and he profoundly modified it. He thus grouped the books to form a single work in nine major parts. Consequently, a great part of Leo's transitions disappeared from the text when they conflicted with the new divisions imposed by Ramusio.

One can already see that Ramusio's endeavor left Leo's work far from intact. His reorganization, division and attribution of titles are elements that greatly influence the reading. The editor did not limit his role, however, to these structural modifications. He intervened even more directly by permanently modifying the content—sometimes the information itself and sometimes, more subtly, the tone and the connotations of the text. Beyond those already examined, one finds transformations varying in length, in importance or even in purpose on almost every page.

Sometimes these changes seem to be inadvertent. For example, Ramusio often changed proper names. It is clear that in most cases the reason for the changes was a simple reading mistake. I will focus only on two of these errors, due to the frequency of the occurrence of the proper names and because such mistakes could not have been made in the manuscript by an author so intimately familiar with the geography and history of North Africa. Evoking the people of Lamtuna, from whom descends the dynasty of the Almoravids,[2] who played a major role in the history of Maghreb and Muslim Spain, the Italian edition and all its translations use the spelling "Luntuna." The manuscript uses "Lumtuna," proving that Leo was not to blame for this mistake. The name of the important city of Tlemcen in today's Algeria also has the bizarre spelling of "Telensin" in all the editions and translations of the *Descrizione*. Because one finds in the manuscript the spelling "Telimsin," this error is only imputable to Ramusio. Many other errors in the use of proper nouns can be found; they are not surprising coming from a non-Arab-speaking editor unfamiliar with North African matters.

One other area in which Ramusio made many transcription mistakes is in his use of numbers. This is a very important aspect.

Indeed, one of the qualities most appreciated by the historians who use the *Descrizione* is the precision of the information it provides about a large part of Africa in the beginning of the sixteenth century. Yet Ramusio's errors in transcribing numbers obliterate the accuracy of elements as important as demography, tax amounts and analysis of general economic life. He made many mistakes of the kind, linked to the presence of slashes accompanying numbers. For example, /50 000/ often becomes 150 000 in the printed text.

Often, however, it is clear that one cannot reduce the modification of the original text to a simple misreading; the analysis of many excerpts proves that Ramusio was not solely concerned with giving the printer a text more readable and grammatically correct. His rewriting is quite slanted, and, as we will see, politicized. The manuscript, dictated by an Arab author to an Arab copyist, was Europeanized by Ramusio in many ways. The distortion can be found in several of the editor's strategies; here I will study some of the most remarkable and visible ones. First, Ramusio added some comparisons with Europe and, at the same time, left out some references to Arab civilization and literature. Thus, he added passages that brought the text closer to its readers and stripped it of elements that stressed the cultural identity of its author. The two objectives, seemingly different, do, in fact, merge. In both cases, the goal is to bring the text closer to its European reader, to remove some of its strangeness and to partially integrate into the *Descrizione* the pre-existing image of Africa that it would do so much to transform.

Ramusio added about fifteen comparisons with Europe, some of which have particularly strong echoes in the Western cultural tradition. However, it must also be said that he eliminated from the final draft three comparisons with Europe that appear in the original manuscript. At the end of the first book, Leo makes two references to a book he calls *The Cento Novelle*,[3] which cannot be found in the printed text. On the other hand, Ramusio also left out a comparison with an Italian city, which appears on folio 51b of the manuscript. These omissions are all the more puzzling when one considers the many cases where Ramusio did exactly the opposite. At the very least, it reminds us that the interpretation of the discrepancies between the original and the rewriting presents many complexities, not the least of which is the difficulty of recognizing cases in which the reason for omissions is mere negligence.

Ramusio's additions seem easier to analyze. I shall examine some of the most significant ones. One of the references added by Ramusio is quite remarkable in terms of its cultural and political connotations. It is found in a chapter of Book One, where Leo describes the character of the inhabitants of Barbaria (as North Africa was called in Europe at this time) and explains that "sonno homini integri non hanno troppo malitia homini virili quel che dicono in absentia confirmano in presentia" (MS, fol. 40b). Ramusio did not content himself with this laudatory appreciation: "ancora che negli antichi secoli, come di cio fanno fede le istorie degli scrittori latini, siano stati altrimenti tenuti" (1978, 63). The printed text adds an allusion to the accusation of perfidy, which had hounded North Africans ever since Sallust alluded to the *fides punica*, to how untrustworthy Punic promises are. Numerous are the European authors who, after reading Leo, never failed to allude to the well-known perfidy of the North African people, especially whenever political circumstances demanded hostility against them, as was often the case. At least one author, however, openly blames Leo for his partiality in favor of his countrymen:

> Quant à ce que Léon a dit de ceux de son pays, qu'ils ne sont pas doubles, il les a véritablement flattés, vu qu'il n'y a gens du monde plus perfides, ni prompts à changer d'avis et renverser toutes les assurances qu'ils auront données (Davity 1637, 40).

Leo's words on the subject have convinced few of his readers. At the very least, the strength of his affirmation has been diminished by Ramusio's intervention.

In other passages, the editor added allusions to the Western tradition and even modified the meaning of the text in order to integrate the cultural memory of European readers. When Leo describes the pre-Islamic religions of Northern Africa, he evokes the cult of fire and, particularly, the necessity for its followers not to let it burn out in temples. He draws the link between this practice and the one that prevailed in ancient Persia. This comparison was not enough for Ramusio; the passage irresistibly evoked a cult that existed long ago in his own country: "nella guisa che nel tiempo della dea Veste si soleva osservare appresso i Romani" (1978, 46). In the description of the city of Bona, the text of the manuscript simply mentions that it was called "antiquamente Orpona" (MS, fol. 310a). Ramusio corrected the mistake and added a detail not mentioned by Leo, perhaps ignored: The old name of the city was "Hippo, dove fu episcopo santo Agostino" (1978, 312). It is understandable that Ramusio could not resist the temptation to add an allusion to such a renowned figure, one of the most important in the Christian tradition and in European culture. It seems difficult, however, to believe that his sole motivation was to provide the reader with more complete information. Here again, the subsequent evolution of the reading of Leo helps us to put this modification in perspective. Many European authors who later, especially in the sixteenth and seventeenth centuries, attempted to write an African history, attached great importance to the Christian past of North Africa and to the saintly figures who became famous during that time, among whom Augustine is undoubtedly the most celebrated. These historical reconstructions had a clear political connotation: The goal was to show that North Africa, having been Christian, could become Christian again through a reconquest that would prolong the "Reconquista" that took place on the Iberian peninsula, as the Portuguese victories on the Atlantic coast and the Spanish victories on the Mediterranean coast seemed to announce. I will return in a moment to the place reserved for the representation of North African history in Ramusio's translation.

Although very important, the insistence on ancient Christianity in North Africa was not the only aspect of this political and ideological endeavor; the authors also turned their attention to the Latin past, or to the past linked to Latinity. One of the symbolic loci through which the writers attempted to demonstrate historical links between Europe and North Africa, which would justify the conquest of the latter by the former, was Carthage, which had the advantage of bringing together two crucial elements: its cultural proximity and its rivalry with Rome. In this light, it is not surprising that one of Ramusio's additions can be found in the chapter concerning Carthage. In the manuscript, Leo signals different theories on the origin of the city, including the following:

> Questa e una cipta antiqua edificata secundo alcuni da una genta venuta da Assiria e alcuni altri dicono che la fu edificata da gente derivata da Armenia la quale passo el Mare de Moria & remanase in quella parte & edificorono la dicta cipta (MS 316b).

Ramusio modified this passage in two different ways. From the handwritten sentence, he kept only the first hypothesis, which, alluding to the Phoenician origin of the Carthaginian people, was acknowledged in the European tradition. On the other hand, he replaced the second hypothesis with the following: "alcuni altri dicono che ella fu edificata da una regina" (1978, 317), which related to the legendary foundation of Carthage by Dido.

Ramusio felt the need to add references to European history and cultural tradition. Correlatively, he erased a certain number of allusions to Islamic civilization and Arabic literature. In the extensive text on Fez, Leo elaborates on the history of Sufism, on the political evolution that marked it and on the most famous Sufi authors. Ramusio eliminated from these pages a certain amount of information. He omitted, in particular, the very name of Muslim mysticism, "Essofia," which appears on folio 179a of the manuscript. Finally, on the subject of popular mystical societies, Leo mentions certain offensive rumors about their meetings and concludes: "& in lo commento di la favola del Hariri sonno narrate mille cose particulari & sonno dishoneste a dirle in questa opera per molti respecti" (MS 182a). This reference to a famous author of the twelfth century was erased from the printed text.

One of the most interesting omissions can be found in the chapter on Tebessa. Leo quotes a poem, insulting for the people of this Tunisian city, by an author named al-Dabbag. Ramusio translated the poem but left out the rest of the chapter. Indeed, Leo does not stop there; he comments with obvious pleasure on certain verses, drawing attention (probably the attention of the copyist to whom he was dictating the text) to the subtlety of the expression. He then talks about another poet, Ibn al-Khatib (fourteenth century), who made himself famous through the same kind of vituperative writing. Evidently, this passage is a digression where Leo gives in to his taste for poetry and shows off his knowledge of Arabic literature. Ramusio erased a good part of it, thus revealing that the cultural dimension of Africa described by Leo did not represent in his eyes an important element of the text.

Both strategies—adding European and Christian references and removing African, Arabic and Islamic ones—obey the same pattern, which relieves the text of some of its strangeness and reduces the gap between the text and its readership. I have tried to demonstrate that this effort cannot be reduced to its cultural aspect, in the narrow sense of the term, and that the political content of this work is very important. One is all the more drawn to the conclusion that some of Ramusio's other interventions lead to the same result, which is to remove the foreign cultural and historical dimension from the text of the *Descrizione* and, by the same token, from the North African reality it describes.

The representation of history in the text, in particular, is subject to many of Ramusio's distortions. Once again, the direction imposed on the text by the Italian editor is closely akin to elements observed in the way European authors have used the *Descrizione* and have represented the history of Africa. Leo's work belongs essentially to the geographic genre. However, historical developments also hold an important place in it. The author tries to ground the geographical descriptions of countries and cities in history. Almost every section of the text starts by recalling, sometimes in a very detailed way, the history of the kingdom, the region, the province, the city. Quite surprisingly, considering the importance of this aspect of the text, these passages are quoted in relatively few historical works, as opposed to the more descriptive parts. The details provided by Leo were probably difficult to use by readers ignorant about the topic and who suffered from the lack of a clear historical thread in the *Descrizione*. It is interesting to notice that in preparing the text for publication, Ramusio foresaw this distrust or lack of understanding. Indeed, he summarized or curtailed a great part of the historical narratives such as those in the chapters devoted to Arzilla, Chesasa, Meggeo, Tilimsan, Mahdia, among others. The number of these omissions leads us to conclude that they are, in fact, one of the main aspects of the work of Ramusio, who ended up reducing the historical depth that Leo wished to give to his text.

In some cases, it is not pieces of information that are eliminated; it is the tone of the text that changes to the point of modifying its significance, and, at a deeper level, to the point of affecting the vision of history developed in the *Descrizione*. The chapter in which Leo refers to Marrakech is a good example of the practice. He retraces the historical evolution of the city, and one of the themes he expands upon most in these pages is the melancholy comparison between the splendor of Marrakech under the reign of the Almohad dynasty[4] and the sadness of a present in which the monuments of the capital city were falling in ruins, and the palaces were overrun by brambles and wild animals. What Ramusio took away from the text is the tone in which one detects Leo's personal engagement with the historical reconstruction, a tone that is almost lyrical. For the author, the consideration of Marrakech, in its present state of decadence, is the concrete image of the history of the Maghreb, which has passed from times of greatness to a state of crisis and dissension that he has witnessed and that he often evokes in the *Descrizione*. For Leo, writing about that history and evoking the feelings that it provokes in him are intimately linked, probably all the more so in that he writes his text from a situation of exile. For these reasons, the difference between personal memory and cultural memory becomes less obvious to him. In one particular case, this confusion reaches its peak. Leo describes the pitiful present state of the royal palace library of Marrakech and evokes the greatness of the empire of Yaqub al-Mansur, the greatest sovereign of the Almohad dynasty:

> il armatoroli de li libri sonno al presente nidi de colombi proprio alla usanza del mundo nel qual non e cosa ferma pero che gia el Mansore signoreggiano in Affrica da Messa fine in Tripoli di Barberia qual viagio el prefato compositore dice non haverlo passato cavaliare in mino de 90 giorni cio e per la longheza e per la largheza in mino de 15 giorni cio tutta la parte nobile de Affrica" (f. 73b).

Ramusio modified that passage considerably, leaving out the melancholy reflection on the instability of this world, which, in Leo's text, provides the link between the contemplation of the ruins of Marrakech and the memory of the past greatness of North Africa. In fact, it is in this description that Leo gives these fallen monuments their symbolic aspect and historical depth. These are precisely the qualities that Ramusio's rewriting stripped from the text. The rewriting removed another essential element: The Italian edition mentions that al-Mansur ruled over a large territory and indicates the number of days necessary to cover it by horse in its width and length. However, this information is given in a general way and is not linked to the figure of Leo. Once again, Ramusio deprived the text of its personal dimension and of the closeness between the author and his topic, a closeness that explains his engaging in the evocation of the past of North Africa.

Ramusio's modifications to the historical developments of the *Descrizione*, in which he eliminated certain passages and rewrote others, are not minor. Their importance becomes all the more clear as one links them to other editorial interventions in the text. Thus, allusions to European civilization and the disappearance of references to Arab culture all contribute to the orientation of the text in the same direction. In fact, Ramusio's aim was to impose on the *Descrizione* itself a vision of an objective that differs from that which appears in the manuscript. In other words, it attempts to modify the vision of African history presented in Leo's work. This history, as it appears in the *Descrizione*, is forced to conform with an image imposed according to European history, as a result of the various means used by Ramusio.

In a rather strange passage, Ramusio made a change that allows us to better grasp the vision of African history that he was advocating. Once again, the conception he offers of African history is all the more interesting in that it can be retraced later in many authors' visions of North Africa. In fact, the importance of this conception would grow and become one of the main aspects of the image of the historical evolution of the Maghreb as depicted by European texts. Leo points out that the ancient name of the city of Begia was Vechia. He tries to explain the evolution of the name by referring back to what he has learned about certain Italian regions: "non e stata mutata cosa alcuna pero che in terra de Lavoro & in Calabria dicono bino per vino & bechio per vechio" (f. 314b). This attempt at linguistic explanation was left out by Ramusio, who replaced it with a passage extremely different in meaning and in possible implications:

Ma io credo che'l nome primo che li poseno i Romani sia corrotto per la gran mutazione de de signori e di fede, vendendosi che questa parola non e araba (1978, 315-316).

Where Leo tries to give a linguistic explanation to the name's evolution, Ramusio referred back to history. The history of North Africa, he writes, was affected by such a change that the names were altered. The "great mutation" to which the Italian editor refers is the Arab invasion after which North Africa was no longer, as some might have thought, an extension of Europe. This disruption was to become one of the great themes of European literature on North African history; more precisely, authors would present this rupture as an event that could not be understood and that led the region to diverge from its "normal" destiny, and to cease to be Christian and Latin.

If one considers this concept, one better understands to what extent any of the manuscript's modifications made by Ramusio cannot be conceived as anecdotal. Analysis reveals a coherent pattern. The addition of allusions to Saint Augustine, to the cult of Vesta or to the *fides punica* is not fortuitous. These seemingly benign alterations lie within the scope of a work that aims to reduce the foreign dimension of the text, and especially of its object. In many sixteenth and seventeenth century European texts, North Africa provides the space for an elaborate ideological construction that, within the study of its past, insists on what brings it closer to Europe, and that, consequently, strives to water down what distances it from Europe. This is not an innocent endeavor: It is about justifying in advance a conquest of North Africa that Europeans were anticipating.

The heavy rewriting of the *Descrizione* given by Ramusio offers precious information on the European vision of Africa in the middle of the sixteenth century and deserves to be studied as a document in itself. However, we are also lucky to have at our disposal a manuscript that allows us to understand Leo's vision of Africa. Only this text deserves to be considered as the original. The scope of this study does not allow for a detailed analysis of the translations of the Italian text published from the sixteenth century on to the twentieth. I shall simply note that the French translation by Jean Temporal in 1556, though generally a good one, still contains many mistakes, and that Joannes Florianus' Latin text, is, on the other hand, very faulty, omitting or summarizing a good number of passages and teeming with mistranslations. This is the very text John Pory used for his English version. The only translator who consulted the manuscript is Alexis Epaulard. He claims in his preface that he corrected the most significant discrepancies between the texts. However, the comparison between his edition, Ramusio's and the manuscript shows that this is far from being the case and, therefore, that to this day, none of the editions of the *Descrizione* have been truthful to the text dictated by Leo to the copyist.

This is a fact to be kept in mind all the more so in that interest in the work of Leo Africanus has increased noticeably in recent years, and no longer exclusively among historians of the Maghreb and West Africa. It has become obvious to many that the *Descrizione* is a text of paramount importance for understanding the evolution of cultural and political relations between Europe and North Africa. Its significance stems from the fact that it has been one of the main sources used by the authors who created the image of modern Africa in Europe. In order to study this aspect of its influence, it is obvious that one need not consult the manuscript, to which these writers did not have access.

In the long and complex history of the relations between Europe and North Africa, Leo's text is a very important document that deserves to be studied in its own right. Here, it is crucial to study the manuscript. This article focuses on only one part of Ramusio's interventions, but one begins to see that the Italian editor has obliterated essential aspects of the text, which goes beyond simply omitting information. Ramusio distorted the one element of the work that might be the most important for us. Leo Africanus' work is a text written by an Arab writer, in Italy, in very bad Italian, for European readers whose knowledge of Africa was almost non-existent. The distance between him and his potential reader was great; on the other hand, as he says more than once, he does not have at his disposal the works that would allow him to most efficiently carry out his task and he must lean on his memory more than he would have had he been writing in his country. The unusual circumstances under which he composed his book are precisely what make it so important to study. The position of this geographer, situated between two cultures with a long common and conflictive history of negotiations, confrontations and misunderstandings, constitutes the essential aspect of the work of interest to us today. Leo Africanus' work is a frontier work, written by a man coming from one culture and addressing another. One of the most important questions it raises is how he negotiated this distance, how he used it and how he may have played with it. It represents a considerable problem that demands that one examine the role and function of the references to Arab geographical and historical literature in his work, as well as other less obvious elements such as the genre to which it belongs or the rich details of its descriptions explained by the fact that he addresses foreigners. One other important aspect to be considered is Leo's reasons for writing this text. We do not know whether he was fulfilling an order from the Pope, his patron, and if the latter had imposed some guidelines to which Leo had to conform his work. Whatever the case, in this text Leo not only tries to describe an object already culturally defined by a long historical and geographical tradition, he creates it knowing full well that his reader completely ignores this tradition and that he himself can only count on his memory to refer back to it.

What seems certain is that the *Descrizione*, to use the title chosen by Ramusio, is a mixed work, a hybrid work, in terms of the ambivalent situation of its author, the ways in which he negotiated that situation, and in terms of his obligation to inscribe in the text both civilizations in question, his and his reader's. However, when the Italian editor adds references to European culture and tradition, when he leaves out a page commenting admiringly on an Arabic poem, when he erases the traces of a profound nostalgia for a period in North African history all the more brilliant for being compared with a threatened present, it is with that very quality that he tampers, and it is that very quality that is altered. When Ramusio rewrote Leo Africanus' text, he betrayed the unique character of a work written on the frontier of cultures.

Notes

1. His reign extended from 1505 to 1524. He was nicknamed "the Portuguese" because of a long forced stay in Portugal.
2. They reigned in the eleventh and twelfth centuries.
3. Maybe a version of the *Novellino*.
4. They ruled North Africa in the eleventh and twelfth centuries.

Works Cited

l'Africain, Jean Léon. *Description de l'Afrique*. Trans. Alexis Epaulard. Paris: Maisonneuve (1956), 1980.

l'Africain, Jean Léon. "Historiale description de l'Afrique." *Historiale description de l'Afrique*. Trans. Jean Temporal. Lyons, 1556.

Africano, Giovan Leo. "Della Descrizione dell'Africa." In Giovanni Battista Ramusio, *Delle Navigazioni e Viaggi*, vol. 1, Turin, Eianaudi, 1978 (1550, 1554, 1563, 1588, 1606, 1613, 1837).

Africano, Joannes Leo. Manuscript, number 953, fund Vittorio Emanuele, Biblioteca Nazionale, Rome.

Africanus, Joannes Leo. *Africae Descriptio*, 1556 (1559, 1632).

Africanus, Leo. *History and Description of Africa*. Trans. from Latin by John Pory, 1600.

Bandello, Matteo. *Novelle*, 1554.

Barth, Heinrich. *Voyages en Afrique* (translated from German), 1860.

Belleforest, François de. *Cosmographie Universelle*, 1575.

—. *Histoire Universelle*, 1570.

Bodin, Jean. *Les Six Livres de la Republique*, 1576.

Boemus, Joannes. *Recueil de diverses histoires*, (Latin original first published in 1536).

Broc, Numa. *La Géographie de la Renaissance*. Paris: Bibliothèque Nationale, 1980.

Burton, Robert. *The Anatomy of Melancholy*, 1621.

Cardano, Hieronimo. *De Subtilitate*, 1550.

Codazzi, Angela. "Leone, Giovan." In *Enciclopedia Italiana di Scienze, Lettere ed Arti*. Rome, 1933.

—. "Il Trattato dell'Arte metrica di Giovanni Leone Africano." In *Studi Orientalistici in Onore di Giorgio Levi della Vida*, vol. 1, Rome, 1956. Pp. 180-98.

Davity. *Description générale de l'Afrique*, 1637.

De Jode, Gerard. *Speculum Orbis Terrarum*, 1578.

Garcia-Baquero, Juan. "Leon el Africano y la cartographia." In *Archivos de Estudios Africanos*. Madrid, 1953. Pp. 31-56.

Marmol Carvajal. Luis Del, *Africa*, 1573.

Massignon, Louis. *Le Maroc dans les premières années du XVI° Siècle, Tableau géographique d'après Léon l'Africain.* Algiers: A. Jourdan, 1906.

Mauny, Raymond. "Note sur les 'grands voyages' de Léon l'Africain." In *Hesperis*, Rabat, 1954. Pp. 379-92.

Mercator, Gerard. *Atlas*, 1595.

Münster, Sebastian. *Cosmographia*, 1544.

Rauchenberger, Dietrich. "Jean Léon l'Africain/Hasan al-Wazzan, un manuscrit et des données complétant la partie italienne de sa biographie." In *L'Occident musulman et l'Occident chrétien au Moyen Age*, 379-92. Rabat: Publications de la Faculté des Lettres, 1995.

Renou, C. *Description géographique de l'Empire de Maroc*, 1847.

Thevet, André. *Cosmographie universelle*, 1575.

Walckenaer, C.-A. *Recherches géographiques sur l'Intérieur de l'Afrique continentale*, Paris, 1821.

Zhiri, O. *L'Afrique au Miroir de l'Europe, Fortunes de Jean Léon l'Africain à la Renaissance*. Geneva: Droz, 1991.

—. *Les Sillages de Jean Léon l'Africain du XVI° au XX° siècle*. Casablanca, Wallada, 1995.

From the Certainties of Scholasticism to Renaissance Relativism: Montaigne, Translator of Sebond

Philip Hendrick
University of Ulster

The *Théologie Naturelle* was first published by Montaigne in 1569, at the height of the religious wars in France.[1] Some eleven years later he wrote in the *Apologie de Raimond Sebond* that he had two main reasons for undertaking the task of translating Sebond. First he claimed that his father, a few days before his death, found a copy of the *Theologia Naturalis* under a pile of abandoned papers and ordered his son to translate it into French. Having by chance, as he says, little else to do at the time and not wishing to refuse the best father who ever was, he managed as well as he could, and the translation was published just after his father's death. The letter of dedication, which precedes the translation, was dated from Paris on the day his father died. Several commentators have pointed out the lack of plausibility of this scenario. The lengthy *Theologia Naturalis*, with a total of 226,000 words, some six hundred pages, would have required a considerable amount of time to translate. Montaigne's work is of the highest caliber and was obviously not completed in haste. It must therefore be concluded that the whole story was fabricated in order to make it appear that the translator was a dutiful son carrying out his father's wishes rather than an enthusiastic proponent of the merits of the original work. The second reason cited for publishing the translation is that the work could be viewed as a useful antidote to the propaganda of the Reformers, referred to as "les nouvelletez de Luther." But even this more plausible reason is couched in terms that refer more to the past than the present, and the view is attributed to his father rather than himself. We must assume that Montaigne had other reasons for translating Sebond but that he did not wish to state them publicly.

I have argued elsewhere that the motivation for undertaking the translation was probably more related to his literary ambitions than anything else (Hendrick 1996). And it is undoubtedly true that translation was viewed at the time as one of the best pathways for the aspiring writer to follow, that it provided an opportunity for developing and refining skills that were required for creative writing. This view was solidly based on texts from Cicero, Quintilian and others and has been well documented and studied by scholars (Rener 1989; Kelly 1979). But as Valéry Larbaud has observed, the translation that is carried out purely as a means of acquiring the skills of writing will not carry conviction. There must also be some primary motivation that inspires the translator and that constitutes an objective in itself (Larbaud 1946, 76). This study will examine Montaigne's translation from the point of view of the political and religious context of his time, and seek to establish to what extent the work was motivated by religious and political considerations.

When Sebond completed his treatise in about 1436, printing had not yet begun, the Turks had not yet taken Constantinople and the Hundred Years War was still raging. Joan of Arc had been burned at the stake only a few years previously, and, in general terms, the Middle Ages, though on the wane, were still informing the thought and attitudes of writers. Not that this implies a homogeneous uniformity among thinkers. Battles raged on many a field over theological and philo-sophical matters of substance. Occam and the Nominalists, Duns Scotus and others had radically differing views over many areas. But they all shared a fundamental world view, which was God-centered, in which humans had a well-defined role. The same world view had existed for many centuries, so that even when scholars disagreed, as they often did, they did so in the context of a stable and largely unchanging world view. Sebond's work, which is an attempt to prove the truth of the Christian religion by purely rational means, without reference either to biblical or Church authority, draws on the writings of many medieval thinkers, as Jaume de Puig has shown in his recent study (Puig 1994). Followers of Augustine, such as Saint Anselm, Saint Bernard, Hugo and Richard of Saint Victor, Saint Bonaventure and Duns Scotus, but also a wide variety of other sources, are followed and paraphrased. The suggestion is made by Puig that the *Theologia* is a first attempt to counter the humanist movement of the time represented by Bernard Metge and that it puts forward a new approach to religion based on the central role of man, both as subject and object of the work.

Montaigne's translation belongs to a period when France was similarly riven by war, this time the wars of religion. But it was a totally different world from that inhabited by Sebond. The 130 years between the completion of the original text of Sebond and its translation by Montaigne had seen some of the most far-reaching and radical changes in human history. It is not surprising, therefore, that Montaigne should write not only in a different language, but that the vision of the world that emerges from his text should be substantially different from that expressed by the Latin original. One of Montaigne's first tasks, then, was to modernize the text so that contemporary readers could recognize the vision that was inherent in the translation. Montaigne does this with great skill and efficiency, subtly changing a sentence here, a word there, the word order in another passage, in such a way that the reader would not necessarily be aware that the original text had not expressed the same point of view.

But Montaigne's process of modernization does not stop at merely making his text more readable for his contemporaries. The evolution of mind-sets that had occurred in the 130-year period was so fundamental that any translation of the images and concepts and ideas of the original into sixteenth-century idiom must necessarily have entailed important consequences for the ideas themselves. These consequences can be seen in matters of theology, philosophy and the very concept of writing itself. Sebond's work deals with man's place in the world, his relationships with God, with other humans and with the rest of creation, and the revolution that was about to take place in human thought and experience could not have been foreseen by the writer. Montaigne, writing over a century later, takes these same subjects and relates them to his own understanding of man and the world about him. Since translation is to a large extent determined by its context, and, as Derrida has remarked, "un contexte n'est jamais absolument déterminable, ou plutôt...sa détermination n'est jamais assurée ou saturée" (Derrida 1972, 369), the influence of the different contexts on the respective texts of Sebond and Montaigne can be very great. While the translation follows the original text faithfully, there is a constant series of choices to be made by the translator that depend on his perceptions of the reality in which he lives.

But since the subject of the Sebond treatise is to a considerable extent theological in nature, the translator, being a declared believer, could not alter the substance of the text in any way that might detract from the correctness of the theological ideas expressed. In spite of all the changes in the intervening century, the Catholic Church, through the Council of Trent, had affirmed the truth of all major doctrines under discussion during the Reformation. The Council had completed its final session when Montaigne began to translate, probably around 1567. And although its conclusions were not widely promulgated in France until later, its main doctrinal decisions had been taken at the first session, 1546-47, and it is inconceivable that Montaigne would not have been aware of the essential points that related to Faith, Justification and the Sacraments. These very points were expressed by Sebond with great clarity, and it would seem plausible to argue that Montaigne saw the translation of Sebond's work as a useful expression of the Catholic faith at a time when it was still being challenged and fought over in his own country. However, it was not enough merely to reiterate the dogmas of the past as they had been expressed prior to the Reformation. The events of the past decades could not be overlooked, and in his translation, Montaigne shows clear evidence of an attempt to reconcile the eternal truths of his religion with the contemporary view of the world, with its changing mentalities in so many areas.

How, then, did the translator set about his task? It is instructive to study his remarks about his own translation in various texts. He writes about his project in two main contexts. In the dedication to his father, he writes:

> J'ay taillé et dressé de ma main à Raimond Sebon, ce grand Theologien et Philosophe Espaignol, un accoustrement à la Françoise, et l'ay devestu, autant qu'il a esté en moy, de ce port farrouche, et maintien Barbaresque, que vous lui vîtes premierement (Montaigne 1581, iii).

The topos of the translation as new clothing was very common in the Renaissance (Rener 1989, 24). It can refer to a multitude of elements, ranging from elegance of style to more sophisticated means of expression and of communicating ideas in the modern idiom of the target language. But surely Montaigne here has more in mind than style and idiom. It all depends on what he means by "ce port farrouche, et maintien Barbaresque." Many commentators have castigated the Latin style of Sebond, though it is perfectly acceptable when judged by the standards of the time in which it was written. The requirement for a precise and accurate language capable of expressing in a universally accepted idiom the theological and philosophical ideas relating to religion meant that there was a great deal of repetition, and many terms were used that were not originally part of classical Latin. This very precision was later to be scorned by the humanists, who only saw in it the decline and corruption of a beautiful and elegant language. And, of course, they in their turn tended to be excessively in awe of classical writers, as is evidenced by the controversy surrounding Erasmus' satirical *Ciceronianus*. In the text cited above, I would argue that Montaigne intends more than purely linguistic characteristics when he uses the words "farrouche" and "barbaresque." His translation pays attention to the precise use of certain philosophical and theological terms, and in many of the 330 chapters the focus of his text is quite different from that of the original. To that extent his redressing of Sebond consists, in part, of a fundamental restatement of the themes of the original in a contemporary idiom. The consequences of this are numerous and of immense importance to the overall import of his text.

The letter of dedication to his father makes some further, somewhat enigmatic, statements. After a modest disclaimer that indicates that the critical reader may find traces of Gascon dialect in his translation, he goes on to say:

> car en eschange de ses excellens et tres-religieux discours, de ses hautaines conceptions et comme divines, il se trouvera que vous n'y aurez apporté de vostre part, que des mots et du langage: marchandise si vulgaire et si vile que qui plus en a, n'en vaut, à l'avanture, que moins (Montaigne 1581, iii).

As Mary McKinley has pointed out, there is a great deal of confusion in this text (McKinley 1990, 175). We are uncertain as to who is being referred to in the use of "vous." Is it the translator or his father? I would argue that the confusion is deliberate in order to create a distance between the original and the translation, and to shed at least some of the responsibility for whatever defects may exist in the translation on either Sebond or Montaigne's father, who ordered his son to translate it in the first place. And the derogatory reference to language as opposed to the "hautaines conceptions" rings false coming from the pen of such a literary craftsman. It is much more probably a device for distancing himself from the sometimes debatable and controversial arguments of Sebond. Montaigne can then say that all he did was translate the book and that he is not responsible for its contents.

The other text in which he writes of translation is the *Apologie de Raimond Sebond* itself. Early in this, his longest essay, he says of the work: "Il faict bon traduire les autheurs comme celuy-là, où il n'y a guiere que la matiere à representer; mais ceux qui ont donné beaucoup à la grace et à l'elegance du langage, ils sont dangereux à entreprendre" (Montaigne 1965, 439-440). This comment shows the degree to which the translator is aware of the pitfalls of the exercise. Most translations are of texts that have inherent literary merit, and it is notoriously difficult to reproduce the qualities of the original in the target language. By choosing a writer whose literary style is basic at best, Montaigne is thus avoiding many of the traps that beset other translators. Notice, however, that he does not condemn Sebond's style absolutely. The modification "il n'y a guiere que la matiere" implies that while it is essentially a question of translating ideas rather than images, there are still a number of difficulties facing the translator and he needs to have a strategy for dealing with them. One final sentence gives an insight into Montaigne's approach to the source text: "Je trouvay belles les imaginations de cet autheur, la contexture de son ouvrage bien suyvie, et son dessein plein de pieté" (Montaigne 1965, 440). The ideas contained in the *Theologia* appeal to Montaigne insofar as their overall organization is esthetically pleasing and elegant, whatever the apparent inadequacies of the language in which they are expressed. Through these remarks we can piece together an attitude that values the intellectual qualities of the work and that suggests that a more elegant expression of them in French would produce a worthwhile and lasting tribute to his father.

Two further comments need to be made before examining some passages of the translation in detail. Like many of his contemporaries, Montaigne was completely bilingual in Latin and French. George Steiner makes some insightful comments about the nature of the bilingual translator:

> It may be that the bilingual has his own private semantic correlation—in effect his private implicit system of analytical hypotheses—and that this is somehow in his nerves.... The polyglot mind undercuts the lines of division between languages by reaching inward, to the symbiotic core. In a genuinely multilingual matrix, the motion of spirit performed in the act of alternate choice—or translation—is parabolic rather than horizontal. Translation is inward-directed discourse, a descent, at least partial, down Montaigne's "spiral staircase of the self" (Steiner 1992, 125).

Viewed from this perspective, Montaigne, in translating, could be seen to be wrestling not only with the problems of practical translation, but also with the very concepts and ideas expressed by the original text. The nature of man, of his relationships with God and other creatures were not simply Sebond's ideas that Montaigne dressed up in a different language. They were the very substance of the text that he was creating in French, and his translation was also a means for him to express his own ideas about some of the most fundamental issues confronting humanity.

The second general comment concerning a feature of Montaigne's translation is that it consistently works toward an elimination of repetition that exists in the source text. It is well known that most translators of Montaigne's time were similarly exercised about the avoidance of repetition in their texts (Rener 1989, 157). This concern for linguistic variety and for creating diversity within the

French language itself is a function of the new perception that views the world not as one, but diverse, not as repeating patterns, but as varied and individual entities, each with its own worth. Thus the repeating patterns of Sebond's text are partly an expression of the static structures that were held to exist in the created world. Sebond does not hesitate to repeat the same word several times in the course of a single passage. And there is a series of chapters (71 to 79) that each begin with the same formula. This is not because the Latin writer was totally devoid of linguistic creative ability or did not value variety of expression in itself. It is far more likely to be the case that he was consciously using repetition as a device to express his own view of the world and of creation as a coherent structure, capable of being understood through the medium of the traditional analytical tools of scholastic Latin and with a familiar shape that was encapsulated by the familiar and repetitive features of the language used.

The translation of Sebond's Prologue has long been the subject of controversy among Montaigne scholars, as it is the text that has been most obviously modified in the translation. Sebond expounds the basis for his whole work, namely that man, unaided by any outside authority, can prove the truths of the Christian religion by the light of his reason alone. The whole *Theologia Naturalis* had been put on the index of forbidden books for a brief period in 1559, but it was cleared, except for the Prologue, in 1564. When Montaigne came to translate it, he made several substantial changes. François Rigolot has argued recently that it is possible that Montaigne was translating a different edition to the one we now know, and that, in fact, Montaigne was translating faithfully without making any major changes (Rigolot 1995). It is an attractive thesis and would solve many problems if proved true. But until such time as we can find the missing manuscript, or edition, it is more plausible to go along with the probability that Montaigne was translating with a view to adapting his text to the acceptable orthodoxies of his day and to his own deeply held opinions. The modifications have been well documented, and it is not necessary to repeat the findings of other commentators here (Coppin 1925). But the modifications to the Prologue have been repeated, to a less dramatic extent, in many other passages of the translated text. The overall effect is to lessen the degree to which certainty can be attained by the light of reason alone.

As well as the specific references to certainty, truth and reason, there are other areas in which the certainties of the past become the moving, unfathomable mysteries of the present. The questions of the nature of Faith, of the relationship between God and man, between man and the rest of creation, and on the very nature of man's identity are posed in very different terms by the translator from those used by Sebond and his sources. The question must then be raised whether Montaigne's modifications are deliberate attempts to subvert the meaning and import of the original text. This is vigorously denied by some critics, who, perhaps fearing that any suggestion along these lines could appear as an attack on the integrity of Montaigne's religious beliefs, prefer to reject the possibility of any divergence between the two texts (Céard 1993). The discrepancies and transformations are undeniably there, but for all that there is no evidence of deliberate and overt subversion of Sebond's message. Instead there is constant interpretation, reworking, and sometimes rewriting, but always an exploration of the original text and its meanings in order to discover other, more acceptable and more understandable ways of expressing the same idea to his audience.

Let us look first at some examples of the translation that do not refer to specific points of theology or philosophy but that give us a general insight into the degree to which perspectives had changed during the 130 years that elapsed between the writing of the original and its translation. Chapter 97 of the translation is a good illustration of this general difference of approach between the two writers.

Vide igitur homo	Or sus homme jecte
istum mundum	hardiment ta veuë bien loing
universum et	autour de toi, et contemple si
considera si sit aliquid	de tant de membres, si de
in eo quod tibi non	tant de diverses pieces de
serviat.	ceste grande machine, il y en
	a aucune qui ne te serve.

The Latin text is transformed to a considerable degree by the translator so as to express the difference in perspective. The simple exhortation "Vide" becomes "jecte hardiment ta veuë bien loin autour de toi." In the same way the little word "aliquid" is expanded so as to become "tant de membres...tant de diverses pieces de ceste grande machine." The effect of these changes is twofold. First, the nature of the universe that man lives in is presented in a different fashion by each writer. The universe of the Latin text is fixed, immobile and a complete whole. In the French text, its diversity and its immensity are stressed. Consequently, the reaction of man in the Sebond text is simply to look and see. However, the French text urges him to be more active, to react to the complexity and movement of the world about him. No longer can man's place in the universe be assumed to be unchanging. He must be an active participant in the changing world about him and actively seek to define his role in it. As the universe itself is perceived as more complex and more diverse, so necessarily must man's role require more participation on his part so as to be discovered and acted upon. This initial perception will help shape a number of other attitudes and interpretations of man toward God and the world he lives in.

A second extract from this same chapter brings us a step further in our analysis of the changes in perspective between the two writers.

Hoc etiam circuitus temporum per quattuor tempora anni innovando et renovando omnia quolibet anno continue ministrant.	Ce bransle divers du Soleil, ceste constante varieté des saisons de l'an ne regarde qu'à ta necessité et à te pouvoir renouveller continuellement des fruicts pour ton usage.

The routine cycle of the Latin text is made more diverse in the translation. But the new element here is that the "fruicts pour ton usage" imply that Man's role in this continually moving, changing universe must be more proactive. Instead of the rather neat and tidy arrangement of Sebond's sentence, we have a more frenetic world in which the only way for man to succeed is to take responsibility for his own actions, rather than wait for the goods of the world to be bestowed upon him. Montaigne will take this initial response to the world around him a step further when he goes on to translate the passages that deal with philosophy and theology.

The problems of translating a philosophical work have been brilliantly analyzed in a recent study by Andrew Benjamin (Benjamin 1989). Taking texts by Plato, Seneca, Heidegger, Walter Benjamin and others, he highlights the way in which philosophical terms have evolved throughout the ages, principally because when the works have been translated, no fully equivalent term existed in the target language. Thus the concept of nature changed in a substantial fashion when the Romans translated the original Greek word "physis" as "natura." Likewise the concept of being is different in Seneca to that implied by the equivalent Greek term used by Aristotle. In each language, a certain concept has a number of possible meanings or connotations, and in the translation it is often only possible to reproduce some of these adequately. This leads inevitably to differences of emphasis when a philosophical work is translated, even from a language that is linguistically close to the target language. George Steiner puts it thus:

> Like all verbal discourse, philosophy is tied to its own executive means. To use Hegel's enigmatic, but suggestive phrase, there is an "instinct of logic" in each particular language. But this gives no particular guarantee that statements on universals will translate. No

less that than of poetry, the understanding of philosophy is a hermeneutic trial, a demand and provision of trust on unstable linguistic ground (Steiner 1992, 256).

Steiner's remarks are particularly relevant in the case of Montaigne, whose translation is in a language that had not yet developed its own philosophical terminology. Thus Scipion Dupleix, writing some twenty years after Montaigne's death, was able to lament that the Latin word "existentia" did not have an adequate equivalent in French (Dupleix 1610, 120). Montaigne tends to use the term "essence" to signify both essence and existence, a usage that immediately poses problems for the translation of a scholastic text where both terms have their own particular signification. In this area, Montaigne's solution appears to have been to ignore the problem, assuming quite correctly that his readers would have no interest in the precise meaning of technical, abstract terms used by Sebond. Thus the translator uses the terms "estre" and "essentia" indiscriminately, in such a way that the precision of the original text is severely blurred. This problem was unavoidable for Montaigne, on account of the level of development of the French language, but there are many other topics that he treats with equal independence from the source text. We have already seen how the Prologue was modified in order to diminish the level of certainty claimed for the arguments put forward. But the very means used by Sebond to express that certainty, namely logic, are also altered by the translator.

One of the more striking differences between the original text and the French translation is the suppression of the vast majority of words indicating direct causality. Latin words like "ideo," "igitur," "per con-sequens," "quoniam," "autem" and "sequitur" are invariably not trans-lated. Not that the argument is fundamentally changed, although that does occasionally happen. Montaigne eliminates the repetitive and classroom-like terms of scholastic logic for many reasons, both esthetic and rhetorical. But the overall effect of his changes is to create a text that is less explicit in its claim for absolute certainty and truth. The argument, far from being highlighted and signposted by the series of linguistic indicators, is often embedded in the more fluid and dynamic prose of the translation in such a way that the very questions being discussed produce a more mobile and a more dynamic form of argument in which the level of certainty is often lowered. Or rather the systematic segmentation of the argument into identifiable premises of the syllogism is suppressed, and the new text, with its fluidity and variety, reflects the real world of change and motion. The rigid and static certainties of the scholastic text are transformed into real, personal and living contingencies of the contemporary world as viewed by Montaigne.

One of the most dramatic features of this new approach by the translator lies in his formulation of the description of the relationship between God and man. In the text of Sebond, as in most medieval texts, God is the Supreme Being, who created an ordered universe consisting of four levels of being in which man is at the top of the scale. Each creature knows its place, and each element of creation relates to the others in strictly defined and clearly identifiable ways. But because of the profound changes in world view that had occurred in the intervening century, such an ordered and predictable universe was no longer credible for Montaigne's readers. Man's place in the universe has now to be won and deserved, rather than granted automatically. Some of the passages translated demonstrate this change very clearly, and, in particular, the section of the work that deals with man's honor. Take this passage from chapter 201:

Primum malum est quia homo qui est factura Dei et opus Dei efficitur capitalis et formatus inimicus Dei factoris sui. Et quid pejus homini est quam proprius honor per quem fit inimicus Dei et per quem destruit quantum in eo est Deum factorem suum quia destruit intentionem suam suum honorem et per consequens elongat seipsum a Deo in infinitum quia tantum distat a Deo quantum sua intentione elongatur ab intentione Dei.

Que nous doit-il estre plus evitable qu'une telle poison qui met en nostre fantasie l'appetit forcené de vouloir destruire la grandeur de nostre facteur? de nous vouloir opposer par une frenetique presomption à ses desseins inviolables et à sa volonté toute puissante? et qui nous esloigne par consequent de sa grace, à mesure que nos intentions sont diverses et differentes à la sienne.

This is very typical of the whole section of the translation (chapters 174 to 222) that seems to strike a particularly personal chord with Montaigne. There is certainly a great deal of variation in the translation, compared with other chapters in which the original text is followed more closely. One of the features of these more lyrical passages is that Montaigne frequently adds phrases in a way that develops certain aspects of the text. In this example he skillfully uses certain concepts from the Latin text and elaborates on them in the translation. For example "qui met en nostre fantasie l'appetit forcené de vouloir destruire la grandeur de nostre facteur" is a semantic development of the abstract term "inimicus." A literal translation would simply have written that man becomes an enemy of God and destroys God. But here Montaigne infuses this notion with additional meaning, indicating that we deliberately act out of greed and self-interest to wish to bring the Creator down to our level. There is an implicit moral condemnation of the selfishness and arrogance of each individual who acts on his own and sets himself up as a rival to God. It is the "frenetique presumption" of man that creates these "intentions... diverses" that are so destructive. Sebond's text deals with an abstract moral problem, that certain characteristics in human nature run counter to God's wishes. In the translation, that abstract notion is transformed into a multitude of strong-willed, selfish and self-important individuals who each are devoted to their own honor at the expense of their religious duty. In other words, the moral responsibility for one's actions is not tied up in abstract moral questions, but in the personal decision of each individual. This attitude is one that runs counter to the notion that any group of people who belong to the true religion can justifiably treat their opponents as the enemies of God.

The theme of the fall is treated in a similar fashion by Montaigne. The dramatic and catastrophic effects of man's fall from grace are accentuated throughout the translation. There is more surprise and dismay expressed in the French text than in the original. The following extract from chapter 236 demonstrates the difference in emphasis:

Post praedicta oportet investigare originem corruptionis et mali ipsius naturae hominis et quomodo intravit et videre quis hominem fecit talem et in tali statu sicut modo est.	Il me faut à ceste heure trouver la cause de nostre corruption, il me faut trouver par où elle s'est insinuee en nostre nature, et par quels moyens nous nous sommes si estrangement eslongnez de nos conditions premieres.

The coldly neutral tone of the Latin, which appears to be presenting an intellectual puzzle to be solved rationally, contrasts with the sense of anguish implied by the French text. The responsibility for finding the cause of our fall is taken on by the first person, thus immediately closing the gap between the writer and the problem. It becomes not an abstract issue, but our own personal tragedy. The word "intravit" is transformed into "elle s'est insinuee en nostre nature," a dramatic and mysterious event. But once the horror of the event is recognized, it is again man who must take responsibility for what follows: "nous nous sommes si estrangement eslongnez de nos conditions premieres," replaces the neutral "quis hominem fecit talem." It is this constant involvement of the writer with the events being described that brings the whole scenario to life and that helps to involve the reader in the drama that is evoked. This emphasis on the individual's participation in and responsibility for the situation he finds himself in is a reflection of the changed perceptions of man in his relationship with God and with others. The increased emphasis on the individual nature of moral choices is a consequence of these changing perceptions and leads in the direction of a deepening awareness of the importance of self-knowledge as a basis for moral decisions.

The very thorny and controversial question of Faith and Justification was at the core of the religious quarrels of the first half of the sixteenth century. Luther and Calvin challenged the traditional view of the Church and in so doing laid the foundations for the establishment of the Protestant religion. Sebond's treatment of the subject is quite traditional and orthodox, but in the translation, Montaigne consistently changes the emphasis of certain passages dealing with key concepts relating to the nature of Faith. There is no dramatic transformation of the ideas of Sebond, as the censors would have quickly identified and condemned such a text. Instead there is a consistent shift of emphasis and a gradual reworking of the original text so that the translation expresses a more personal view of Faith. First, in chapter 72 he translates the quality "summe fidelem" attributed to God as "plein...de foy," thereby setting up the word "foy" as not being limited to belief alone, but also expressing the notions of faithfulness and commitment. And then in chapter 78 he translates the simple Latin sentence "Item est necessarium homini credere et affirmare si vult esse bonus" with a much more convoluted version: "Ce bien nous touche à la contemplation de nostre liberal arbitre, veu qu'estant en plaine liberté de choisir le bien ou le mal, et estant obligez par raison à faire le bien...." According to the French text, belief alone is not enough if man wishes to be good. He must freely and willingly choose good or evil and be impelled by reason to choose the good. Just as in the examples we have already analyzed, man's actions count for more than his passive situation in the world, and he himself must be actively involved in all his major decisions. In subsequent texts Montaigne continues to refine the notion of Faith and is always careful to distinguish between the notion of belief and that of commitment and choice. In doing so, he was often treading a difficult path between affirmation of Catholic orthodox doctrine and the expression of his understanding of Faith in a modern idiom, which took account of the debates that had been raging over the preceding fifty years.

The question of Justification by Faith is similarly adapted by Montaigne in such a way that the import of his text is quite different from that of Sebond. Chapter 295 offers a significant example of the difference in emphasis of the two texts:

Et ideo prima reparatio hominis per Baptismum fit gratis et absque poenitentia exteriori sed sufficit fides propria et interior poenitentia seu displicentia et applicatur ei tota mors Christi gratis ad satisfaciendum pro omnibus suis peccatis ac si ipse sustinuisset pro seipso mortem illam.	Nostre premiere reparation au baptesme se faict gratuitement et sans nostre exterieure repentance, la mort de Jesus Christ nous y est liberalement appliquee, et nous purge entierement de toutes nos fautes. Tout ce que nous avons failly jusques lors par ceste propension vicieuse, qui estoit originellement en nous, nous y est effacé et aboly, pourveu que ceux qui sont en aage de vouloir ayent affection de se joindre à Jesus Christ, et soient marris interieurement du passé.

This translation shows an awareness of the debate over the nature of Justification by Faith. If the Latin text tends to imply that Justification is automatic for the person who believes "sufficit fides propria," the French text is much more nuanced, by the addition of the phrase "pourveu que ceux qui sont en aage ayent affection de se joindre à Jesus Christ," which once again implies the active participation of those who wish to be justified. The consistent switch of emphasis from passive to active, from static to dynamic, which is observed throughout the translation, is seen here at work in the very interpretation of theological doctrine.

Montaigne's translation of Sebond is not political in the sense that Montaigne had an overt agenda such as combating Protestantism or maintaining the credibility of the Catholic faith at a time when it was under fire in his own country. There is no clear evidence that he used the text of Sebond in order to further his own particular political or religious point of view. There is, however, abundant evidence of an implicit goal or goals. One can identify, throughout the whole of the translation, many examples where Montaigne is involved in the issues dealt with by the text of Sebond. He is not concerned only with producing faithfully the ideas of Sebond's text. He is in constant dialogue with these ideas and constantly seeks to express them in an idiom and within a perspective that he himself can recognize and that his readers will likewise accept. The Reformation has taken place, and its political consequences in all their horror are unfolding before his eyes. The Catholic faith, as expounded by Sebond, is a reflection of the rigid dogma built on an intellectual system that was no longer universally accepted. In order to make this faith acceptable to his contemporary readers, Montaigne uses all his skill as a writer to dress up his text in an ideological perspective that takes into account the massive changes in world view, and the way in which Catholic theology was expressed, so as to communicate his own, deeply personal, deeply individual version of religious experience to his readers. His rational approach to religion is based more on personal conviction than on an all-embracing system. The emphasis in his translation on diversity and the responsibility of the individual, rather than on homogeneity and the structures of the universe, is an indication of the ideas of tolerance and breadth of vision that would emerge in the course of the *Essais*. At the same time, his own ability to write about the world around him in all its complexity was without doubt developed to a higher level as a result of his translating activity. And while there is no overt political or religious intent to his work, many aspects of the translation can be viewed as an implicit plea for tolerance and broadmindedness in the middle of raging religious wars.

Notes

1. There is only one modern edition of the translation (Montaigne 1932, 1935). The text quoted here is the one published in Montaigne's lifetime (Montaigne 1581), which includes the author's own corrected version of the first edition published in 1569.

Works Cited

Benjamin, Andrew. *Translation and the Nature of Philosophy*. London: Routledge, 1989.

Céard, Jean. "Montaigne traducteur de Raimond Sebond." *Montaigne Studies* 5, 1-2 (1993): 11-26.

Coppin, Joseph. *Montaigne traducteur de Raymond Sebond*. Lille: Morel, 1925.

Derrida, Jacques. *Marges de la philosophie*. Paris: Les Éditions de Minuit, 1972.

Dupleix, Scipion. *La Métaphysique, ou science naturelle*. Paris: Dominique Salis, 1610.

Hendrick, Philip. *Montaigne et Sebond: l'art de la Traduction*. Paris: Champion, 1996.

Kelly, Luke. *The True Interpreter*. Oxford: Blackwell, 1979.

Larbaud, Valéry. *Sous l'invocation de Saint Jérôme*. Paris: Gallimard, 1946.

McKinley, Mary. "Traduire, Écrire, Croire : Sebond, les Anciens et Dieu dans le discours des *Essais*." In *Montaigne, Apologie de Raimond Sebond, De la Theologia à la Théologie*. Ed. Claude Blum. Paris: Champion, 1990.

Montaigne, Michel de. *Oeuvres Complètes*, vols. 9-10. Ed. A. Armaingaud. Paris: Conard, 1932, 1935.

—. *Essais*. Ed. Villey-Saulnier. Paris: PUF, 1965.

—. *La Théologie Naturelle de Raymond Sebond*. Paris: Michel Sonnius, Guillaume Chaudière and Gilles Gourbin, 1569 and 1581.

Porcher, Jean. "La *Théologie Naturelle* et les théories de la Traduction au XVIe siècle." In *Oeuvres complètes de Michel de Montaigne*, vol. 10. Paris: Conard, 1935.

Puig, Jaume de. *Les Sources de la pensée philosophique de Raimond Sebond (Ramon Sibiuda)*. Paris: Champion, 1994.

Rener, Frederick M. *Interpretatio: Language and Translation from Cicero to Tytler*. Amsterdam: Rodopi, 1989.

Rigolot, François. "Editing Montaigne's Translation of Sebond's *Théologie*: Which Latin Text Did the Translator Use?" *Montaigne Studies* 7 (1995): 53-67.

Sebond, Raymond (Raymundus de Sabunde). *Theologia naturalis sive Liber creaturarum, specialiter de homine*. Deventer: Richardus Paffroed, 1485.

Steiner, George. *After Babel: Aspects of Language and Translation*. 2nd ed. Oxford and New York: Oxford University Press, 1992.

Montaigne's *Traduction* of Sebond: A Comparison of the *Prologus* of the *Liber creaturarum* with the *Préface* of the *Théologie Naturelle*

Edward Tilson
Yale University

"It nigrum campis agmen"
—Aeneid IV

There is a great deal at stake in the longstanding critical debate surrounding the *Théologie Naturelle*, Montaigne's 1569 translation of Raimond Sebond's *Liber creaturarum* (*The Book of the Creatures*). On the interpretation of Montaigne's intent in his translation hinge arguments about the meaning of his most important essay, the *Apologie de Raimond Sebond*. Moreover, as this central essay is a microcosm of the *Essais*, these arguments concern the nature of Montaigne's project in them. To define Montaigne's relation to Sebond at the outset of his literary career is, in some degree, to define what it is that he will go on to assay.

Sebond, or Sebeydem, or Sibiude, was a professor of theology, the arts and medicine at the University of Toulouse, where he composed, between 1434 and 1436, a manuscript that was originally entitled *Scientia libri creaturarum seu naturae et de homine*. In this work, the study of the Book of Nature, understood to be a hierarchical reflection of the divine will, leads to a proper understanding of the nature of man as the capital letter of the book, and from there, by analogy, to the understanding of God. Montaigne undertook the translation of this work at the behest of his father. He claims to have tossed it off in a matter of months but can be shown to have been interested in Sebond, if not in translating him, as early as 1562 (Coppin 1925, 37). The great question about the translation is whether Montaigne deliberately undermined the thesis of the Catalan theologian or, as Donald Frame put it in his 1947 article "Did Montaigne Betray Sebond?"

Modern critical attention to the question of Montaigne's translation really begins with the abbé Reulet's 1875 study, *Un inconnu célèbre. Recherches historiques et critiques sur Raymond de Sebonde*. Reulet considered the *Théologie Naturelle* to be primarily an exercise in style, a view which has been largely, though undeservedly, overlooked in later criticism.[1] Reulet was succeeded by Joseph Coppin, whose claim that Montaigne's translation was essentially faithful to the text of Sebond but that Montaigne had gradually grown away from his medieval predecessor defined the debate in terms that persist to this day.[2] This evolutive thesis was flatly contradicted by Armaingaud, who asserted that the skeptical and libertine hand of the 1588 *Essais* had been at work already in the early translation (Montaigne 1932). The controversy continued to simmer, with articles in support of both camps appearing regularly. Recently, it has again been the subject of a great deal of critical attention in which an effort is being made to go beyond the construction of scenarios that feature Montaigne either as the faithful disciple or as the treacherous villain, as a catholic or as a skeptic, and to focus on the detailed comparative analysis of the two texts.[3] A corollary of this new textual emphasis has been the realization of the need to establish which Latin text Montaigne worked from.[4]

The first known edition of the theologian's work came from the presses of Guillaume Balsarin between 1487 and 1492. It was entitled *Liber creaturarum sive de homine*, and the author was given as Raymundo Sebeydem (Rigolot 1995). These are crucial details since they formed the basis for Coppin's judgment that the Balsarin edition could not have been the text used for Montaigne's translation (Coppin 1925, 26) and for his consequent decision to use a text based on the Deventer edition entitled *Theologia naturalis sive liber creaturarum, specialiter de homine* as the basis for his comparative analysis (Coppin 1925, 69), a judgment and a decision that have been accepted by successive critics.[5] As Rigolot has recently shown, however, Coppin's decision to exclude the Balsarin text was a hasty and possibly mistaken one (Rigolot 1995, 63-64).

Sebond's work had been put on the Index in 1558-9, with a renewal of the condemnation for the *Prologus* only in 1564. Since Coppin, it has been widely held that Montaigne knew of the prohibition and deliberately altered the ideas of the Prologue to bring it more into line with Catholic orthodoxy.[6] Thus some critics exculpate Montaigne from the charge of perverting Sebond's text on the grounds that it was a necessary expedient and take the changes as proof of Montaigne's religious nature. Others point out that it is unclear why the *prologus* was condemned.[7] However, since the alterations to the content of the *prologus* chiefly entail the reduction of Sebond's claims for the certainty of his doctrine, and since these critics see the *Liber creaturarum* as an ode to reason, they take the changes as evidence that Montaigne's subsequent attack on reason in the *Apologie* was an assassination of Sebond foreshadowed by a treacherous translation.

More recently, Jean Céard has suggested, in an attempt to exonerate Montaigne based on the differences between the *préface* and the Latin of the available editions of the *Liber creaturarum*, that he may have been working from a manuscript that has not come down to us and that already contained the changes in question (Céard 1993). François Rigolot dismisses the anonymous *réviseur* hypothesis and instead claims that Montaigne may be vindicated by the fact that some of the changes first pointed to by Coppin had already been made in the Balsarin edition (Rigolot 1995, 61-67). In comparing the opening paragraph of the *prologus* with that of the *préface*, we will address the textual question and that of the most obvious emendations concomitantly before proceeding with an analysis of the more subtle stylistic and semantic differences between the Latin and French texts:[8]

Prologus	*Préface de l'auteur*
In laudem et gloriam sanctissime trinitatis et gloriose virginis marie. In nomine domini nostri jesu christi ad utilitatem et salutatem omnium christianorum sequitur scientia libri creaturarum seu liber naturae et scientia de homine quae est propria homini. Inquantum homo et qui est necessaria omni homini et est ei naturalis et conveniens per quam suum conditorem cognoscit et diligit et ad cognoscendum seipsum homo illuminatur et ad omne debitum ad quod homo tenetur: Inquantum *homo* et de iure nature et per consequens cognoscet **omnia** ad que obligatur naturaliter *tam deo quam proximo.* Et non solum illuminabitur ad cognoscendum immo per istam scientiam voluntas movebit et excitabitur cum laeticia et sponte ad volendum faciendum et operandum bonum ex amore. Et non	A la louange et gloire de la tres-haute et tres-glorieuse Trinité, de la vierge Marie, et de toute la cour céleste: au nom de nostre Seigneur Jésus Christ, au proffit et salut de tous les Chrestiens, s'ensuit la doctrine du livre des creatures, ou livre de Nature: doctrine de l'homme, et à luy propre en-tant qu'il est homme, doctrine convenable, naturelle et utile à tout homme, par laquelle il est illuminé à se cognoistre soy-mesme, son createur et **presque** tout ce, à quoy il est tenu comme homme; doctrine, contenant la reigle de Nature, par laquelle aussi, *un chacun* est instruit de ce à quoy il est obligé naturellement *tant envers Dieu qu'envers son prochain*, et non seulement instruict, mais esmeu et poussé à ce faire de soy-mesme par amour et par une allaigre volonté.

solum hoc sed etiam *ista scientia docet omnem hominem cognoscere realiter* **infallibiliter** *sine difficultate et labore omnem veritatem homini necessariam tam de homine quam de deo et omnia quae sunt homini necessaria ad salutem et ad suam perfectionem ut perveniat ad vitam eternam.* Et per istam scientiam homo cognoscit **sine difficultate et infallibiliter** quicquid continetur in sacra scriptura. Et praecipue per hanc scientiam cum magna certitudine intellectus humanus adheret et credit absque dubitatione toti scripture sacre. Quoniam removet hominem ab **omni** errore et dubi-tatione. *Item in ista scientia et per istam potest solui omnis quaestio que debet sciri ab homine tam de deo quam de homine et hoc sine difficultate* et cognoscuntur **infalli-biliter** omnes errores anti-quorum philosophorum paganorum ac infidelium. Et per istam scientiam tota fides catholica **infallibiliter** cognoscitur et pro-batur esse vera. Et omnis secta quae est contra fide *[...]* cognoscitur et probatur esse falsam et erroneam. *Et ideo nunc in fine mundi summe necessaria est ista scientia omni christiano ut quilibet sit munitus certus ac solidatus in fide catholica contra impugnatores fidei ut nullus decipiatur et sit quilibet paratus mori pro ea* (Sebeydem).

En outre *ceste doctrine apprend à tout homme de veoir à l'oeil sans difficulté et sans peine la verité,* **autant qu'il est possible à la raison naturelle** *pour la cognoissance de Dieu et de soy-mesme, et de ce dequoy il a besoing pour son salut, et pour parvenir à la vie eternelle:* luy **donne grand accez** à l'intelligence de ce qui est prescrit et commandé aux sainctes escritures, et fait que l'entendement humain est deslivré de plusieurs doubtes, et *consent hardiment à ce qu'elles con-tiennent concernant la cognoi-ssance de Dieu, ou de soy-mesme.* En ce livre se descouvrent [...]les anciennes erreurs des payens et philosophes infidelles, et par sa doctrine se maintient et se cognoist la foy Catholique: toute secte qui luy est contraire y est descouverte, et convaincuë faulse et men-songere. *Voylà pourquoy en ceste decadence et fin du monde, il est besoing que tous les Chrestiens se roidissent, s'arment et s'a-sseurent en ceste foy là, contre ceux qui la combattent, pour se garder d'estre seduicts et s'il en est besoing, mourir allaigrement pour elle.*

Coppin provides a succinct and much cited analysis of the alterations that most obviously affect the opening paragraph:

Ainsi, dans la traduction de Montaigne, le Livre des Créatures ne nous apprend plus tout ce à quoi nous sommes tenus, mais seulement *presque* tout, *autant qu'il est possible à la raison naturelle*; Il ne nous enseigne plus toute vérité, mais la vérité; il ne le fait plus *infaillible-ment*; il ne nous délivre plus de tout doute, mais de *plusieurs* doutes; il ne fait plus que *donner accès à l'Ecriture...* (Montaigne 1932, 9:v).

Comparison of the Balsarin edition with the text cited by Coppin, and of both with the 1569 translation, shows that *presque* does indeed replace *omne*; that *autant qu'il est possible à la raison naturelle* is an addition; the *infallibiliter* in question is already absent from the Balsarin text, although there is an additional one in the previous sentence that is absent from the Deventer text used by Coppin; *plusieurs* does replace *omni*; *donne grand accez* replaces the phrase *sine difficultate et infallibiliter* which contains yet another *infallibiliter*.[9]

Thus, while there may be some grounds for preferring the Balsarin text, it does not relieve Montaigne of the charge that, for whatever reasons, he weakened Sebond's claims for the certainty of reason through additions and omissions.

This is not, however, sufficient evidence to convict the translator of betraying the sense of his source. These charges of infidelity are immaterial in that they rest on the assumption, originating, perhaps, with the neglect of Sebond's original title and compounded by the uncritical acceptance of Montaigne's report that Turnèbe had pronounced the work to be some "quintessence" drawn from Thomas Aquinas,[10] that Sebond's *Liber creaturarum* is a natural theology in the Thomist sense of a demonstration of the existence of God conducted in terms of logic, or reason, and based on the study of physics, or nature.[11] In fact, Sebond's theology shares much of its vision with that of Augustine, for whom natural theology is a contemplative science, the study of the fundament of being, and is defined in opposition to rational philosophy.[12] The deprecatory tone with which Montaigne, behind Turnèbe, refers to the *Liber creaturarum* bespeaks an ambivalent reaction to the hybrid nature of a doctrine in which developments inspired by the introspective tradition of Augustine and of Anselm are juxtaposed with rationalistic, exterior arguments that focus on the hierarchy of beings.[13]

In the fight against the Averroïst doctrine of separate truths, Sebond pledges allegiance to both camps: The reader is to be *non seulement instruict, mais esmeu*; reason and faith are to be reunited through the combination of psychological insight with physical observation. The alterations we have already considered, though they tend to slant the translation toward one side of Sebond's equation, should not be taken as evidence of a travesty. Obviously, Montaigne has a penchant for highlighting pessimistic and ultimately skeptical traits at the expense of Sebond's claims for reason, but these traits are inherent in the makeup of the *Liber creaturarum* itself.

Our next task is to examine the stylistic changes Montaigne made to the text. Again, there are two critical camps: On the one hand, there are those who say that in divesting Sebond of his barbarous garb to fit him with an *accoutrement à la françoise*, Montaigne merely shows a concern for his reader's sensibility, that he remains faithful to the theologian's meaning.[14] On the other hand, there are critics who claim that even where there is an appearance of equivalence in the two texts, Montaigne's style insidiously but intentionally saps Sebond's text of its meaning (Hendrick 1990), or that while the translation might not be a deliberate betrayal, Montaigne's style contains subtle changes in perspective and tone that quite transform the message conveyed.[15]

There are three capital *chefs d'accusation* here: that Montaigne particularizes the universal nature of Sebond's *homo*; that he introduces concrete images in speaking of abstract concepts, and vice versa; and that his text develops a dynamism that contrasts with the static aspect of Sebond's. A glance at our section of the *préface* is sufficient to convict the text on the first charge: *Un chacun* does indeed particularize Sebond's *homo*.[16] If we take the concluding sentence of the paragraph as a case in point to examine the second and third charges, we can see that the passage contains a number of concrete images that serve to enliven the idea it conveys. To begin, a gratuitous *decadence* is introduced. The series of verbs, *se roidissent, s'arment, et s'asseurent*, puts the phrase in the active voice and greatly develops the *soldatesque* metaphor contained in germ in the *sit munitus certus ac solidatus* of the *prologus*. Perhaps most telling of all is the substitution of *estre seduicts* for *decipiatur*: The doubling of the martial metaphor with the erotic overtone of the *viator* metaphor is, as Sainte-Beuve would say, *du Montaigne pur*.

But why is it that critics equate what they acknowledge to be stylistic improvements with a *traduction* in the sense of a betrayal, rather than that of a translation? This persistent rhetoric of accusation is linked to what is perhaps the central conflict in Montaigne studies, the debate over the essayist's conception of the self and of the self's relation to God. From Pascal's condemnation of Montaigne's foolish project of self-portraiture through the influential peroration of Sainte-Beuve's Jansenist persona in *Port-Royal* runs a critical current that accuses Montaigne of jettisoning Faith in favor of a shallow narcissism, or *philautie*.[17] More recent studies tend to discern in the translation the traces of a modern *sujet de l'énonciation* incompatible with the medieval doctrines developed in the summa. Behind the detail of the stylistic liberties Montaigne takes with the Catalan theologian's text, this current of criticism sees a sort of surrender, if not an attack: The translator is accused of a reductionism that eliminates the relation of dependence between the source text and his own version (between Creator and Creation), and of usurping for himself the status of autonomous subject. Montaigne's disregard of Sebond's Latin functions for these critics as an analog of the freedom Montaigne will later arrogate himself in writing a secular confession that they see as self-indulgent posturing.

These views miss the particularity of Sebond's work, just as they overlook the complexity both of Montaigne's practice of translation and of the relation between being and writing in his subsequent work. In order to understand the reasons for Montaigne's alterations to Sebond's text, it is necessary to grasp the links between the style of the two versions and their tenor.

Neither Sebond's rationalism nor his Augustinianism are particularly novel, nor can these features explain by themselves why Montaigne should have gone through with the translation of a thousand-page tome. What distinguishes the *Liber creaturarum seu liber naturae et scientia de homine* from earlier theological summae is its anthropocentrism. As Jaume de Puig has pointed out, the *Liber creaturarum* is neither about natural philosophy, nor is it, in the accepted sense of the word, a theology (Puig 1994, 71). The subject is man, and the method, the appeal to human experience, corresponds with the subject:

> Et ideo ipsemet homo et sua natura propria debet esse medium, argumentum, testimonium ad probandum omnia de homine, scilicet, quae pertinent a salutatem hominis, vel damnationem, vel felicitatem, vel ad bonum vel ad malum eis (Sebeydem, fol.i).

This focus on man is striking enough that some critics have even been led to present Sebond as a harbinger of humanism (Colomer 1990).

Nevertheless, if the subject of the *Liber creaturarum* is man, he is still *homo*, not *vir*, and the author, whose work the abstract phrases of Sebond translate, is God. While Sebond relies on experience, and more particularly on introspection, to demonstrate his claims *tam de homine quam de deo*, he is still working within an analogical parenthesis that assumes man is made in the divine image. His psychological study leads to the affirmation that the fundament of being is that unity of will and judgment that he calls the *liberal arbitre*, but this is a faculty characterized by its universality both in the sense that it is not subject to the constraints of time or space and in the sense that it is what defines all men as such. In terms of being, the individual content of this faculty is of no importance: Men are both self-identical and essentially identical the one to the other in their formal dependence on the Creator. Knowledge of man is inconceivable independently of the knowledge of God yet the two are neither interchangeable nor are they distinct; rather, they are analogically guaranteed, and it is this connection that allows Sebond to develop his anthropological theses in the context of an apologetic work.

The connection between God and man, reason and faith, and between the logical and psychological components of Sebond's doctrine is expressed syntactically in the opening paragraph of the *Liber creaturarum* by the repetition of the separable conjunction *tamquam*. One can see in the *préface de l'auteur*, however, that Montaigne severs the link between the two aspects of Sebond's philosophy. Of the three uses of *tamquam*, only the first, *tam Deo quam proximo*, in which both elements concern an objective knowledge, is rendered with the equivalent French structure *tant envers Dieu qu'envers son prochain*. Where the conjunction is used to link knowledge of God with knowledge of the self, Montaigne suppresses the correlative, translating *cognoissance de Dieu et de soy-mesme* in the first instance, and then disjoins the terms: The promise that all questions as much about God as about man will be resolved is translated as a claim that the reader will go along with what is said regarding knowledge either of God or of the self, *cognoissance de Dieu, ou de soy-mesme.*[18]

If we allow ourselves a proleptic glance at the *Essais*, it seems likely that what Montaigne experienced in the interrogation of his own judgment (and in the process of translating) was not his dependence on a pre-existing and immutable form but rather the mobility of his self (and of his text) and the particularity that set him apart from other men, most notably from the all-too-human author of the *Liber creaturarum*. Given the undermining of the analogical parenthesis that guarantees Sebond's anthropocentric reflections, it is tempting to see in the *Théologie Naturelle*'s insistence on Augustinian traits over scholastic rationalism and its replacement of the *Liber creaturarum*'s static universalism with a concrete, individual and mobile style, an aggressive humanism that inverts the relation between author and translator, between man and God.

But this would be an exaggeration of the opposition between the two texts. As we have seen, Montaigne's alterations are anchored in the content of his source, and it is a simplification to portray the *Théologie Naturelle* as the inauthentic *traduction* of an authentic original. The differences between the French and Latin texts can more usefully be understood as the product of two different ideas of translation.

A theologian, Sebond presents his work as the "translation" of the divine Verb, effacing his own role behind the topos of the *liber mundi*. His constant repetition of adverbs of necessity, his endless logical concatenations and analogical comparisons are a function of this conception and serve to cement the link between the content of the summa and the form of its expression. For Sebond, the *Liber creaturarum* is a "translation" that provides its reader with direct access to the truths of religion.

Montaigne, on the other hand, begins by separating the content of the *Liber creaturarum* from the form of the *Théologie*.[19] He presents the product of his own labors as a pale imitation of the Catalan's inspired text. Indeed, it would hardly behoove him to present his French version as an analogical version of the Verb: A translation in the second degree, by its very existence, the French is placed at a further remove from the truths it is meant to communicate. Montaigne's more pessimistic attitude with regard to the powers of reason (and his more developed use of language) reflects a more modest conception of the possibilities of translation, but this is not to say that he attacks these truths, or that they are absent from the *Théologie*, any more than the relation to an Origin will be evacuated by the author of the *Essais*. Though no longer a simple analogical equivalency, the relation between the two terms of Sebond's equation, God and man, remains the central concern of a translator and a writer whose texts distance the very truths they are meant to communicate.

Notes

1. With the exception of Hugo Friedrich's treatment of the matter in his magisterial *Montaigne*. Cf. 113 et infra.
2. "On ne saurait admettre le jugement de Reulet: 'En sa double qualité d'artiste et de sceptique, Montaigne est moins curieux du vrai que du beau.' [...] C'est une vraie traduction, mais c'est la traduction élégante d'un original à peine lisible." (Coppin 1925, 80).
3. See the studies in the volume edited by Blum (1990), those in Rigolot (1993) and Hendrick (1996).
4. For a treatment of this complicated question, see Rigolot (1995) and Guy (1990).
5. Cf. Guy (1990, 18).
6. Cf. Coppin (1925, 67): "Il devait connaître les condamnations de l'Index, puisque sur un autre livre, le catéchisme de Bernardino Ochino, il a porté de sa main la mention: *liber prohibitus*." Also, Rigolot (art. cit., 62). Montaigne notes in his *Journal de Voyage*, when his books are returned by the Roman censors, "[...]et Sebon, ils me dirent que la préface estoit condamnée" (1992, 120), which seems to suggest, contrary to Coppin's supposition, that he was previously unaware of the condemnation.
7. The condemnation may have been because of his neglect of patristic and traditional authority. See Coppin (1925, 66).
8. Words and phrases relating to the textual argument are in bold. The additional *infallibiliter* cited in connection with Rigolot's philological demonstration are in bold italics. Elements treated in the discussion of style are italicized.
9. Coppin (1925, 70). *Vide* the Deventer text as given by Coppin (1925, 67): "Ad laudem et gloriam altissimae et gloriossimae Trinitatis, virginis Mariae et totius Curiae caelestis, in nomine Domini Nostri Jesu Christi.: ad utilitatem et salutem omnium Christianorum, sequitur scientia Libri Creaturarum, sive Libri Naturae: et scientia de homine quae est propria homini in quantum homo est; quae est *necessaria* omni homini, et ei naturalis, et conveniens, per quam ipse illuminatur ad cognoscendum se

ipsum et suum Conditorem et omne debitum ad quod homo tenetur, in quantum est homo; et de regula naturae per quam etiam cognoscit quilibet [omnia] ad quae obligatur naturaliter, tam Deo quam proximo. Et non solum illuminabitur ad cognoscendum, immo per istam scientiam voluntas movebitur et excitabitur sponte, et cum laetitia, ad volendum et faciendum ex amore. Et non solum haec; sed ista scientia docet omnem hominem cognoscere realiter sine difficultate et labore [omnem] veritatem [homini necessariam], tam de homine quam de Deo, et omnia quae sunt necessaria homini ad salutatem et [suam perfectionem], et ut perveniat ad vitam aeternam. Et per istam scientiam homo *cognoscit, sine difficultate et realiter, quicquid*, [in Sacra Scriptura continetur, et quicquid] in Sacra Scriptura dicitur et praecipitur, [per istam scientiam cognoscitur infallibiliter, cum magna certitudine] ita ut intellectus humanus, [cum omni securitate et certitudine], *omni* dubitatione postposita, [toti] sacrae scriptura assentiat, [et certificatur, ut non possit dubitare quaestionem in ista scientia. Et per istam scientiam potest solvi omnis quaestio quae debet sciri] tam de Deo quam de seipso, [et hoc sine difficultate]. Et cognoscuntur in hoc Libro [omnes] errores antiquorum philosophorum et paganorum ac infidelium; et per istam scientiam [tota] fides catholica [infallibiliter] cognoscitur et probatur esse vera. Et omnis secta quae est contra fidem catholicam cognoscitur et probatur [infallibiliter] esse falsam et erronea...." We have retained Coppin's system of notation, according to which italics are used to indicate words that have been changed, and suppressions are signalled by square brackets.

10. "[...] je m'enquis autrefois à Adrien Tournebu, qui sçavoit toutes choses, que ce pouvoit estre de ce livre; il me respondit qu'il pensoit que ce fut quelque quintessence tirée de S. Thomas d'Aquin" *Apologie de Raimond Sebond* (Montaigne 1962, 417).

11. Cf. Thomas Aquinas, 1969, vol. 1, *The Existence of God*, 1A. 1, 1: "The diversification of the sciences is brought about by the diversity of aspects under which things can be known[....] Accordingly there is nothing to stop the same things from being treated by the philosophical sciences when they can be looked at in the light of natural reason and by another science when they are looked at in the light of divine revelation. Consequently the theology of holy teaching differs in kind from that theology which is ranked as a part of philosophy" [natural theology].

12. Following Plato, Augustine divides philosophy into three parts: "first, moral philosophy which pertains to action; second, natural philosophy whose purpose is contemplation; third, rational philosophy which distinguishes between truth and error. These are all subsumed in theology since[...]in God is to be found the cause of all being, the reason of all thinking, the rule of all living. The first of these truths belongs to natural, the second to rational, and the third to moral philosophy." (Augustine 1958, 149-150).

13. The first fifty chapters, which serve to establish the existence of God and thus create the framework for the ensuing analogical arguments, are largely derived from Anselm's ontological argument; chapters 130 to 175, which anchor Sebond's theology in human psychology, are inspired by the *City of God*. In general, the first half of the summa, the exposition of the Book of the Creatures, stands in an analogical relation to the second half, which explains the Sacrements in light of the Bible. Cf. Puig (1994).

14. Cf. Coppin (1925, 80); Céard (1993, 21).

15. Cf. Habert (1993); Hendrick (1993); Worth-Stylianou (1993). Hendrick's extensive and sedulous treatment of Montaigne's translation attributes some of the differences between the two texts to the very nature of translation and concludes that the translation is at once faithful to and divergent from the Latin (1996, 229).

16. Interestingly, this *homo* is replaced by *quilibet* in the Deventer edition. Cf. Coppin (1925, 68).

17. Commenting on the *Apologie*, Sainte-Beuve's persona suggests that Montaigne may have begun his defense of Sebond in earnest but that he got carried away by the process of writing and ended up modeling his individuality in the mirror of his style. Sainte-Beuve (1953, 1:475 et inf).

18. The alternative reading, which takes the conjunction *ou* to mean that knowledge of God is conflated by Montaigne with knowledge of the self, cannot be sustained. Montaigne's compression of this section has the effect of attributing this knowledge to an understanding of Scripture rather than to the *Liber creaturarum* itself, a distinction of little importance for Sebond since the Bible is another analogical expression of the same truth.

19. In his dedication, Montaigne attributes the translation to his father, as patron of the work: "[...]en eschange de ses excellens et tres-religieux discours, de ses hautaines conceptions, et comme divines, il se trouvera que vous n'y aurez apporté de vostre part, que des mots et du langage: marchandise si vuolgaire et si vile, que qui plus en a, n'en vaut, à l'aventure, que moins." (Montaigne 1932, 9:iv).

Works Cited

Augustine. *City of God*. New York: Image Books, 1958.

Blum, Claude. *Montaigne – Apologie de Raimond Sebond: De la Theologia à la Théologie*. Paris: Champion, 1990.

Céard, Jean. "Montaigne, traducteur de Sebond: Positions et propositions." In Rigolot 1993. Pp. 11-26.

Colomer, E. "Raimond Sebond, un humaniste avant la lettre." In Blum 1990. Pp. 49-67.

Coppin, Joseph. *Montaigne, traducteur de Raymond Sebond*. Lille: H. Morel, 1925.

Frame, Donald. "Did Montaigne Betray Sebond?" *Romanic Review* 38 (1947): 297-329.

Friedrich, Hugo. *Montaigne*. Trans. Robert Rovini. Paris: Gallimard, 1968.

Guy, Alain. "La *Theologia Naturalis* en son temps." In Blum 1990. Pp. 13-47.

Habert, Mireille. "L'Inscription du sujet dans la traduction par Montaigne de la *Theologia Naturalis*." In Rigolot 1993. Pp. 27-47.

Hendrick, Philip. *Montaigne et Sebond: l'art de la traduction*. Paris: Champion, 1996.

—. "Montaigne's Translation of Sebond: Towards a Reassessment." In Rigolot 1993. Pp. 49-64.

—. "Traduttore traditore: Montaigne et Sebond." In Blum 1990. Pp. 139-65.

Montaigne, Michel de. *Oeuvres complètes*, vols. 9 and 10. Ed. A. Armaingaud. Paris: Louis Conard, 1932.

—. *Oeuvres complètes*. Ed. Maurice Rat and Albert Thibaudet. Paris: Pléïade, 1962.

—. *Journal de Voyage*. Ed. François Rigolot. Paris: Presses universitaires de France, 1992.

Puig, Jaume de. *Les Sources de la pensée philosophique de Raimond Sebond (Ramon Sibiuda)*. Paris: Champion, 1994.

Reulet, l'abbé. *Un inconnu célèbre. Recherches historiques et critiques sur Raymond de Sebonde*. Paris: E, Palmé, 1875.

Rigolot, François. "Editing Montaigne's Translation of Sebond's *Theologia*: Which Latin Text Did the Translator Use?" *Montaigne Studies* 7 (1995): 53-67.

Rigolot, François, ed. *Montaigne Studies* 5 (1993): 1-2.

Sainte-Beuve. *Port-Royal*, vol. 1. Paris: Pléïade, 1953.

Sebeydem, Raymundo de. *Liber creaturarum sive de homine*. Lyon: Balsarin, n.d.

Thomas Aquinas. *Summa Theologiae*, vol. 1: *The Existence of God*. New York: Image

Books, 1969.
Worth-Stylianou, Valerie. "'S'il vous palist de conter avec luy': les trois personnes dans la traduction de la *Théologie Naturelle*." In Rigolot 1993. Pp. 65-75.

"Entreat her hear me but a word": Translation and Foreignness in *Titus Andronicus*

Adam McKeown
Clarkson University

And even the Latins, who profess not to be so licentious as the Greeks, show us many times examples but of strange cruelty, in torturing and dismembering of words in the midst, or disjoining such as naturally should be married and march together, by setting them as far asunder as they possibly can.

—Samuel Daniel

"Entreat her hear me"

Toward the close of act 2 of *Titus Andronicus*, Tamora and Lavinia stand face to face in a conversation neither understands very well. The two women—one a Goth, the other a Roman; one treacherous, the other faithful; one a captive become queen, the other a princess become captive; each in her turn a victim and accomplice in an internecine and self-replicating plot of murder and revenge—find they cannot communicate. The scene is rich with the drama's most important rhetorical and epistemological concerns, but however it obviously works on that level, I want to propose that the scene also stages a problem with language in its most basic sense: Two people from completely different cultural backgrounds are running up against a language barrier.

Lav.	Sweet Lords, entreat her hear me but a word…
	O, be to me, though thy hard heart say no,
	Nothing so kind, but something pitiful.
Tam.	I know not what it means; away with her!
Lav.	O, let me teach thee for my father's sake,
	That gave thee life when well he might have slain thee.

	Be not obdurate, open thy deaf ears.
Tam.	Hadst thou in person ne'er offended me,
	Even for his sake I am pitiless....
Lav.	O Tamora, be called a gentle queen,
	And with thine own hands kill me in this place.
	For 'tis not life that I have begged so long...
Tam.	What begg'st thou then, fond woman? Let me go!
Lav.	'Tis present death I beg; and one thing more...
	tumble me into some loathsome pit...
	Do this, and be a charitable murderer (2.2. 137-178).[1]

Perhaps they need a translator. Someone who could have spared Lavinia the trouble of having to "teach" Tamora what she means by "pity" or explain to Tamora how in the Roman lexicon "pity" means something other than "kind" or how a "gentle queen" is one who might kill with her own hands. A translator might have helped Lavinia avoid such clumsy constructions as "charitable murderer" and prevented the two from arriving at the end of their impassioned dialogue having to re-explain what they were discussing in the first place. "Confusion fall—" is Lavinia's final utterance before her tongue is severed shortly after this scene, the pathetic irony of the language barrier having run its ghastly course.

Among Shakespeare's Roman plays, only *Titus* is so concerned with the confrontation of cultures, with the foreignness of the Latin language, and with the constant and irreconcilable presence of foreignness in general—the inevitable suspicions, misunderstandings, intermarriages, confused allegiances, and dissolutions of tradition that always seem to accompany it. *Titus* very pointedly enacts the most infamous confrontation of cultures Elizabethan society knew, a confrontation already loaded with the dark promise of the end of empire, of a world era and of an order of things broadly conceived. But to discuss these issues as matters of translation is to engage the reader in one of those games of academic three-card monte in which a term is introduced and shuffled about without much explanation of how it differs from less gimmicky ways of describing the same phenomenon. *Titus* is not, after all, a translation. Moreover, the centuries of critical outcry against this troubling play make it too ready a cause for well-intentioned scholars seeking the simple key that will manumit a great drama from the prison of bloody sensationalism in which this one is bound.[2] I propose instead to examine translation in terms of the play. Translation, both of language and of culture, emerges in *Titus* with all the creative energy and cultural pride, as well as all the misgivings and feelings of cultural vulnerability, appropriate to an England that was aggressively but anxiously fashioning a global presence and emulating the continental Renaissance.

This argument begins and ends with a culture's attitude toward the foreign. Ostensibly, translation is an expression of value for another culture's intellectual products, but it is a far more complicated matter than that. Friedrich Schleiermacher explains that translation appeals to a connoisseur audience for whom "the foreign is familiar, but yet always remains foreign"; it is something for which one develops a "taste" but a taste in which one is never invested to the point of expertise:

> We see that, just as the inclination to translate can only come into being when a certain ability to use foreign languages is widespread among the educated public, so the art will increase in the same manner...but this can occur only when a taste for and knowledge of foreign intellectual works spread and increase among those in a nation who have exercised and educated their ear without, however, making the knowledge of language their actual business (Schleiermacher 1992, 44).

It follows that the educated palette savors translation precisely because it promises to be foreign. It also follows that for translation to have this appeal, its foreignness must announce itself in some appreciable way. We might, for example, praise a translation that offers an English text with elusive turns of phrase or syntactical peculiarities that we associate, perhaps even arbitrarily, with the conventions of the source language. For the connoisseur, such a translation is intriguing and charming because it is extraordinary and recognizably foreign.

Fittingly, the play in which "Shakespeare translated for the first time Imperial Rome to Elizabethan London" is obsessed with displaying its own foreignness (Suzuki 1990, 104). Generic expectations of Elizabethan drama account for part of this display. Only one of Shakespeare's plays is set in his own time and place, and much of Elizabethan drama at large is set in places remote in time or distance. These facts only emphasize to what extent Elizabethan society had cultivated a market for the foreign; people went to the theaters in part to witness the spectacle of foreignness, just as they gobbled up accounts of exploration and exotic marvels. But even in a genre in which foreignness is expected, *Titus* stands out, mostly in how it uses the Latin language. Latin is organic to much early modern drama, of course, whether it is cast magnificently (as in *Tambourlaine*) or risibly (as in *Epicoene*). *Titus*, however, presents Latin metatheatrically. It is fastened to arrows, it is pointed out from printed pages, and when it is spoken it is grafted crudely to English.

The first instance of grafted Latin comes in act 1 when Lucius embarks on a human sacrifice, uttering some carefully scripted Latin poetry as he goes: *"Ad manes fratrum* sacrifice his flesh" (1.1.101). It may be too much to expect audiences who would have only heard these words to note the stylistic confrontation contained in them. The Latin poetry is characteristically vocalic and relies on its rich *a's*, upon which the English intrudes with the alliteration of *s's* and *f's*. As awkward as it sounds, the juxtaposition succeeds in drawing the audience's attention to the foreign words and their incompatibility with the English ones. For those who knew Latin, this incompatibility would have been even more palpable. "Sacrifice his flesh to the spirits of our dead brothers," the line might read in English. For those who did not know Latin, Lucius' subsequent report of off-stage sacrifice would have had a comparable effect, identifying the grizzly enterprise as a "Roman" custom and describing it in words that seem grossly unsuited to the actions. Note how the alliteration intensifies:

> See, lord and father, how we have performed
> Our Roman rites. Alarbus' limbs are lopped
> And entrails feed the sacrificing fire,
> Whose smoke like incense doth perfume the sky (1.1.145-148)

On stage, we might imagine Lucius returning with his jacket or robes soaked red—a dagger yet dangling from his hand—while the mother and brothers of the victim listen to the gleeful, panting account of the sacrifice in all its nauseating detail. The audience is made party to a disemboweling that scarcely seems in concert with the solemn Latin words that initiate it or the sensuous English that describes it.

In an effort to provide some explanation for this sort of impossible juxtaposition of action and word that litters the play, Albert H. Tricomi (1974, 13) suggests that *Titus* "continually investigates the chasm between the spoken word and...actual fact." Jane Hiles (1995, 233-34) has similarly observed that *Titus* turns on a series of "rhetorical failures" that occur when "characters' contexts shift without their realizing it, so that they fail to answer the occasion with the appropriate mode of discourse [or] adopt an inappropriate style of diction." But perhaps these rhetorical failings perform some other function. To an audience largely familiar with classical poetry, these halts might have served to help recall to mind the sensuous depictions of violence characteristic of poets like Ovid. In other words, the "rhetorical failures" on which the drama turns call attention to the presence of foreign sensibility. The Latin and purple English suspend the drama and transform it into a bloody diorama with an Ovidian voice-over. The play has stopped here for a moment, and we are asked instead to look at and listen to a poem.

For those in the audience who learned their Latin through imitation and verse writing, these awkward breaks would have held special interest. Though Locke and Milton, among others, renounced the practice of teaching Latin through these means, the practice continued well into the twentieth century, and in Tudor England it was a pedagogical mainstay. Schoolmasters would instruct scholars to compose Latin verse according to the style and diction of a designated classical writer (White 1932). For scholars who lacked a poet's ear, this must have been an especially daunting exercise, but even they would have been inculcated to associate each classical poet with certain regularities of diction, syntax, and especially theme that could be applied methodically to new verse. Anyone with a grammar-school education in Elizabethan England was likely to have had a sensitivity to the stylistic and thematic concerns of classical poetry, which would have made the conspicuous appearance of such poetry on stage particularly resonant.

However, such a familiarity with Latin coincided with an equally palpable sense of distance from it. Even for those who knew and were extremely comfortable with Latin, it remained another language, one reserved for specific functions, or, as Roger Ascham described it, one "kept not in common talk but in private books." For the lower classes and for many women of all social strata, the foreignness of Latin would have been exacerbated by the social fact that the language was employed and dispensed by institutions from which they were often systematically excluded. In any case, the distance from Latin was very different than it might be for modern audiences. For Elizabethans, it was a distance that had to be measured (or a "de-distanced" distance, in Heidegger's terms[3]); for us it is simply not a feature of our cognitive landscape. For an Elizabethan audience, however, Latin and classical poetry were very much a presence, but an ever alien one.

The haunting description of the maimed Lavinia in act 2 draws on this sense of familiarity and distance. The familiarity is provided by a Latinate poem, which would have struck the chords of many schoolhouse memories; the alienation is provided by a juxtaposition of sweet words and bloody images that just cannot work on stage. Over a tongueless, handless girl, motionless and bleeding, Marcus cants,

> Speak, gentle niece, what stern ungentle hand
> Hath lopped and hewed and made thy body bare
> Of her two branches, those sweet ornaments
> Whose circling shadows kings have sought to sleep in
> ...

Why dost not speak to me?
Alas, a crimson river of warm blood,
Like a bubbling fountain stirred with wind,
Doth rise and fall between thy rosed lips,
Coming and going with thy honey breath (2.4.16-25).

For the audience willing to have the dramatic integrity jeopardized by this ghastly annunciation of foreignness, these words could be as seductive as this obviously influential passage from Ovid that tells of the rape of Philomela:

> Then, openly confessing his horrid purpose, he violated her, just as a weak girl and all alone, vainly calling, often on her father, often on her sister, but most of all on the great gods. She trembled like a frightened lamb, torn and cast aside by a grey wolf, cannot yet believe that it is safe; and like a dove which, with its own blood all smeared over its plumage, still palpitates with fright, still fears those greedy claws which that have pierced it (6:523-530).

For those audience members who might have missed the allusion informing the beautifully awkward description of Lavinia here, in act 4 Shakespeare has her gesture with her bloody stumps toward what is presumably this very passage from the *Metamorphoses*.

"Hear me but a word"

Not enough critical work has explored the tension surrounding the strange cameo of "Ovid's *Metamorphosis*" (4.1.42) in act 4 of *Titus*. Jonathan Bate's recent argument typifies the evenhanded critical treatment to which I want to propose an alternative:

> *Titus Andronicus* is a prime exhibit in the case for Shakespeare's artfulness: to put it simply, the play is an archetypal Renaissance humanist text in that it is patterned on the classics.... The "quoting" of the leaves of Ovid's book by Lavinia tells the audience this is the case. Her reading signals that the play is both a revisionary reading of the Ovidian text and an examination of the efficacy of humanist education (Bate 1993, 104).

Bate's assessment identifies but does not enlarge upon the central issues at stake. Of course, Lavinia, having had her tongue removed, is not "quoting" Ovid's poem but enacting it, and to adopt Bate's own language, Marcus "tells the audience this is the case" in no uncertain terms: "See brother, see: note how she quotes the leaves" (4.1.50).

Reading "how" as *in what way* as opposed to *that*, Marcus' statement is not a simple declaration, but an invitation for the audience to "see" in what way the drama commandeers Ovid and translates his words into dramatic action. While this move is, as Bate says, "revisionary" it is also confrontational. To see how Lavinia quotes is thus to see how she does not quote, to see how she and Ovid are both merely players in somebody else's drama.

A century after *Titus*, John Dryden (1987, 112) calls Shakespeare "the Homer, or father of dramatic poets." Though we tend to dismiss Dryden's statement as inflated compliment, he saw that something akin to a struggle for cultural identity was at issue in Shakespeare's plays. But rather than the battle Dryden envisioned, one fought with bright banners and Greek words streaming across the fields of time, the struggle I propose is more along the lines of what Michel Foucault describes in his analysis of Nietzsche's term *Entstehung* or "emergence." Says Foucault (1984, 92-93): "[*Entstehung*] is not the unavoidable conclusion of a long preparation, but a scene where forces are risked in the chance of confrontations, where they emerge triumphant, where they can also be confiscated." If we imagine *Titus* as a place of emergence—a particularly appropriate concept for this early drama that was both Shakespeare's first attempt at tragedy and first Roman play—we should expect to find forces risked in the chance of emerging victorious, and we should equally expect the unremitting anxiety arising from the possibility that those forces may be confiscated. The confrontation with Ovid thus bears both the ecstasy of possible victory and the terror of possible loss. To see how Lavinia does not quote Ovid is not only to see an Ovid subordinated to an English tragedy, but also to see a girl with her tongue cut out by savage foreigners.

The prevailing approach to translation during the Elizabethan period underscores these two possibilities. Unlike the method of translation practiced almost universally today, which is based on the eighteenth-century model of "movement toward the original" (Friedrich 1992, 14-15), many late Renaissance translators operated under the assumption that thought content is independent of language and can—or even should—be wrested from foreign words and impressed into the service of the translator's language. Hugo Friedrich (13) explains:

> This approach is based on the premise that the purpose of translation is to go beyond the appropriation of content to a releasing of those linguistic and aesthetic energies that heretofore had existed only as pure possibility in one's own language and had never been materialized before. The beginning of this premise can be traced

back to Quintilian and Pliny; it was to become the dominant characteristic of European translation theories of the Renaissance. Its most striking hallmark is its effort to "enrich" (*enrichir, arricchire, aumentar*). Again, one does not move toward the original in this case. The original is brought over in order to reveal the latent stylistic possibilities in one's own language that are different from the original.

Although Andrew Gurr (1996) has recently entered a long-overdue word of caution against the indiscriminate application of the colonizer/colony paradigm when envisioning Renaissance foreign relations, the idea of seeking out the products of other cultures in order to enrich the host culture has a certain imperial resonance that becomes even louder when the classical sources underlying this model of translation weigh in. Says Friedrich (12):

> The classical and early Christian precedents for this ethnocentric approach to translation are worth hearing, as they reveal its underlying imperiousness. Cicero says of his translation of Demosthenes, "I translate the ideas, their forms, or as one might say, their shapes; however, I translate them into a language that is in tune with our conventions of usage (*verbis ad nostrum consuetudinem aptis*). Therefore, I did not have to make a word-for-word translation but rather a translation that reflects the general stylistic features (*genus*) and the meaning (*vis*) of the foreign words."

Saint Jerome's discussion of the translator's art is even more startling: "The translator considers thought content a prisoner (*quasi captivos sensus*) which he transplants into his own language with the prerogative of a conqueror (*iure victoris*)" (Friedrich, 12).

But the risk of importing the foreign is that it will not stay where it is put, that it will challenge the host culture, or even that it will itself become the conqueror. In *Titus* there exists a more sinister and pervasive instance of this kind of struggle than the one Ovid's *Metamorphoses* presents. It involves the Latin *pietas*, a term, synonymous with Aeneas himself, that combines duty, patriotism, goodness, and devotion to family, gods, and country.[4] I will suggest that *Titus* enacts—with all the expected moments of pride and anxiety—the appropriation of this Latin word and the subsequent attempt to release its linguistic energies into the English words "pity" and "piety."

Heather James remarks that "Vergilian *pietas* has ossified over the centuries Titus' religious, patriotic, and familial observances conform to the letter rather than the spirit of the law" (1991, 286). But how does one communicate "Vergilian *pietas*" in a language that has no word for this concept? Even "piety," the logical English equivalent, not only fails to capture the meaning of the Latin term, but also introduces serious ideological and aesthetic problems when it is asked to do so. "Piety" is encoded with the idea of kindness, sympathy and humanity. "Piety" and "pity"—as well as their adjectival forms "pious" and "piteous"—were often interchangeable through the seventeenth century, though their discrete meanings as we understand them today were also in use widely.[5] To an Elizabethan audience, "piety" was associated with "pity" down to the basic level of its linguistic existence; so while *pietas* does not necessarily embrace the qualities known to the English as "pity," "piety" almost always does. The sanctioning of such rapes, land-grabbings and murders as Aeneas and his men commit under the auspices of *pietas* has everything to do with a social order that values familial and patriotic duty over sympathy for those human beings who fall outside the boundaries of family and country. Elizabethan England committed its share of atrocities in the name of country, but it was nonetheless a society in which Christianity was the religious and moral law of the land. However arbitrarily Elizabethan England might have observed the imperatives of mercy and sympathy for one's fellow human being in its foreign relations, the importance of these virtues in the overall scheme of social formation and religious obedience is unquestionable.[6] "Piety," for the Elizabethans, could not connote duty in general since it is etymologically entwined with "pity" and often signifies the performance of duty toward God and, by extension, the observance of Christian virtues in general. Indeed, it would be difficult for any speaker of modern English from Shakespeare's time to our own to imagine how an individual replete with "piety" could also be hard-hearted, violent and vengeful. Eugene M. Waith's observation (1995, 106) seems telling in this regard. "The integrating force of the drama," he says, "though too weak to impose itself upon the chaos, appears in the guise of friendship, brotherly love, justice, and gratitude." I suggest that these qualities are precisely what distinguish English "piety" from Roman *pietas*. In "piety" brotherly love, justice and gratitude are assumed values; in *pietas* they are, at best, incidental.

What complicates this problem is, again, the practice of translation an educated Elizabethan would have learned in school. We know from Roger Ascham (1967, 14-15) that double-translation was a common means of teaching Latin. Boys would translate passages from Latin into English, put their work aside for several hours, and then translate their English back again into Latin. The work would be judged by how closely the new Latin retranslation of the English translation came to the Latin original. Given the notorious severity of Tudor pedagogues, the symbol of whose profession was the birch rod,[7] we can imagine to what extent scholars hoping to return painlessly to a correct Latin retranslation might have Latinized their English, especially with words such as *pietas* that have neat cognates. Small as Shakespeare's Latin may have been, we know he was intimately familiar with the practice of double-translation. In *The Merry Wives of Windsor*, Sir Hugh Evans drills a young boy— conveniently named William—and chides him for failing to perform the double-translation correctly:

> Evans. What is *lapis*, William?
> Will.   A stone.
> Evans. And what is "a stone," William?
> Will.   A pebble.
> Evans. No, it is *lapis*: I pray you remember in your Prain (4.1.26-30).

Less obvious are infelicities like "We'll bring him to his house with *shouts* and *clamours*" (my emphasis) that point to the more subtle linguistic turbulence present in poems conceived in a mind raised on a diet of double-translation (Dorsch 1995). In some ways, *Titus* may be thought of as a failed exercise in double-translation. Just as William cannot get back to *lapis* from "stone," we cannot get back to *pietas* from "pity" and "piety." We do not find that virtue circulating through Titus' bloodthirsty actions. Within the play, it is appropriately Tamora, an outsider unfamiliar with Roman custom, who does most of the work of alerting the audience to the problem with this translation.

The Andronici present themselves as careful observers of some set of obligations that the play asks us to understand as "pity" and "piety" while what they really observe is *pietas*. Tamora discovers this problem only too late. Says she to Titus:

> O, if to fight for king and commonweal
> Were piety in thine, it is in these.
> Andronicus, stain not thy tomb with blood.
> Wilt thou draw near the nature of the gods?
> Draw near them in being merciful.
> Sweet mercy is nobility's true badge:
> Thrice-noble Titus, spare my first born son (1.1.113-123).

But Titus cannot understand her—or he imagines that she misunderstands the purpose of the sacrifice he is about to direct. "Piety" is precisely what compels him to destroy Tamora's son, and staining his own "tomb with blood" is precisely the act of mercy and kindness he has offered twenty-five of his own children. His response to her frantic appeal is frighteningly calm and dismissive:

> Patient yourself, madam, and pardon me.
> These are their brethren whom your Goths beheld
> Alive and dead, and for their brethren slain
> Religiously they ask a sacrifice (1.1.124-127).

Though complying with a sacrifice "religiously" asked makes sense to Titus, Tamora's response suggests that his sense of piety does not include pity. But rather than thinking of the problem as a failure in translation, she sees it as a naked hypocrisy: "it is a cruel irreligious piety" (1.1.133).

True to her role as a subjugated foreigner, Tamora will eventually turn the language of her oppressor against him. In the scene with which I opened this paper, Titus' daughter asks for pity when she begs Tamora to murder her and leave her in a ditch. Tamora's glib response coldly echoes her own frustration with the Andronici's notion of "piety" and "pity": "I know not what it means" (2.2.157).

There is no doubt that Aaron, the most skillful and manipulative translator throughout, is aware of how uncomfortably *pietas* rests in the words "piety" or "pity." Ascending his makeshift proscenium, the ladder from which he believes he is about to meet his own violent end, he delivers an appropriately misplaced prologue to the muddled drama we have just seen:

> 'Twil vex thy soul to hear what I shall speak;
> For I must talk of murders, rapes, and massacres,
> Acts of black night, abominable deeds,
> Complots of mischief, treason, villainies
> Ruthful to hear, yet piteously performed (5.1.62-66).

Once again, the pivotal location in the speech is occupied by a word that we cannot immediately make sense of, given what we have seen. By "piteously performed," Aaron may be saying that the horrors of the drama are performed in the spirit of mercy, according to the mandates of duty, or for the purpose of evoking sadness. All possible definitions fit the contexts we have encountered, but none seems to mitigate, subsume or subvert the other, often contradictory, meanings. It is a problem similar to the one Mrs. Ford and Mrs. Page discover in *The Merry Wives*:

> Mrs. Page. Trust me, he beat him most pitifully.
> Mrs. Ford. Nay, by th'mass, that he did not: he beat
>   him most unpitifully, methought (4.2.188-190).

Maybe if we had a word like *pietasly* it would all make sense, but we do not, and as Aaron implies, a word like "piteously"—loaded as it is with notions of vengeance, of open-ended duty, of Christian obedience, of kindness and of sympathy—confounds any effort to identify the action that suits this word. We cannot know in what precise way the performance of horrible deeds may be piteous, and, as long as we cannot, any effort to comprehend those horrors will fail. What Titus' Rome sees as piteous is something that we literally cannot express in English, and it is thus no surprise that the drama ends with a deliberate play on the possible meanings of "pity." As Lucius says of Tamora, "Her life was beastly and devoid of pity, / And being dead, let birds on her take pity!" (5.3.199-200).

Fig. 1. A scene from *Titus*; drawing attributed to Henry Peacham. Copyright the Marquess of Bath, Longleat. With permission.

"Confusion fall"

The only drawing we have depicting a Shakespeare play as it might have been performed during Shakespeare's own lifetime is the one attributed to Henry Peacham (Fig. 1). The scene is from *Titus* but not from any version of the play known to have been performed in England. The drawing's peculiar arrangement of characters and costume begs explanation, and usually that explanation has involved emblems. Jonathan Bate (1995, 43) comments on its "emblematic quality, which exactly fits the way in which the characters in the play so often seem to become emblems, to be frozen into postures that are the very picture of supplication, grief or violent revenge." Bate's assessment does not exclude but downplays the possibility that the drawing is as schematic as it is emblematic. That is, the apparent inaccuracies may be visual cues for recalling the overall play as it appeared onstage.[8] If we allow the sketch to communicate on that level, it suggests that Roman and Elizabethan cultural markers competed for the same theatrical space *and* that at least one observer found this mixture both exciting and unsettling.

At a glance it may be easier to recognize the heady optimism of the humanist goal of synthesis—or at least continuity—with the classical past. Standing near the center of the sketch in Roman garments is Titus. A laurel crown and a spear complete his costume, appropriate symbols of both his political and intellectual authority. Behind him yeomen of the Elizabethan guard wait at his command. Kneeling before him in "vaguely medieval" garments is Tamora (Bate 1995, 43), unmistakably a great lady of some northern kingdom—pious, gentle, supplicating.[9] One of her sons wears Elizabethan clothing, along with the fashionable locks and whiskers of the day.[10] His brother, however, is a marble statue from the classical past—bleached and expressionless with a flat nose-bridge and cropped Roman hair. If not a meet and happy union then at least *discordia concors*: The classical past and early modern England may confront one another uneasily in this scheme, but the final effect is an equilibrium figured almost as a marriage.

But there is another story here. On the right margin stands Aaron the Moor, an unwelcome fourth on the Gothic side of a drawing that desperately seeks balance around Titus' spear. A rival authority, he holds a sword at port-arms, and it, like his accusatory finger and haughty chin, points at Titus and Tamora both. The sword also dangles menacingly over the heads of Tamora's children. Or is Aaron knighting the two? In one way, the awkward figure of the Moor functions almost as an orienting device—like the perspective skull in Holbein's much discussed *French Ambassadors*—that directs the observer toward the mood and attitude proper for understanding the image as a whole.[11] The immediately recognizable foreignness of the stark, black figure—both defensive and arrogant—sabotages any enthusiasm for cultural gain the drawing may express. The foreign in *Titus* operates, after all, by seduction, force and subterfuge—not as a marriage, but as a rape. If we could make this picture speak, it would almost seem to share Samuel Daniel's warning "not so soon [to] yield our consents captive to the authority of antiquity...all our understandings are not to be built by the square of Greece and Italy."[12] But if it were only so simple. Without the authority of antiquity, the square of Greece and Italy, a play like *Titus* could not exist at all. And that is where the sketch and the drama leave us—stuck in a moment of confrontation and wondering what will happen next.

Notes

1. Throughout this essay, I have used the Arden editions of Shakespeare's plays.
2. Waith (1995, 99) provides as good a synopsis of the tragedy's legacy of critical reception as any: "It is surprising to find Shakespearean critics in agreement, yet almost to a man they have concurred in their verdict on the merits of *Titus Andronicus*. The word which most nearly sums up the play is 'disgust'. Ravenscroft called the play 'a heap of rubbish'; Coleridge said that it was 'obviously intended to excite vulgar audiences by its shocking scenes of blood and horror—to our ears shocking and disgusting'; Dover Wilson recently called it a broken-down cart laden with bleeding corpses from an Elizabethan scaffold. Only a few critics have had so much as a word of praise for this early Shakespeare tragedy."
3. Heidegger's term in chapter 23 of *Being and Time* is *Ent-fernen*. As distances become apparent only when things are discovered, the ability to establish distance between ourselves and other beings depends on other beings having a place in our *In-der-Welt-sein*, a mode of being defined by our sense of relationship to the things around us. By identifying things as having distance from us, we identify them as having a relationship to us and vice versa—otherwise we do not recognize their existence at all. It would support my argument, at the expense of its readability, I am afraid, to add that once another being has been de-distanced (as I suggest Latin was for Elizabethans) it nevertheless remains *another* being. However near a thing becomes, we cannot close the gap that makes it other. *Diese Ent-fernung...kann das Dasein nie kreuzen.*
4. Throughout the epic he is *"pius Aeneas."*
5. Oxford English Dictionary, New Edition, s.v. "piety" and "pity."
6. Quinn (1982). It is difficult to generalize the relations between Elizabethans and other cultures—or, for that matter, the relations between classes and genders within Elizabethan society. The tendency has been to see pragmatic and ethnocentric concerns overriding moral and ethical ones, but the Quinns' compilation of writings from the Roanoke voyages reveals a more complicated picture. Thomas Harriot's narrative is particularly interesting in this regard.
7. Ascham's book is in part intended to promote a less oppressive educational environment where children might enjoy learning. In any case, we easily lose sight of how demanding the Tudor classroom must have been. Beatrice White (op. cit.) says of the schoolmaster, "He was a man of terror, and Shakespeare's allusions to 'breeching scholars' and 'heavy looks' have all too loud an echo in other writers" (xii). She goes on to quote Nash, whose comments in *Summer's Last Will and Testament* are worth repeating for any reason: "Nouns and pronouns, I pronounce you as traitors to a boy's buttocks" (xiii).

8. See Gombrich (1960).
9. Students of iconography will no doubt recognize that Tamora's position here is that of the donor, suggesting that however humble she may appear, she holds a place of great honor within the scheme of the drawing. See, for instance, Filippo Lippi's *The Coronation of the Virgin*.
10. See Strong (1977). His discussion on the identity of Hilliard's *Young Man amongst Roses* ventures into an interesting exploration of gentlemen's hair fashions.
11. Carruthers (1998), especially chapter 3, "Cognitive images, meditation, and ornament," 116-170.
12. Daniel (1930, 139). Here and in the epigraph I have followed Stephen Greenblatt's example and "modernized the spelling in quotations from Renaissance texts, since it seemed odd to cite Shakespeare in a modernized edition wile leaving his contemporaries to look quaint and timeworn" (xi).

Works Cited

Ascham, Roger. *The Schoolmaster.* Ed. Lawrence V. Ryan. Ithaca: Cornell University Press, 1967.

Bate, Jonathan. *Shakespeare and Ovid.* Oxford: Clarendon Press, 1993.

Bate, Jonathan, ed. *Titus Andronicus*, by William Shakespeare. New York and London: Routledge, 1995.

Carruthers, Mary. *The Craft of Thought: Meditation, Rhetoric, and the Making of Images, 400-1200.* Cambridge: Cambridge University Press, 1998.

Daniel, Samuel. "A Defence of Ryme." In *Poems and A Defence of Ryme.* Ed. Arthur Colby Sprague. Chicago: University of Chicago Press, 1930.

Dorsch, T. S., ed. *Julius Caesar*, by William Shakespeare. London and New York: Routledge, 1955.

Dryden, John. "Essay of Dramatic Poesy." In *The Oxford Authors: John Dryden.* Ed. Keith Walker. Oxford: Oxford University Press, 1987.

Foucault, Michel. "Nietzsche, Genealogy, History." In *The Foucault Reader*, ed. Paul Rabinow, 76-100. New York: Pantheon, 1984.

Friedrich, Hugo. "On the Art of Translation." In *Theories of Translation*, ed. Rainer Schulte and John Biguenet, 11-16. Chicago: University of Chicago Press, 1992.

Gombrich, E. H. *Art and Illusion: A Study in the Psychology of Pictorial Representation.* Princeton: Princeton University Press, 1960.

Greenblatt, Stephen. *Shakespearean Negotiations: The Circulation of Social Energy in Renaissance England.* Berkeley: University of California Press, 1988.

Gurr, Andrew. "Industrious Ariel and idle Caliban." In *Travel and Drama in Shakespeare's Time*, ed. Jean-Pierre Maquerlot and Michele Willems, 193-208. Cambridge: Cambridge University Press, 1996.

Heidegger, Martin. *Being and Time.* Trans. Joan Stambaugh. Albany: State University Press of New York, 1996.

Hiles, Jane. "A Margin for Error: Rhetorical Context in *Titus Andronicus*." In *Titus Andronicus: Critical Essays*, ed. Philip C. Konlin, 223-248. New York: Garland, 1995.

James, Heather. "Cultural Disintegration in *Titus Andronicus*: Mutilating *Titus*, Vergil, and Rome." In *Violence in Drama*, ed. James Redmond, 123-140. Cambridge: Cambridge University Press, 1991.

Oliver, H. J., ed. *The Merry Wives of Windsor*, by William Shakespeare. London: Methuen and Company, 1971.

Ovid. *Metamorphoses*. Loeb Classical Library. Trans. Fank Justus Miller. Ed. G. P. Goold. Cambridge, Mass.: Harvard UP, 1974.

Quinn, David B., and Alison M. Quinn. *The First Colonists*. Raleigh: North Carolina Division of Archives and History, 1982.

Schleiermacher, Friedrich. "On the Different Methods of Translation." In *Theories of Translation*, ed. Rainer Schulte and John Biguenet, 36-54. Chicago: University of Chicago Press, 1992.

Shakespeare, William. *Julius Caesar*. Ed. T. S. Dorsch. London and New York: Routledge, 1955.

—. *The Merry Wives of Windsor*. Ed. H. J. Oliver. London: Methuen and Company, 1971.

—. *Titus Andronicus*. Ed. Jonathan Bate. New York and London: Routledge, 1995.

Strong, Roy. *The Cult of Elizabeth*. Berkeley: University of California Press, 1977.

Suzuki, Mihoko. "The Dismemberment of Hippolytus: Humanist Imitation, Shakespearean Translation." *Classical and Modern Literature: A Quarterly* 10, 2 (1990).

Tricomi, Albert H. "The Aesthetics of Mutilation in *Titus Andronicus*." *Shakespeare Survey* 27 (1974): 11-19.

Waith, Eugene M. "The Metamorphosis of Violence in *Titus Andronicus*." In *Titus Andronicus: Critical Essays*, ed. Philip C. Konlin, 99-114. New York: Garland, 1995.

White, Beatrice. Foreword to *The Vulgaria of John Stanbridge and The Vulgaria of Robert Whittington*. Ed. Beatrice White. London: Kegan Paul, Trench, Trubner, 1932.

Contributors

Renate Blumenfeld-Kosinski received her Ph.D. at Princeton University and is Professor of French and Director of the Medieval and Renaissance Studies Program at the University of Pittsburgh. Her publications include *Not of Woman Born: Representations of Caesarean Birth in Medieval and Renaissance Europe* (Cornell UP, 1990); *Images of Sainthood in Medieval Europe* (ed. with T. Szell, Cornell UP, 1991); *The Selected Writings of Christine de Pizan* (W.W. Norton, 1997); *Reading Myth: Interpretations of Classical Mythology in Medieval French Literature* (Stanford UP, 1997); as well as numerous articles on medieval French literature. She has also translated the works of Margaret of Oingt (Newburyport, Mass., 1990) and co-edited *Translatio Studii*, a volume in honor of Karl D. Uitti (Rodopi, 2000).

Dolores Buttry is currently Assistant Professor of French and German at Clarion University of Pennsylvania. She holds a Ph.D. in Comparative Literature from the University of Illinois and a Ph.D. in French from the University of Pittsburgh, where she studied with Renate Blumenfeld-Kosinski. Her area of academic interest is French literature of the twelfth century. She is particularly interested in the Norman chronicler, Wace, and has presented numerous papers on that author at the Kalamazoo International Courtly Literature Society, and Leeds medieval conferences, as well as at the Kentucky Foreign Language Conference. A short article about Wace has appeared in *Romance Notes* and other articles are pending.

Luise von Flotow translates literary works from French and German into English, most recently completing works by Herta Mueller, Martin Walser, Emine Sevgi Oezdamar and Madeleine Monette. She is Associate Professor for Translation Studies at the University of Ottawa in Canada, and works on gender and translation, ideological and cultural issues in translation, and media translation.

Edwin D. Floyd received his B.A. in Greek from Yale University, and his M.A. and Ph.D. in Classics from Princeton University. He also studied at the American School of Classical Studies at Athens. After teaching at the College of William and Mary, he joined the University of Pittsburgh faculty in 1966, where he is currently chair of the Classics Department. His areas of specialization are Greek poetry, Greek and Indo-European linguistics and Sanskrit. Among the authors on whom Professor Floyd has published are Homer, Sappho, Parmenides, Pindar and Nonos, and, on the Latin side, Vergil; he has also published on Linear B and on Greek phonology, morphology and etymology. The current focus of his work is the development of Indo-European formulas in the Rig-Veda and in Homeric and post-Homeric Greek, from archaic times into the Byzantine era.

Cristiana Fordyce received a Laurea in Linguistics from the University of Pisa, Italy, in 1987. She is a doctoral candidate in the Department of Romance Languages and Literatures at Boston College where she is completing her dissertation on rhetoric entitled "Between Personal Value and Common Repute: Rhetoric of Self-Defense in the Merchant Era." She has published and worked on Dante, Boccaccio, Raimbaut d'Aurenga, Poggio Bracciolini, Boethius and Peter Abelard. Presently, her research deals with the expression of conflict between the individual and the communal society in the context of Guelf prose and poetry. Beginning in September 2001, she will be director of the NEH-funded Decameron Web Project in the Department of Italian Studies at Brown University.

Philip Hendrick is Senior Lecturer in French at the University of Ulster. After studying French and Latin at University College Galway, he obtained his doctorate from the University of Pennsylvania, completing a thesis on Montaigne and Lucretius. His research has centered on Montaigne, with occasional excursions into computer-assisted language learning and the French media. His book *Montaigne et Sebond: l'art de la traduction*, was published by Champion in 1996.

Kenneth Lloyd-Jones is the McCook Professor of Modern Languages and chair of that department at Trinity College, Hartford, Ct., where he has taught French and Italian since 1978. Earlier, he taught at the University of Maryland and the University of Wales. He has a Ph.D. in French Renaissance poetry from the University of Wales, and a Doctorat en Lettres in Renaissance Latin oratory from the Université de Saint-Etienne, and has published extensively in the fields of neo-Latin literature, humanist translation, and the classical tradition in the French Renaissance.

David A. Lopez received his B.A. from the University of Notre Dame and his Ph.D. from Yale University, both in Medieval Studies. His main interests are in the social and intellectual history of Christianity in Late Antiquity and the Early Middle Ages. His dissertation offered a new paradigm for the significance of martyrdom, apocalyptic expectations, and apologetic writings in the second and third centuries. He is currently Assistant Professor of History at Deep Springs College (Nevada), where he teaches ancient and medieval history, theology and languages, and continues his research into the development of early Christianity.

Adam McKeown received his B.A. and M.A. in English Literature from the University of New Hampshire and his Ph.D. from New York University. His research interests include rhetoric and the visual arts, translation and magic. Currently, he is a visiting assistant professor of Liberal Studies at Clarkson University in Potsdam, N. Y.

Daniel Russell received his Ph.D. at New York University and is Professor of French at the University of Pittsburgh, where he has taught for the past thirty years. He has chaired the Department of French and Italian and directed the Medieval and Renaissance Studies Program. He has written widely on the French Renaissance, and has a special interest in emblems and other emblematic forms in early modern Europe. He has published numerous books and articles on emblems, among them *Emblematic Structures in Renaissance French Culture* (Toronto 1995), and he is co-editor of the journal *Emblematica*.

Zrinka Stahuljak received her Ph.D. at Emory University. She is currently Assistant Professor of French at Boston University, and specializes in medieval French literature and historiography, having recently completed a dissertation entitled "Bloodless Genealogies. Alliance and Kinship in the French Middle Ages." She has also published articles on the medieval *Roman d'Enéas* and on contemporary issues of translation, testimony, and the relation between neutrality and violence.

Andrew Taylor teaches in the English Department at the University of Ottawa. He is the author of *Textual Situations: Three Medieval Manuscripts and Their Readers* (University of Pennsylvania Press, 2001), and one of the co-editors of *The Idea of the Vernacular: An Anthology of Middle English Literary Theory, 1280-1520*. His current research focuses on medieval reading practice.

Edward Tilson has studied at the University of Toronto and Carleton University, and is currently a doctoral candidate at Yale University.

Oumelbanine Zhiri began her career at the University Hassan II, Mohammedia, Morocco. Since 1992, she has been teaching French and Comparative Literature at the University of California, San Diego. Her research focuses on the literature and culture of Europe in the Early Modern period, and its relationship with Arab and Islamic civilization. She is particularly interested in historiography and geography. She is the author of three books: *L'Afrique au Miroir de l'Europe, Fortunes de Jean Leon l'Africain* (Geneva: Droz, 1991), *Les Sillages de Jean Leon l'Africain du XVIe au XXe siècle* (Casablanca: Wallada, 1995), and a study of François Rabelais, *L'Extase et ses paradoxes. Essai sur la structure narrative du* Tiers Livre (Paris: Champion, 1999). Her current project is an in-depth study of the unpublished manuscript of the description of Africa by Leo Africanus.